GLASGOW BIBLE COLLEGE

GROWING UP

(OASIS)

INTERI

CHRISTIA

D0866072

3DL
4 FEB 2000
9.30 am

24 FEB 2000
9.30 AM

14.4.2000
9.30 am

1 May 2000
9.30 am

1 0 OCT 2000

- 6 MAR 2002

- 6 JUN 2002

23 APR 2007

13 MAR 2003

1 8 MAR 2004

30/1/06

0 7 NOV 2006

29 Feb 08.

3 0 JAN 09

Gospel & Culture is a movement of Christians from many different Churches and traditions. We are united by our commitment to Jesus Christ and by a determination to engage with today's culture and to communicate the gospel to it.

We work together to create resources which help Christians relate their faith to the real world. They include...

- Touring lectures, workshops and weekend conferences. Led by some of the Church's leading thinkers and communicators, these are designed to sharpen and inform the faith of Christians and local churches.

- Books such as this one, tapes, occasional papers, and our regular newsletter.

- Our twice-yearly journal, *Leading Light*, which tackles the major cultural issues facing Christians today. Written with wit and style, and in clear, accessible language, *Leading Light* is a valuable resource for anyone who wants to communicate the gospel in our culture.

For more information about Gospel & Culture and *Leading Light*, please write to Lavinia Harvey, Gospel & Culture, Dept. of Theology & Religious Studies, King's College London, The Strand, London WC2R 2LS.

GROWING UP EVANGELICAL

Youthwork and the Making of a Subculture

Pete Ward

First published in Great Britain 1996
Society for Promoting Christian Knowledge
Holy Trinity Church
Marylebone Road
London NW1 4DU

Copyright © Pete Ward 1996

All rights reserved. No part of this book may be reproduced or
transmitted in any form or by any means, electronic or mechanical,
including photocopying, recording, or by any information storage and
retrieval system, without permission in writing from the publisher.

British Library Cataloguing-in-Publication Data
A catalogue record of this book is available
from the British Library

ISBN 0-281-04840-1

Typeset by Pioneer Associates, Perthshire
Printed in Great Britain by
Redwood Books, Trowbridge, Wiltshire

Contents

Preface

This book was born out of my own sense of frustration in seeing young people come to faith, but then fail to find a place in evangelical churches. Reaching out to unchurched young people is almost unbearably demanding and tough. It has therefore been disappointing to discover that even when young people accept Jesus, they might not choose to accept the Church as well. What has been even more disturbing has been the realization that most evangelical congregations find acceptance of these young people to be equally difficult.

My feeling that these were essentially 'cultural' issues led me to reflect on the nature of evangelical church and the role that youthwork itself has played in its history and development. Over the last two years in which I have been working on this material, I have come to feel that we should probably speak of two different styles or 'disciplines' in Christian youthwork: one style would be work within the Church and the other would be work with the unchurched. To make this distinction is not, as far as I am concerned, a value judgement of any kind. Both disciplines of Christian youthwork are desperately needed, both have the ability to be evangelistic and should be concerned to see young people grow in the faith. The point is that they operate in different ways and have different rules, so the term 'discipline' has helped me to clarify these distinctions.

This book is an examination of how work within the discipline of church-based youth fellowship work has evolved. Much of what is written here deals in a fairly analytical and sometimes critical way with this kind of youthwork. I am aware that most of my work has been with young people beyond the fringes of church groups, but I am also committed to church-based youthwork. I am not setting out to undermine the youth fellowship approach to youthwork. My chief concern is to stimulate theological reflection so that we can do youth fellowship work better. We need to have good, healthy and spiritually alive youth groups in our churches. If we are to achieve this, then along with the considerable investment in effort and money which we are at present seeing within the evangelical constituency, we also need to take time to reflect and learn.

Youthwork shapes the Church, and it is my desire that some of the issues raised in this book will stimulate new initiatives and attitudes. Young people and those who minister among them change the culture of the Church and this book shows some of the ways this has happened in the past. Youthwork now needs again to lead the way in building a Church which is able to welcome a diversity of young people who want to follow Jesus and to grow up evangelically.

The Limitations of the Book

This book was written as an attempt to start the discussion on the cultural impact of youthwork on the evangelical church. This is, however, a new area of study and I am aware of the limitations of what I have written. I have tried to maintain a focus on the developments which are particular to an English context, as I recognize that while there may be much which is of relevance to the British Isles in general, I am aware that Northern Ireland, Scotland and Wales also have distinctive religious traditions and histories. I have also wanted to avoid the use of Britain when I mean England and England when I mean Britain.

There are a number of gaps in the material gathered, not least a full account of the interconnections between the United States and England. The historical aspects of the book are more of the nature of case studies than a definitive study. I have chosen to highlight what I consider to be the mainstream of church-based work. The effect of this is, I realize, that notable traditions of youthwork, such as that represented by the uniformed organizations, have been largely ignored. I have also given only brief consideration to para-church agencies such as Youth For Christ or Youth With a Mission. The extent to which the picture I have developed is tempered or changed by an examination of other youthwork organizations or traditions awaits further work. I have, however, attempted to trace the history and development of the youth fellowship in evangelical church life. The material gathered might also be seen to indicate a bias towards the Anglican Church. In part this represents the availability of sources, in part it also indicates my view that Anglicans have often been in the forefront in developing the predominant forms of youthwork in this country. I was tempted to limit the scope of this book to youthwork within the evangelical wing of the Church of England, but as my work progressed I could see a wider picture emerge. I am more than willing to accept, however, that my generalizations concerning evangelical youthwork might be vulnerable to the insights of those better connected to churches other than the Anglican Church. If my view of things is found to be wanting I will await with interest significant work on the distinctive traditions of evangelical youthwork within the Free Churches.

A number of friends have read either all or parts of the manuscript and have offered their thoughts and encouragement. For this I am very grateful; they include: Graham Cray, Kenneth Habershon, Anna Scott-Brown, Michael Eastman, Michael Baughen, Colin Fletcher, John Buckeridge, Chris Irvine and Steve Tilley. I am also very grateful to my editor at SPCK, Naomi Starkey, for her encouragement and support as I have worked on this project. In pulling together the research for the book I have been sent, or lent, materials by some very kind and generous people: Gill Brentford, David Bishop, Bruce Gillingham, Simon Law, Crusaders, CYFA and Dean Borgman. I have been very privileged to be able to interview some of those directly involved in the developments which

I describe and to these people I want to express my particular thanks: Nick Stone, Pete Meadows, Malcolm Doney,
David Winter, Kenneth Habershon and Michael Eastman.
I want to say a big thank you to my assistant Anna Scott-
Brown for her work, particularly in helping with the editing
of the songbook sections; also to Michael Eastman, whose
detailed comments on chapters two and three were invalu-
able, and to Phil Moon and Steve Tilley, who have made the
CYFA archives freely available to me. I would like to express
my thanks to Archbishop George Carey and the Lambeth
Partners for their support for me over the last year or so. I
am honoured to work as advisor to the Archbishop of
Canterbury, but this does not mean that the ideas expressed
in this book can necessarily be taken as reflecting his. Lastly
I should thank Tess, my wife, and Eleanor and Callum who
have tolerated a book-obsessed husband and father for too
long.

PETE WARD
Oxford

Introduction

The Place of Youthwork within Evangelicalism

It was an experience of failure in youthwork which led to the writing of this book. For the last seven years I have been involved in training Christian youthworkers with an organization called 'Oxford Youth Works'. The focus of our training course has been work among young people who are unconnected to the Church. Given our outreach focus, it is encouraging when one of our graduates is employed in a church context. Unfortunately these appointments do not always work out. This book came about as I reflected on the experience of one young youthworker who was taken on by an evangelical church to reach out to young people in the local area.

Everything started extremely well. The church had a good history of youthwork with a fair-sized youth fellowship and an open youth club one night a week. The appointment of a youthworker was considered and discussed in some depth by the church and the PCC and it was agreed that work should focus on outreach in the local school. Using the training gained at Oxford Youth Works the youthworker quickly began to build relationships with a group of relatively 'tough' working-class young people who lived on an estate close to the church. Within a year or so relationships had developed to such an extent that a good few of the young people would regularly drop by the youthworker's office at the church. In addition numbers in the open youth club had grown from ten regulars to around sixty young people, most of whom were contacts made by the new youthworker. There was evidence that the outreach was working with a small group of around five or so of these young people meeting on a weekly basis in the church building to worship and pray.

The work was obviously going extremely well. The problem was that the church found it difficult to come to terms with the young people who were now starting to affiliate themselves to the youthworker and to the church building. They were regarded as 'trouble' and something of a threat. One of the volunteer leaders at the open club even asked the youth leader, 'Why have you brought this lot here? We've just got rid of a group like them.' Clearly they were seen as a problem. This label was also applied to the young people who had become Christians. It was seen as an issue that the group were meeting on their own in the church rather than joining up with the existing youth fellowship. At the same time parents saw good things happening with this new group and they wanted their own children to benefit. So there was significant pressure from church members to 'do something for our young people'. The solution was to run joint worship events for both of the groups once a month. When these got started it was clear that the presence of the working-class young people was resented by the youth fellowship.

The story did not end terribly well. After two years the youthworker decided to move on. During lengthy discussions concerning the future of the work, the initial desire to continue the ministry among the working-class young people on the part of the church leadership was slowly eroded by pressure from church members, some of whom had children in the youth fellowship. It was from among this group that the support for the employment of a youthworker had first come. Eventually the church appointed a new youthworker but substantial changes to the job description placed much greater emphasis on work within the church with the existing youth fellowship. Meanwhile the original group of working-class young people, including those who used to worship in the church building, were left with little or no contact with the church and were somewhat puzzled as to what had happened.

Extensive discussions with the church leaders and the youthworker concerned left me with a number of questions. Why did this experiment in mission not succeed? How can a church have the imagination to plan such an appointment but then fail to deal with the consequences of success? Why should a church which has paid so much money for a youthworker not seemingly want local young people even when they come to faith? These questions were less directed at this one individual church than at evangelical churches in general. As I pondered these questions I was convinced that the answers lay in an understanding of the mind set or 'subculture' of the evangelical church.

By subculture I mean that those within the evangelical church are a minority group in the population who share a number of behaviours, values and lifestyles.[1] The young people with whom the youthworker had made contact clearly did not fit in with this shared church subculture. Even those young people who had expressed interest in the faith and attended worship were still seen as difficult or a problem. Despite the fact that they had come to faith, the church appeared to find it difficult to accept them. Much as a human body might reject a donated organ of the wrong type, these young people had been effectively excluded from church life. The striking thing to my mind was that church members' resistance to these young people appeared to transcend their obviously deep desire to reach out with the gospel. There was a contradiction between the stated official line of this evangelical church, namely to share the faith with everyone in the local community, and the actuality as experienced by this group of young people. This contradiction seemed to indicate a strong undercurrent of values and motivations which were powerful enough to cut across the official theological position of the church.

It was with these questions in mind that I came to *Evangelical Anglicans*, a collection of essays written by the

staff and associates of Wycliffe Hall, Oxford. In the introduction to the book Dick France and Alister McGrath are
concerned to point out the differences between evangelicalism and fundamentalism:

> ... sociologically, fundamentalism is a reactionary
> counter-cultural movement, with tight criteria of mem-
> bership and is often associated with a 'blue collar' con-
> stituency. Evangelicalism is a cultural movement with
> increasingly loose criteria of self definition, which tends
> to be associated with a professional or 'white collar' con-
> stituency.[2]

The distinction between evangelicalism and fundamentalism is an important one to make. However, the question
which this observation raised in my mind was what is the
nature of the 'cultural' movement of evangelicalism?
Fundamentalism may well have tight criteria for membership, but in my experience the 'white-collar' nature of
English evangelicalism imposed its own restrictions on
membership. Fundamentalism might well be a 'separatist'
movement, but how 'open' was evangelicalism? If evangelicalism was a 'cultural movement' then something within the
'culture', or to use my term, subculture, of evangelicalism
was resistant to outreach to young people. This observation,
however, paradoxically led me back to youthwork.

It was the omission of youthwork from the picture of
evangelicalism painted by *Evangelical Anglicans* which caused
me to reflect further. I was frustrated that the book examined and categorized various aspects of evangelical church
life but failed to treat evangelical youthwork in a similar
fashion. It would have been easy to put this down to the
usual marginalization of youth and children's work in theological circles. At this point, though, it occurred to me that
perhaps this aspect of evangelical life was hidden from view
for more interesting reasons. Perhaps the examination of
evangelical youthwork was a sensitive issue, which was 'close
to the bone'. It was not only in this book that youthwork
was largely unconsidered; it was hard to find one serious

investigation into evangelical work with young people in an English context which could grace a university library's shelves. A full-blown conspiracy was probably putting things a little strongly, but could it be that the lack of consideration of evangelical work among young people indicated just how important it was?

Since the Second World War evangelicalism in England has experienced a remarkable renaissance. With growth has come a considerable broadening of the evangelical constituency. We now have a bewildering array of new brands of evangelical from conservative, or open, to radical and even post-evangelical. With organizations such as Reform coming into existence the question of evangelical identity has become something of a hot potato. My own experience of theological colleges, and in particular Wycliffe Hall, had shown me how evangelicalism easily divides into tribes. When examined closely, allegiances, and indeed theological positions, could be connected to youthwork of one kind or another. It is my contention that there are close correlations between particular camps, houseparties and festivals and the various divisions which characterize the contemporary evangelical scene. Youthwork is close to the culture-carrying heart of the various factions within the movement. It is its centrality to the maintenance of existing positions which makes youthwork a sensitive and therefore largely unexamined area of evangelical activity.

The 'hiddenness' of evangelical youthwork may well be a figment of my overactive imagination. It seems clear, though, that the place where young people are brought to faith and then nurtured in the early years of their Christian lives must have some influence on the eventual shape of the Church. The nurture of children is a key place where the values of any community are focused. The existence of so many evangelical bodies devoted to youthwork is an indication of the attention which work among young people has received. This importance is especially strong among the armies of volunteers who have run beach missions and camps year in year out all around the country. The importance increasingly being placed on youthwork within the church, as evidenced by the rapid rise in full-time youthworkers employed in parishes, also indicates how pivotal this aspect of church life has become.

Evangelical Origins

Evangelicalism is a diverse and complex movement but according to Noll, Bebbington and Rawlk there are four characteristics which hold true throughout the movement: 'Biblicism (a reliance on the Bible as ultimate religious authority), conversionism (a stress on New Birth), activism (an energetic, individualistic approach to religious duties and social involvement), and crucicentrism (a focus on Christ's redeeming work as the heart of essential Christianity).' [3] Although McGrath traces such characteristics back to the fifteenth century,[4] these writers see the true origins of evangelicalism in the eighteenth-century revivals in English-speaking countries. Wells, in contrast, concentrates attention on the much more recent past of the 1940s when he says that the movement took on the form which we would characterize as 'evangelical'.[5] This modern period of evangelical history corresponds closely to the emergence of strong, and I would argue influential, developments in work among children, young people and students. In an English context there is a good deal of agreement that modern-day evangelicalism has emerged as a powerful force within the Church and that this resurgence is in no small way due to the efforts of those engaged in work among young people and students.

McGrath identifies three main factors which led to the renewal of evangelicalism in the postwar period. The first of these is the ministry of E. J. H. Nash (known as Bash), whose camps for boys from the top public schools 'formed a new generation of evangelical thinkers and leaders'. This was complemented by the spreading influence of the Inter-Varsity Fellowship Christian Unions for university students and in particular by the establishment of the Tyndale Fellowship for Biblical Research which fostered a new generation of evangelical biblical scholars. The third factor he identifies was the influence of the ministry of John Stott who was appointed as Rector of All Souls, Langham Place in 1950. Stott was converted through the ministry of E. J. H. Nash and was closely linked to developments in the IVF.[6]

Saward also focuses on the importance of Bash's Iwerne Minster camps, the work of the IVF biblical research committee and the ministry of John Stott. Alongside those following the lead of Randle Manwaring he also notes the importance of 'the Crusader Union of Bible Classes'. He observes that 'Through regular Sunday afternoon Bible Class teaching and summer camps the Crusaders reached young men and boys who, in many cases, rarely went to church'. A good many leaders within the Church of England were led to faith through the work of Crusaders; Saward counts himself among them, along with Bishops John Taylor and Keith Sutton who came to faith in this way. There were also, according to Saward, a number of leaders within the Church who had first been drawn to the Christian faith through Crusaders, who had since moved to more liberal or catholic traditions.[7]

In *Evangelicalism in Modern Britain* Bebbington also sees youthwork as being of central importance in the growth and development of modern evangelicalism. He points to a range of organizations and activities including Bash Camps, Pathfinders, Filey Holiday Crusades and Operation Mobilisation.[8] Elsewhere Bebbington mentions the importance of the British organization 'The National Young Life Campaign' and the US-based 'Youth For Christ':

> The other strength (of evangelicalism) was the vitality of evangelistic organisations targeting young people, most notably 'Youth For Christ' and (in Britain) 'The National Young Life Campaign'. From their ranks emerged some of the most dynamic figures in a postwar resurgence of evangelical religion.[9]

Not least among these leaders was the evangelist Billy Graham. Graham's roots lay in a close association with Youth for Christ. In 1945 Graham joined Torrey Johnson to work with 'Chicagoland Youth for Christ'. Johnson, who was the founder of YFC, made it clear to Graham that young people were the key to the renewal of the Church. According to Graham's biographer, 'Torrey Johnson convinced Billy that if they could sweep young people into a tide of revival, they could place Evangelical Christianity at the heart of a movement to revitalize American culture.'[10] The importance of Billy Graham to evangelicalism in England is widely acknowledged.[11] The evangelistic campaigns of 1954–5 and 1966–7 were to make a significant impact on church life in this country, such that even the originally critical Archbishop of Canterbury, Michael Ramsey, came to accept that 'every time Graham came to England on a mission, more young men had vocations to be priests'.[12] Graham's first visit to England was in 1946 and in October of that year he returned with the soloist Cliff Barrows and together they embarked on a tour of twenty-seven towns and cities.[13] The tour was under the general banner of 'British Youth for Christ'. Graham's host was the British evangelist Tom Rees who had been running 'Youth for Christ' meetings for a while before he made contact with Torrey Johnson and Graham.[14] At the end of the tour 250 youth leaders were gathered in Birmingham to hear Graham. Johnson flew over from Chicago especially to attend this meeting.[15]

The view that youthwork has played a decisive role in the development of modern-day evangelicalism in England is therefore widely supported. The consensus is that youthwork was one of the key ways whereby people were introduced to the Christian faith. Through camps, houseparties and missions a generation of leaders emerged who were themselves able to influence the Church. Yet the role of youthwork in shaping and forming the mind, methods and spirituality of the Church has been largely ignored. Despite the fact that every year thousands of young people are involved in evangelical youth activities, the eventual influence that this might have on the future shape of the Church has been relatively unexplored.[16]

Youthwork and the Shape of Evangelicalism

The central thesis in this book is that modern evangelicalism has been decisively shaped by work among young people. The study of youthwork therefore sheds light on some of the core issues affecting evangelicalism today, including such questions as culture, class and spirituality.

The Question of Culture

There is at present considerable debate within evangelical circles concerning the right response of the Church to modern culture. The extent to which the gospel is to be adapted or contextualized within culture is a key question in outreach not only within the United Kingdom but also around the world. At the same time there is an understandable concern to maintain the distinctiveness and transformational aspects of the relationship of gospel and culture.[17]

The twists and turns which characterize evangelical reflection on this issue are well displayed in McGrath's *Evangelicalism and the Future of Christianity*. In a reprise of his piece with France in *Evangelical Anglicans* McGrath defines evangelicalism over and against fundamentalism by noting how the former has generally sought to interact with culture, while the latter has tended towards separation from culture. He quotes Francis Shaeffer who saw evangelicalism as 'Bible-believing without shutting one's self off from the full spectrum of life, and in trying to bring Christianity into effective contact with the current needs of society, government and culture.'[18] Later on in the same book, when he is discussing the ill effects of modernizing attempts to adapt the faith to secular culture, McGrath takes a slightly harder line: 'Evangelicalism believes that to be right is to be relevant. It is too easy to produce a spurious relevance in response to secular pressures, which are often localised and transient in their nature.'[19]

Evangelicalism relates to modern culture by being resistant to secular pressure, while at the same time offering 'an attractive alternative to it'.[20] The words 'resistant' and 'alternative' seem to break down the previous distinction from fundamentalism; however, McGrath later employs a much more 'contextual' approach to culture when he explains how an unchanging gospel should be 'particularised in context'. He is concerned to affirm that the way in which the gospel is proclaimed must change as the context changes.[21]

Alister McGrath is a leading evangelical academic, and the variety of response to the question of evangelical faith and culture which his work displays indicates how sensitive this issue is for contemporary evangelical Christians. The impulses which led McGrath to affirm the role of evangelicals in relation to culture, remaining separate, whilst also seeking to contextualize the gospel, are illuminated to a considerable extent by the history of Christian youthwork. When arguing for the distinctiveness of evangelicalism McGrath quotes Peter Berger with some approval, making the point that in the modern world, every accommodation to culture is destined to be relevant to only one social class. Thus:

> Every attempt to accommodate Christianity to the beliefs of one social grouping proves to make it irrelevant to another. The paradox underlying any attempt to make the gospel 'relevant' is that for everyone to whom the gospel is made relevant, there are probably dozens for whom it is made irrelevant – needlessly.[22]

The limitations with this argument are clear when the history of Christian ministry among young people is considered. Evangelicalism in an English context has been dominated by a prevailing public school and university (indeed Oxbridge) educated ethos. The primary reason for this bias has been that outreach among young people has been most successful and enduring in these areas. The study of youthwork reveals that it has been the primary means by which a faith contextualized within the upper middle class and educated university world predominated among modern-day evangelicalism. A close examination of who came to form the leadership of postwar evangelicalism, of how these people came to faith, how they were initially nurtured in their faith, and where they received their first, and possibly most formative, lessons in Christian leadership, points directly to the contextualizing role of youth and student work.[23]

As we shall see, youthwork has been the means by which the cultural ethos of evangelicalism has come into being and is then maintained. I have used the word 'subculture' to express the particular set of behaviours, values and beliefs of the movement. The reality, however, is that there are a great many groups within evangelicalism, and each of these is a subgroup of the larger movement. The study of youthwork offers vital clues as to how these subgroups have come into existence. While indicating some of this diversity I have tried to demonstrate the broad flow of ideas by referring to evangelicalism in general as a subculture.

The Failure to Reach the English Working Class

The class-specific nature of English evangelicalism is well accepted. This aspect of the movement in England is however particularly remarkable when compared with the United States, where traditionally evangelicalism has been a much more working-class phenomenon.[24] Hatch has offered strong evidence that American forms of evangelicalism, since the revolution, have carried within them strong egalitarian and populist tendencies: 'American Protestantism has been skewed away from central ecclesiastical institutions and High culture; it has been pushed and pulled into its present shape by a democratic or populist orientation.'[25] The democratic impulse within American evangelicalism has, according to Hatch,[26] less to do with the specifics of 'polity and governance' and more to do with the 'incarnation of the Church in popular culture'.

It is such an 'incarnation' of the faith among the majority of the people that English evangelicalism has so far failed to achieve. Much energy has gone into attempts to bridge the divide in reaching 'the unchurched', but it is within the atmosphere and methods of Christian youthwork that we see the key to the resistance of English evangelicalism to egalitarianism and populism. In the first instance the ident-ification of evangelicalism and those from the educated classes was reinforced and maintained by camps, houseparties and university CUs. In the 1960s, however, pioneers such as David Sheppard and those associated with Frontier Youth Trust sought to spread the Church's impact down the social scale. The story of this work illustrates the extent to which evangelical mission was hidebound firstly by the terms within which the faith was expressed, secondly by the methods of outreach and nurture which had been developed in the universities and public schools, and thirdly by the resistance of the existing members of the Church to young people who failed to 'fit in' socially.[27]

One aspect of this history is the story of how English evangelicalism has been able to draw inspiration from its American counterpart while maintaining its class-bound nature. In a good many of the most influencial US imports to these shores there has been a strong populist and egali-tarian ethos. With comparative ease English evangelicals have consistently managed to feed off American innovation whilst largely subverting the egalitarian feel which is common in the United States. I shall argue that vital clues as to how this has come about are to be found in the history of Christian youthwork.

Why do Teenagers and Young Adults Leave the Evangelical Church?

Peter Brierley's research in *Reaching and Keeping Teenagers* indicated that churches were losing contact with their young people in significant numbers as they passed through ado-lescence and on into adulthood.[28] Brierley's findings were greeted with a good deal of concern and heart searching by many evangelicals. The discussion of the reasons for this drop-off, however, has probably fallen short of a concerted examination of the nature of Christian youthwork. Such an examination raises important questions and reveals tendencies within evangelicalism which perhaps explain why young people in their later teenage years find association with the Church problematic.

Contemporary evangelicalism has been characterized by a number of features which might be termed 'adolescent'. Holloway draws attention to the adolescent 'arrogance and intemperateness' of many student Christian Unions. Some of this he puts down purely to age, but some of it he sees as being 'systemic to the evangelical experience'.[29] He identifies three main criticisms of evangelicalism, the first being that evangelicals have a tendency to simplify Christian truth. There is, according to Holloway, a 'passion for interpretative theories that offer single explanations for complex realities'.[30] Mark Noll, writing in an American context, and from within evangelicalism, agrees with this analysis, and quotes N. K. Clifford:

> The evangelical mind has never relished complexity. Indeed its crusading genius, whether in religion or in politics, has always tended toward an over simplification of issues and the substitution of inspiration and zeal for critical analysis and serious reflection. The limitations of such a mind set was less apparent in the relative simplicity of the rural frontier society.[31]

As we will see, simplicity and certainty are elements which have also tended to be central to evangelical ministry among students and teenagers. Perhaps linked to this is Holloway's second criticism and his chief frustration, which is a sense that evangelicals are intolerant of the diversity which is to be found within the Anglican Church. In extreme cases, he claims, evangelicals separate themselves from other members of the Church by defining others as not being Christians.[32] Once again the lack of appreciation of a plurality of frameworks of belief can be a characteristic of the more adolescent or teenage mind set.

Holloway's third criticism concerning evangelicalism is

with what he terms 'moralism'. He points out how a significant number of Chief Constables appear to be evangelicals,
and he is unsympathetic with what he describes as the
'successful, sober-suited authoritarians, who are convinced
they have the answer to society's problems'. It is what appears
as a preoccupation with moral success which gives him
problems.[33] Again it could be argued that what Holloway
says concerning the issue of morality and authoritarian leaders within evangelicalism finds its origins in the formative
influences of work among teenagers at camps and houseparties. Firm and clear moral boundaries are, of course, an
essential part of work among all kinds of young people. The
down side of this is that authoritarian leadership is all too
easily bred in the training of the young. Added to this, the
implicit pressure placed on those involved in youthwork by
Christian parents who are concerned for the safety of their
children should not be underestimated.[34] The moralism and
authoritarian tone of evangelicalism may also be a by-product
of youthwork, with leaders schooled in working with young
people finding it difficult to make the transition to shared
patterns of leadership more appropriate to ministry among
adults.

Closely linked to the critique offered by Holloway is the
observation by McGrath that evangelicalism has what he
terms a 'dark side'. One of the features of this dark side of
evangelicalism is the tendency to rely on individual personalities. He then shifts his analysis to the slightly safer
ground of American TV evangelists. Yet in an English context it also seems to be the case that some people experience
evangelicalism as fostering an unhealthy relationship with
Christian leaders. The relationship between authoritarian,
strong and attractive leaders and dependent followers is an
essential one. To have one you need to have the other.
Youthwork is constructed from the relationships and trust
built up between leaders and young people. Evangelical
camps and houseparties have trained successive generations
of leaders within the Church. The problem comes, in any
youth ministry, when a young person wishes to move on and

grow up. There is a need for relationships, which may foster a healthy degree of dependence on supportive leaders, to move gradually to one of mutual interdependence. Such a movement should form the relational agenda of youth ministry.[35]

Within the university CUs and youth fellowships a culture of progressive responsibility and leadership has been developed. There is a link between growing up as an evangelical and leadership which youthwork has carefully fostered. To be a leader is to be adult. Youthwork has tended to create roots to maturity which involve acting as leaders and therefore expecting increased involvement. The rewards for such activities are great, while the sanctions for a gradual lessening of involvement are also fairly strong. This pattern, it could be argued, has evolved a two-class system within evangelicalism: the leaders and the led. There is a serious problem when the primary root to maturity and therefore adulthood is through increased responsibility and leadership within the structures of youthwork. The young Christian who wishes to be accepted as 'adult' while being active in other spheres, such as sport or music, experiences considerable tension between the demands of leadership within the Church and their outside interests. With a choice between being a responsible leader or a pliant and accepting follower – the only two well defined roles within the evangelical community – the independently minded young adult is faced with a significant problem. With models of leadership which have emerged from a long tradition of youth and student work the evangelical church, it would seem, has stored up significant problems for itself. All the time youthwork remains off the agenda of serious theological reflection these patterns will continue to plague evangelicals.[36]

If these observations have any truth in them, then one of the main reasons why young people are leaving the evangelical church in such droves may be because they simply have to. The need to 'grow up' militates against an approach to faith which is so deeply rooted within the structures of teenage life and a subsequent adolescent mind set. Far from seeking to find ways to 'keep' teenagers in safe and possibly dependent programmes, evangelicals need to examine more closely how youthwork might allow for a steady growth and development of young people.

The Quest for an Evangelical Spirituality

It is clear that a good many young adults who have grown up within the evangelical fold have felt the need to experiment with an ever increasing diversity of spiritualities. The issue is being treated with good deal of seriousness by English evangelicals. As McGrath puts it: 'The perceived lack of a credible, coherent and distinctive spirituality is one of the greatest weaknesses facing evangelicalism today.'[37]

In response to this problem McGrath advocates the need for evangelicals to reassess their own history and traditions to see how from within these resources there might be the fuel for future developments. In the course of his discussion of evangelical spirituality McGrath indicates two associated issues. The first is that the mainstay of evangelical spiritual life, the 'quiet time', has become somewhat of a problem for busy business executives or medics.[38] The second is that many people are turning away from evangelicalism to other forms of spirituality because, he says, there has been a failure to 'address the realities of the human situation'.[39]

These two issues in evangelical spirituality could also be seen to arise from the context within which most evangelical Christians have learned the faith. Student life, camps and houseparties are temporary communities. As temporary and therefore relatively artificial experiences of community life they share a common dislocation from the on-going and long-term realities which characterize everyday life. It is a distinctive feature of adolescence that the teenager and the student are divorced from the mainstream of economic life. The limited range of considerations associated with evangelicalism, to which McGrath draws attention, have been fostered in adolescent environments. The comparatively sheltered world of the teenager and student does not lend itself to the more complex issues of later life. The 'quiet time' also can be seen to be a product of the more leisured existence of the adolescent. If this observation is even partly true, then an understanding of evangelical spirituality will require more than the journey back to the sixteenth century advocated by McGrath. There will be a need to develop an understanding of the importance of work among young people and students and how this work has shaped evangelicalism. Patterns of association and spiritual life which have become familiar and cherished in adolescent years will need to be reassessed. In a context where at least one commentator can speak of the 'perpetual adolescence' of evangelicalism there is a need to examine the extent to which evangelicalism is finding itself wanting because it has evolved its spirituality within the context of youthwork.[40]

The Evolution of Evangelicalism

Evangelicals may well advocate an unchanging gospel, but our own activities are often characterized by considerable innovation. A brief survey of music used by evangelicals, or styles of liturgical worship, or even the range of organizations spawned by the movement, is evidence of constant change. This is what Bebbington speaks of as the 'activism' of evangelicals.[41] It is, of course, through creative and imaginative actions that the movement progesses and moves forward, but it is popular culture which has, more often than not, formed the atmosphere and provided the materials for this evolution.

Holloway amusingly, but also a trifle dismissively, remarks that, 'More people go to discos than to high opera, and one of the courageous things about evangelicals is their ability to embrace bad taste for the sake of the gospel.'[42] He is right to point out the tendency within evangelicalism to incorporate elements of popular music and leisure activities as part of its programme for evangelism. It is this characteristic more than any other which has shaped modern-day evangelical religion. There is nothing unusual in this because, 'Evangelicalism

has always been profoundly shaped by its popular character.'[43] Hatch describes how early evangelicalism in the United
States used forms of popular mass culture to spread the
gospel. The advent of cheap and accessible printing led,
during the 1830s, to the publication of evangelical newspapers and periodicals which became 'a burgeoning religious
culture'.[44] Along with printing, the popular spirit of American evangelicalism was also carried by the creation of the
'gospel song':

> At the turn of the nineteenth century a groundswell of
> self-made tunesmiths, indifferent to authorized hymnody,
> created their own simple verses and set them to rousing
> popular tunes. This outpouring of native folk lyricism, or
> what George Pullen Jackson has termed 'indigenous
> country religious songs', borrowed indiscriminately from
> a wide variety of secular tunes of love, war, home-sickness,
> piracy, robbery and murder. The melodies and rhythms of
> fiddle tunes, marches, reels, and jigs were adopted as
> well.[45]

Similar observations could, of course, be made of the hymn-
writing of Charles Wesley or of William Booth. The key
issue is that while, at times, evangelicalism shows itself
capable of affecting the wider culture, the traffic usually
goes the other way. When it is observed that the 'religious'
form of evangelicalism is probably best seen as 'a persistent
mixing of innovation and tradition',[46] then it is clear that the
partner in this innovation is more often than not an aspect
of popular culture.

In the postwar era evangelicalism has undergone significant changes. At the heart of these are innovations which
have to a large extent arisen from work among young
people. Two examples of this would be the enduring impact
of festivals such as Greenbelt or Spring Harvest, both of
which have strong connections with youth culture and in
particular the Jesus Movement.[47] A further example is the
way that worship songs have changed over the last thirty
years. The analysis in Chapter 5 of *Youth Praise*, *Sound of*

Living Waters and *Songs of Fellowship* draws attention to the way that the thought-forms of evangelicalism have developed in recent times. The use of particular musical forms and styles has been as much an influence in the evangelical world as it has been a reflection of emerging theologies. In either case the use of popular music, be it of the rock, pop or 'Classic FM' variety, is rarely, if ever, symbolically neutral. The use of such music profoundly affects the shared spiritual lives of thousands of evangelical Christians.

Maintaining the Evangelical Tribe

The growth in youthwork in present-day parishes has a direct link to the anxiety of Christian parents. It is possible to regard youthwork as an attempt to keep Christian young people 'safe' within the faith. Much of this is, of course, right and proper. Who would choose for their children to be unsafe or at risk? But the question which this raises is the extent to which the right and proper exercise of Christian nurture becomes laden with an emotional charge because of the fears of Christian people.

There is a good deal of evidence that aspects of modern society and youth culture are seen as being very threatening and in some cases downright evil by some evangelicals.[48] These worries, which generally focus on issues such as drugs, sex and the occult, are common among a good many parents. The Christian faith, and in particular that piece of it which impacts on your own child, the youthwork, suddenly becomes very important indeed. Evangelical concerns extend beyond the personal issues of young people. There is considerable discomfort with aspects of the modern media. Mark Noll sees the formative impact of MTV, movies and TV as being deeply threatening of what he terms the 'evangelical mind'.[49]

The force of such evangelical concerns has fallen primarily on the teenager. The fear of the media and of popular youth culture is generally linked to a feeling that young people are particularly in need of protection from such forces.[50] The effect of these sentiments on the shape, atmosphere, and effectiveness of evangelical youthwork cannot be underestimated. One example of this might be the growth of a Christian music industry. It is possible to argue that the separate existence of a Christian 'subculture' owes much of its energy to the desire on the part of Christian parents, adults and young people to have a safe alternative to the more risky and uncontrolled secular youth subcultures. Thus Christian imitations of Rap bands, Heavy Metal bands and so on are generated to feed the needs of a scared Christian public.[51]

The creation of Christian magazines, bands, record labels, concerts, festivals, plays and art in the postwar period, fuelled by the concerns of Christian parents and adults, and, it must be said, encouraged by the enthusiasm of many Christian young people, continues to generate change within the evangelical community. The desire to influence and control young people has been one of the key innovative forces within evangelicalism.[52] The issues raised above have indicated the importance of considered reflection on evangelical work among young people. Youthwork is by no means marginal to the study of evangelicalism. Indeed, it is one of the chief formative influences within the subculture.

PART I

Case Studies in
the History of the
Youth Fellowship

Chapter 1

The Origins of
Christian Youthwork

Those of us involved in Christian youthwork are the inheritors of a long tradition. This tradition will most probably have been passed on to us by word of mouth as we go about our business. Experience and wisdom in Christian youthwork has more often than not simply been shared from one youthworker to another as good advice. Leaders on houseparties or on missions will see it as an important part of their role to help younger helpers learn the ropes. In this sense ours is an oral tradition often rich in custom and mythology. It is rare indeed to find a church where at one time there was not a period of 'wonderful' youthwork when Revd A. N. Other was curate, while virtually every camp has particular games or songs or other customs which are repeated year in, year out. In this way methods of evangelical youthwork and a large part of its wisdom have been generated and kept alive.

The varied and complex history of youthwork is also seen in the legacy of institutions which preceeding generations have spawned. In most towns it is not unusual to encounter a bewildering array of youthwork and most of it will have, or have had at some time, some Christian connection. The different styles of work, groups and Christian ministry among young people have been both energetic and innovative. A new approach to youthwork or one targeted at a particular group of people has more often than not led to the creation of a new body to carry the work forward. In this way evangelical innovation has led to evangelical organizations.[1]

Despite the variety of youthwork styles and methods developed over the years, within the present-day Church there has been an enduring commitment to the importance of the 'youth fellowship'. This chapter sets the scene for the emergence of 'youth fellowship' as a method of Christian youthwork and describes the influences which have shaped this style of work.

Gathering the Young Together

Early Beginnings

Youthwork in an English context is really a nineteenth-century invention.[2] As awareness of the needs of children and young people grew in the popular consciousness, Christian people, with characteristic Victorian energy, set about the task of creating youth and children's organizations. Christian work with children, of course, already had a significant history. In the late eighteenth century Sunday schools were started which taught reading, writing and religious knowledge.[3] But it was during the early part of the nineteenth century that the Sunday school movement was to expand and consolidate its position.[4] The Sunday school was an influence upon the development of youth fellowship work because it set a pattern for a separate gathering for children to receive religious instruction. It was also to have an important role in giving birth to and supporting a number of new initiatives to reach young people which were to evolve during the nineteenth and early twentieth centuries.

George Williams and his friends who joined together to form the first YMCA on 6 June 1844 were well acquainted with Sunday school work.[5] The origins of the Young Men's Christian Society also lie in the evangelical convictions of this group of young shopworkers who were in the drapery trade in London. With clear links to American revivalism, the YMCA grew out of meetings for prayer and Bible study which were held by young men who were living 'above the shop'.[6] The original aims of those who formed the society can be seen to be entirely evangelical when the founders agree to establish

> . . . a society which should have for its object the arousing of converted men in the different drapery Establishments in the metropolis to a sense of their obligation and responsibility as Christians in diffusing religious knowledge to those around them either through the medium of prayer meetings or any other meeting they think proper . . .[7]

The Sunday schools also gave rise to the development of the first uniformed youth organization in Britain. It was the experience of a rowdy Sunday school class in Glasgow which prompted William Smith to found the Boys' Brigade.[8] His basic plan was to create an organization which introduced a military-style drill to boys whom he saw as rough and rowdy. The Boys' Brigade started in 1883 at North Woodside Mission Hall in Glasgow. Always attached to a church, each Brigade was to include a Bible class in its activities. Indeed the Bible class could be seen as the main reason for the work in the first place.[9] When the boys had grown too old for the Boys' Brigade Williams envisioned that they would find a place in the local YMCA, of which he was an enthusiastic supporter. Williams was to provide much inspiration and encouragement to Baden-Powell at the start of the Scout movement. Baden-Powell, however, was less committed to the evangelical stance of the Boys' Brigade and was even less enthusiastic about military-style drill.[10] Baden-Powell's new movement was enormously succesful but despite early co-operation Smith was clear that his Christian commitment and his belief in discipline and drill precluded a merger of the Scouts and the Boys' Brigade.

The creation of the Boys' Brigade came about because of the perceived limitations of the Sunday school. It was the realization that the existing good work needed to be supplemented by new initiatives which gave an impetus to the development of evangelical youthwork organizations over the next hundred years or so. The main driving force behind these initiatives was the conviction that there was a need to provide some continuing Christian fellowship for young people after they had left Sunday school. Following the missions of the American revivalist D. L. Moody, a number of Sunday schools began to run meetings for older young people who had been touched by what they had heard. The groups which met on week-night evenings were generally known as 'Christian Bands'.[11] In 1888, to encourage the development of these groups, the Sunday School Union brought Frances E. Clark, an American congregational pastor, to England. A few years earlier, when Clark was the minister in a church in Maine, he had called all the young people of the church together for a new kind of meeting. This was the start of one of the first church-based youth ministry programmes and it was known as 'The International Christian Endeavour Society'. Dean Borgman lists the organization's six main characteristics:

> All members must strictly commit themselves to:
>
> 1. The pledge – an active commitment to the service of Jesus Christ as Lord and actively participate in the Society's prayer meeting.
> 2. The monthly experience or consecration meeting.
> 3. Systematic, definite and regular committee work – training by doing.
> 4. Private devotion; daily prayer and Bible reading.
> 5. Denominational loyalty including attendance at mid-week prayer and Sunday evening services.
> 6. Interdenominational fellowship – an early Protestant and evangelical ecumenism described as 'a very complete and beautiful system of unions'.[12]

Clark's organization was to prove very effective in seeing young people become actively engaged in Christian life and the whole purpose of the organization was to encourage spiritual growth.[13] On arrival in England the movement, through the support of the Sunday School Union, soon spread. Young people found in Christian Endeavour an emphasis on active service and 'committee work' which was evidently at the time very attractive. Cliff is clear that the importance of Clark's influence in this country was that it moved the emphasis of work among young people away from 'telling' to 'discovering, training and sharing'.[14]

The YMCA and Christian Endeavour arose from the historical tendency within evangelicalism and particularly revivalism to form 'religious societies'. American revivalists from Charles Finney to Billy Graham were to exercise a surprising influence on the formation of Christian youthwork in England. Charles Finney and D. L. Moody were deeply influential in the emergence of George Williams' YMCA. Christian Endeavour was born out of Clark's familiarity with the principles laid down by the eighteenth-century evangelist Cotton Mather and the basic shape of the work was derived from his ideas.[15] Thus Christian youthwork is in this sense the direct application of ideas concerning religious societies to children and young people. Just as the YMCA originated as a religious society for shopworkers and the university Christian Union was a religious society for students, so the emergence of the youth fellowship can be seen as a movement of religious societies for teenagers and young people. It is this movement as it was developed by four organizations which forms the main focus of this chapter.

The Children's Special Service Mission

The Children's Special Service Mission or CSSM originated in 1867 when Josiah Spiers took a group from his Sunday school class to a service run by the American evangelist Payson Hammond in St John Street Chapel, London.[16] He was the first evangelist to hold special meetings for children.[17] At these meetings there were hymns with simple words and lively tunes, an informal style of preaching, and, most importantly, an expectation that children could, and should, respond personally to Christ.

Inspired by what he had seen, Spiers decided to hold

similar services in connection with his own local Sunday
schools in Islington. Others, it seems, were similarly inspired
by Hammond's work and a number of children's services
were started around London. Within a very short time these
groups got together and formed an organization for their
work which they called 'The Children's Special Service
Mission'.[18] The use of the words 'special service' is explained
in part because an Act of Parliament had recently been
passed which allowed the Church of England to hold
'special services', which were not specified by the Book of
Common Prayer. Spiers and the others took advantage of
this Act to create a new kind of service especially designed
for children. Despite the religiosity of the Victorian age
there was a desperate need for this kind of work:

> In spite of all their piety and their respect for family life,
> the Victorians had little understanding of children, and
> less of how to bring them up in the Christian life. Chil-
> dren from wealthier homes were expected to go with their
> parents to church dressed in their 'Sunday best', and sit
> quietly through the long adult services. In most homes
> there would be family prayers but again they would be
> formal and tedious, mostly very difficult for children to
> understand.[19]

To begin to cater for the special needs of children outside
regular church services and Sunday school was a significant
turning point in the Church's ministry. The Christian youth
group is in this respect a direct descendant of CSSM. To
begin to separate young people off from formal church
structures and create something uniquely for them was a
great step forward.

The work started with a broad appeal, but within a comparatively short space of time it became orientated toward
upper middle-class children. For while Spiers was able to
communicate with both rich and poor, as time went on
he began to concentrate his efforts on the more wealthy
sections of society. This development arose because it was
felt that much of the work current in the mid-nineteenth

century was focused on the poor and the needy. Ragged schools, Dr Barnardo's and Sunday schools were all aimed at the less well off, and it was felt that the rich also needed a special mission.[20]

A concern to cater for the particular needs of upper middle-class and wealthy people features regularly in the reasons for the development not only of CSSM but also Crusaders and Varsity and Public School (VPS) camps. It was on holiday that Spiers and his colleagues found the children of the wealthy to be most accessible and open to the preaching of the gospel. Work began to grow on the beaches of the seaside resorts which had recently become popular with the English upper middle classes. Spiers was

> . . . equally able to make friends with the children from wealthy homes whom he met on the beaches in the summer, or in the increasing number of 'drawing room meetings' arranged for them. As time went on he felt more and more called to work with these 'neglected children of the upper classes'.[21]

The services attracted, along with the children, a number of young people as well. Tom Bishop, one of Spiers' helpers, makes this clear:

> So often the Sunday School class leads the child to a certain point, and no further. They come regularly to Sunday School, but they do not come to Christ. At thirteen or fourteen they go to work, and fancy themselves to be too big for Sunday School – and so we lose them. It seems as if we have come to a time when the results of the past years of labour have to be gathered in. The work in these Children's Services is a reaping work.[22]

A good many of the 'special services' were held in the drawing rooms of the upper classes. These gatherings were strictly only for the invited, for it was felt that parents would object if they found their children sitting beside 'the rough and the ragged'.[23] So while Spiers and others continued to communicate with both the rich and the poor, the character

of CSSM was more and more moulded by what was acceptable in the drawing rooms of the wealthy. In Bayswater Dr
Gladstone, a relative of the Prime Minister, was host to a
meeting of one hundred boys in his drawing room. Pollock
quotes one observer as saying that 'everything unsuited to a
drawing room is avoided and the graceful courtesies of the
Christian life are encouraged'.[24]

CSSM was later to change its name to Scripture Union
and this change perhaps points to one of the most important characteristics of this ministry among children and
young people, the commitment to daily Bible reading. From
the late 1870s CSSM had produced Bible reading cards for
children. These Bible reading cards were to be seen as bringing about a 'Scripture Union' of children reading the same
portions of the Bible. In a short space of time the cards were
to spread throughout the world. It is the Scripture Union
which has perhaps been one of the chief ways in which the
evangelical spirituality based on daily reading of the Bible
has been maintained. In this respect innovation in the area
of youth and children's work has quite clearly shaped the
character of evangelical religion and spirituality more widely.

From the earliest days there was a link between the work
of the beach missions and evangelical student groups, especially those from the Cambridge Inter-Collegiate Christian
Union (CICCU) who would regularly work as helpers. One
of the pioneers at Cambridge, W. F. T. Hamilton, came into
contact with Spiers and CSSM while on holiday in Ilfra-
combe. He invited the CSSM worker Edwin Arrowsmith
to visit Cambridge and the result was that during the summer
of 1880 a full team of undergraduates were to lead a beach
mission. Thus began a long-honoured tradition of association between CSSM and university CUs. Douglas Johnson
refers to the three weeks of mission on the beaches with
CSSM as 'recognized' activities for CICCU students during
the long vacation.[25] The presence of these students, especially those who were athletes of one kind or another, drew
many children and young people to the Christian ministry
on the beaches. A rowing blue, in particular, had the drawing

power of a present-day pop star.[26] Arrowsmith along with his teams of Cambridge men was to create a pattern for the beach missions which was to continue well into this century.[27]

For the students and the growing movement in the universities and colleges these summer activities were becoming an essential part of their leadership development. In time it was to be widely recognized that involvement in work with children and young people was the best kind of training for Christian leaders. It was on these activities that patterns of preaching, sharing the faith one to one, and pastoral care were established.[28] One of the Cambridge men helping on a beach mission in 1885 was to remark that it was difficult to overestimate the influence that CSSM had on Christian life at the universities:

> Its robust manliness, which showed that the simplest form of presentation of the Gospel message was compatible with a delight in every healthy form of sport; its absolute allegiance to the Bible; not to speak of the truly non-denominational character of its work, gave it an influence which was remarkable.[29]

In the 1890s Tom Bishop, seeing the current changes in biblical scholarship, felt the need to create a clear declaration of faith. His long but lucid explanation of the basis of evangelical belief was a major factor in preserving CSSM in the more stormy years to come. When the Student Christian Movement (SCM) and CICCU were engaged in difficult discussions in the early 1900s, Sylvester believes that the existence of the CSSM declaration of faith proved to be very influential in helping the fledgeling IVF into a clear evangelical stance.[30]

CSSM was certainly a significant organization; in John Pollock's words, it was 'slowly changing an aspect of British religion'.[31] Not least, this work was to spawn the now popular form of song known as the chorus. Spiers was behind the original hymnbook for children, *Golden Bells or Hymns for our Children*, which was published in 1890.[32] In 1921 the *CSSM Chorus Book* was published and through this book chorus-singing became a recognized part of Christian work among young people across the world.[33] Through the songbooks, Bible reading notes, beach missions and special services, CSSM and later SU were to be at the forefront of evangelical youthwork. These innovations which were designed to reach out to young people, and most particularly to the children of the educated and the wealthy, were to do much to shape the culture of modern-day evangelicalism not only in England but also worldwide.

The Inter-Varsity Fellowship

Groups for evangelical students at universities have, according to Johnson, existed for over 300 years. In the United States, student-led groups owe their origin to the influence of Cotton Mather, who gathered young people together in 1716 in his church in Boston. In eighteenth-century Oxford the story of the Methodist Church and John Wesley is closely linked to the formation of a Holy Club.[34] The IVF, however, was to start life in Cambridge.

The roots of the Christian Union movement lie early in the nineteenth century when a group of Cambridge students started a Sunday school. For over fifty years the Jesus Lane Sunday School effectively acted as an informal Christian Union within the University bringing young men together for prayer, Bible study and service. Ministry among children and young people acted as the focus for evangelical life in the University. In 1877 the first Cambridge Inter-Collegiate Christian Union or CICCU came into existence.[35] The history of CICCU was not without controversy; conflict with the Student Christian Movement led to the refounding of the group and it was from this specifically evangelical union that the work spread to all the universities and colleges in the United Kingdom. In the early part of the twentieth century the Inter-Varsity Fellowship (later to be called the Universities and Colleges Christian Fellowship or UCCF) came into being to act as a support organization, linking the evangelical student groups which were mushrooming around the country. The activities at CICCU were largely to set the model for the other Christian Unions. The constitution was based on college-centred units joining together for joint prayer and witness to the university. A daily prayer meeting was supplemented by a Sunday evening 'evangelistic meeting' and a Saturday evening 'Bible reading'. Occasionally a 'missionary breakfast' would be held where a visiting missionary would talk about Christian work overseas.[36]

A much more detailed account of the origins and spread of the IVF is given elsewhere.[37] The growth of evangelical Christian Unions is mentioned here because it is an important piece of the puzzle in explaining not only the resurgence of evangelicalism in this country, but also the general character of the movement. University CUs were also to act as a pattern for the development of youthwork. The nature of evangelical youthwork has been greatly influenced by the work of the IVF. Douglas Johnson draws attention to the scale of the impact of CUs on British church life:

> Some of those prominent in leadership of churches, missionary societies and other Christian institutions of many varieties were first spiritually awakened and led to Christ in a university or college Christian Union. They learnt first to take responsibility in active service for Christ when serving on the committee of their student Christian Union.[38]

Some no doubt came to faith through other means, but given the fact that most clergy have until recently been expected to be graduates, it could probably be said that the majority of evangelicals ordained in the twentieth century have been to some extent influenced by their contact with a university CU. As with CSSM the work of the IVF is by its very nature focused on the educated and relatively privileged. Evangelicalism has its roots firmly placed in the rarified atmosphere of successful ministry amongst the English professional classes. Johnson is typical of many evangelical leaders in saying:

From twelve years' residence in Christ's College, Cambridge, and from many personal and official contacts since then with students of London and other Universities, I have come to regard the Christian Unions as in the front rank of the Christian forces of today. I do not see anywhere else, even in the Mission Field, more direct, personal and valuable spiritual work being done for the conversion of others, or for deepening the spiritual life: . . . I thankfully recognise that, in God's providence, I owe my own conversion and the most formative influence of my life to the Christian Union at Cambridge [the CICCU]; and I possess many college friends who could say the same.[39]

It is extremely common for evangelical clergy to acknowledge that it was within the Christian Union setting that they were not only brought to Christ, but also nurtured in that faith and then encouraged into leadership. As a nursery for Christian leaders the CU has had few rivals in the twentieth century. The university Christian Union needs to be seen therefore as one of the primary culture formers and carriers of English evangelicalism. It has been the atmosphere of the university and particularly of Oxbridge that has given the movement its particular accent within this country.

The Crusader Union of Bible Classes

At the start of the twentieth century it was the drawing rooms of the upper middle classes which again gave birth to another influential evangelical youth movement. In 1900 a young ordinand, Mr A. C. Kestin, was being entertained by a Mr and Mrs Saffery in Crouch Hill, North London. The Safferys were concerned for the young boys in the local area who were not being reached by the local Sunday schools.[40] They asked Kestin if he would be willing to run a Bible class for these boys. He agreed and in preparing the class he stumbled on what was to be the name of the future organization. As he was searching for suitable publicity Kestin came across a printing block with a medieval crusader etched upon it. This not only solved his printing and publicity problems, it also provided the inspiration to call his gathering 'The Crusaders Bible Class'. In 1901, when Kestin left for missionary work in India, he passed the Bible class to his friend and helper Herbert Bevington.

Within a very short period of time Crusader classes were started in other parts of the country. One of these was soon to boast over a hundred members. Bevington kept in contact with the growing number of groups and when Kestin returned in 1906 informal links were cemented into a more solid organization by the formation of 'The Crusaders' Union of Bible Classes'.[41] Crusaders was started with the explicit aim of reaching the comparatively wealthy and educated sections of society. The founding group were fairly blunt concerning the groups they wished to work among: 'Crusader classes aim at upper middle class boys attending public and private schools, and do not accept board school boys.'[42]

Following the lead of CSSM one of the first decisions of the Crusaders' Union was that there was a need for a joint chorus book for use in the classes. Joint activities between classes were soon starting and these included an annual rally in London and a regular programme of camping. The growth of the organization was very dramatic. In 1906 there were eleven classes with a membership of around 500 boys; by 1936 there were 224 classes with over 15,000 members. On the occasion of their first fifty years (1956) around 18,000 attended classes.

The early Crusader Bible classes tended to follow a regular pattern. Most would meet on what they described as neutral ground, not in premises owned by any one church. A hymn would start events, followed by a Bible reading. After a few notices there would be a gospel talk. This aspect of the work was seen as being of the utmost priority because it was the

> . . . opportunity for presenting the clear message of the Bible; and it is here that the experience of the leader tells most, as he seeks to put across great truths in a clear and systematic way, and to ensure a balance of Christian truth, in as wide a measure as possible is made plain.[43]

The classes were seen as a major evangelistic opportunity and boys brought to faith through the work were to be encouraged to form a connection with a local church. Crusaders was always meant to be non-partisan and inter-denominational, remaining independent from churches. Links were forged with CSSM, however, and in the early days *Crusader News* was sent out wrapped around the CSSM *Boys Magazine*.

The Crusaders' Union has had a considerable impact on evangelical church life. In the 1950s it was estimated that 259 former Crusaders had been ordained into the ministry in Great Britain and a further 2,500 were known to be actively engaged in Christian work outside Crusader classes. These figures indicate a significant influence in developing leaders within evangelicalism.

Varsities and Public School Camps

From a relatively early stage CSSM was to initiate Christian work among public school boys in England. In the 1880s a number of men from the University CUs of Oxford and Cambridge began to develop a concern for public schools. A magazine called *Our Boys Magazine* which was only for boys at prep schools and public schools was published in 1886. Two years later George Pilkington, or 'Pilks' as he was affectionately known, was appointed by CSSM to conduct missions to public schools.[44] The work was to move several steps further in 1892 when two Anglican ordinands studying at Ridley Hall in Cambridge decided to hold a camp for boys from public schools. They immediately set about appointing a president for their work along with a camp commandant and and a chaplain. The first camp was held at Rustingham near Littlehampton on the Sussex coast. The work was soon to grow and by 1895 around 400 boys were spread between a total of five camps. University camps for public schools quickly became an accepted part of the summer activities for CSSM.[45]

The university camps did not survive the devastation of

the First World War, but camps and houseparties were soon restarted in the 1920s and a number of these were for girls. In 1921 there was a successful camp in Switzerland and it was from this and other endeavours that 'Varsities and Public School Camps' was eventually formed as a part of CSSM in 1924. The key figure in the development of this work was a young Anglican clergyman called Eric Nash. Not being fond of his first name he was generally referred to as 'Bash'. He held his first camp in Seaford in 1929[46] and in 1932 he was appointed by CSSM to carry this work forward. During the Second World War the camps were moved away from the vulnerable south coast to Iwerne Minster in Dorset.[47]

Bash was convinced that there was a need for Christian work which focused on public school boys. It was felt that these young people were out of reach from the on-going pastoral work of a church and had been left uninspired (and perhaps unredeemed) by their experience of public school religion. In this sense the camps filled a gap in the existing Christian youthwork.[48] Bash's prayer was to claim the leading public schools for God's Kingdom[49] and to this end he concentrated his ministry on a small number of elite schools. Over time the camps were to multiply and spread their net a little wider to include prep school boys and groups from other less well-known public schools as well as including girls. The policy throughout was to create an atmosphere on the camps which echoed the prevailing culture of the wealthy classes:

> He aimed to concentrate his mission on a highly select clientele, the privileged and largely speaking the rich, who made up perhaps five per cent of our school population; not just the public schools but the top thirty or so. . . . Why this intense concentration? The first answer is a simple one. These schools contained a high proportion of the future leaders of the country. Therefore to reach them with the gospel opened the possibility of reaching future rulers, men with an immense influence over their contemporaries. A phrase often used was that our converts could be a 'multiplication table'.[50]

It has to be said that this policy was immensely successful. Large numbers of wealthy young people were to find
faith through 'Bash camps'. With pastoral care later
extended by Bash's helpers into university life many of these
young people were to go on in the faith and attain positions
of influence. Bash openly encouraged young men to seek
ordination in the Anglican Church and many of the
major figures in the postwar revival of evangelicalism within the Church of England were deeply influenced by his
work, including John Stott, Michael Green, David Watson
and Dick Lucas. At the time of his death *The Times* paid
tribute to this remarkable man:

> Bash . . . was a quiet, unassuming clergyman who never
> sought the limelight, hit the headlines or wanted prefer-
> ment; and yet whose influence within the Church of
> England during the last fifty years was probably greater
> than any of his contemporaries, for there must be hundreds
> of men today, many in positions of responsibility, who
> thank God for him, because it was through his ministry
> that they were led to a Christian commitment.[51]

Michael Green speaks for many when he says 'That single-
minded dedication to his Lord, which I saw so clearly in
Bash, has been the greatest single influence on my own
life.'[52]

Bash camps were thus not just a means of bringing public school boys to Christ: they were also a training ground
for the future leaders of the Church of England. Dick Lucas
makes it clear that in his mind the training offered by Bash
camps was far in advance of anything offered in the Church
of England's training colleges.[53] The meticulous attention to
detail, which is so often mentioned in reference to Bash,
stretched from the messages given in the daily Bible read-
ings, to the length of people's prayers, to the way in which a
person was dressed and even to the suitability of their future
wife. In all of these things Bash was far from being a tyrant
or autocratic character, but he had a firm hand on the way

that the camping ministry would introduce boys to the Christian faith. One of his great contributions to Christian youthwork was his emphasis on quality relationships, not only in the 'personal work' which helped many into the Kingdom, but also in the on-going care and support of young Christians and leaders. He made it clear that the difficult part of Christian work lay not so much in leading people to Christ but in nurturing them in the faith.[54]

Through the ministry of these camps Bash was to have a long and pervasive influence on the character of modern evangelicalism. In 1982 it was estimated that around 7,000 boys had passed through the Iwerne Minster camp alone.[55] An entire generation of evangelical leaders learned their trade by ministering on the camps. David Watson in his biography gives some clue as to the way that Bash camps formed his own approach to ministry in the Church:

> Undoubtedly the most formative influence on my faith during the five years at Cambridge was my involvement with the boys' houseparties, or 'Bash Camps' as they were generally known. Over these five years I went to no less than thirty-five of these camps: two at Christmas, two at Easter and three in the summer each year. They were tremendous opportunities for learning the very basics of Christian Ministry. Through patient and detailed discipling (although the word was never used) I learned, until it became second nature, how to lead a person to Christ, how to answer common questions, how to follow up a convert, how to lead a group Bible study, how to give a Bible study to others, how to prepare and give a talk, how to pray, how to teach others to pray, how to write an encouraging letter, how to know God's guidance, how to overcome temptation, and also most important, how to laugh and have fun as a Christian – how not to become too intense, if you like. I also gained excellent grounding in basic Christian doctrines, with strong emphasis being placed on clarity and simplicity. All this was constantly being modelled by those who were much more mature in

the faith, and I may never fully realise how much I owe to
the amazing, detailed personal help that I received over
those five years.[56]

The impact of this kind of training on someone like
David Watson is clear, but it is also true to say that large
numbers of church leaders and prominent lay people were
similarly affected. As youthwork in the Church of England
began to grow in the 1950s and 60s, it was inevitable that
lessons learned at Iwerne were applied in many parishes
around the country. Along with the method learned on the
camps, a set of behaviours, attitudes and values was also
passed on. What is also fairly clear is that the ethos of
public school life was deeply engrained in this particular
ministry. One example is the way that Bash steered clear of
what he called 'intensity'. Public schools were anxious that
the boys were not put under emotional pressure of any kind.
This anxiety must be seen in the context of what these
schools were originally set up to achieve. The upper middle
classes expected these schools to turn out boys who would
eventually become the future political and military leaders
of the country. Emotionalism, it was felt, was suspect in a
military commander or a Home Secretary. The public school
system is closely associated with the famous 'stiff upper lip'
of the English upper classes. Religion of the ecstatic or
mystical kind was seen as being deeply threatening to such
attitudes. Bash understood this and so any hint of emotional
intensity on the camp was immediately discouraged. As
Eddison tells it:

> How he disliked intensity! I still have a picture in my
> mind of an occasion at some conference, just before or
> after the war, when some soul-quaking talk had sent us all
> back to our rooms to think through what we had heard.
> Somehow it was comforting to learn that Bash had been
> found, propped up in bed, and reading 'Punch'.[57]

Perhaps it was because of this emphasis that when the
charismatic movement was to start to develop in the late
1960s and on into the 1980s despite the fact that many of

the leaders had their roots in Iwerne, Bash and the camps as a whole remained opposed to the new movement. The split within evangelicalism between those who are in favour of charismatic renewal and those who remain opposed to it can be explained to a certain extent by these allegiances. The public school suspicion of intensity has continued to prevail in Iwerne and at present its leaders are very much against the charismatic movement.

An Emerging Pattern

The style and the methods of today's evangelical youthwork have emerged from a rich and exciting history. The origins of the youth fellowship in particular are closely linked to the work of CSSM, IVF, Crusaders and VPS. These four organizations share a number of features and it is these common factors which shed a good deal of light on our present situation.

Success with the Educated and Middle Classes

Evangelical youthwork finds its origins and its most natural context among the wealthy and the educated. While it is wrong to say that evangelicals have chosen to work solely with the educated and wealthy sections of the population, it is also the case that a number of influential and formative ministries have intentionally concentrated on the relatively privileged, arguing that the 'rich' were in some way neglected by the Church. At the time there may have been some justification for this. Evangelical work among the poorer groups in society, however, has failed to thrive or gain very much momentum, despite a good deal of effort.[58] We are therefore left with methods and patterns of youthwork which have evolved almost exclusively in the rarified context of public school and Oxbridge life.

The revival in postwar evangelicalism has happened primarily among the middle classes because of the success of organizations such as CSSM, IVF, Crusaders and VPS.

Where youthwork has been successful it has bred distinctive traditions which are intimately connected to the context from which they have emerged. These traditions therefore carry the particular 'accent' of the educated upper-class context from which they emerged. While there is great deal to celebrate and embrace in this history it has to be said that our inheritance leaves us with a good many problems. We currently find ourselves in a situation where the predominant method of work among young people, the youth fellowship, seems to be ill-suited to outreach beyond a relatively narrow group. In seeking to reach young people who do not fit the current social mix of the Church, we need a fresh wave of creativity. Our task is to work with a variety of social groups and in doing this we could do little better than to follow the example of the pioneers of evangelical youthwork. It was the genius of people like Spiers, Kestin, Bash and the students at CICCU that they found the most natural and appropriate ways to share the faith in particular social contexts. The way ahead lies less in copying their methods than in learning from their creativity. We, like them, need to be willing to take risks and imagine new patterns of work in response to the opportunities provided by the culture of the people we seek to evangelize and according to the guidance of the Holy Spirit.

Temporary Communities

The activities of Christian youthwork have been characteristically camps, mission, houseparties and university life. In more recent times festivals and large celebratory gatherings have been added to this list. Evangelical spirituality has been formed outside the flow of mainstream life. The patterns of worship, prayer, service, fellowship and organization which have grown in the temporary communities have had a great influence on the subculture of evangelical church life. The stresses and strains which evangelicalism is experiencing at present are not entirely unconnected to the context in which the spirituality of the movement was developed. The study of youthwork is therefore essential to any enterprise which seeks to address the young people falling away from the Christian faith as they enter adult life. Young people and students are marginal to the everyday economic realities of life. Is it any wonder that a spirituality which has been so deeply influenced by work among adolescents is experiencing problems when it seeks to be relevant to older people?

Developing a Tradition

From the earliest times there has been a strong link between the training of leaders and evangelical youthwork. CSSM, IVF, Crusaders and VPS have all laid considerable emphasis on helping young people to grow into leadership roles. The Church in general has clearly benefited enormously from this aspect of their work. Many clergy and lay leaders have grown into ministry through their involvement in youthwork. The values, attitudes and behaviours of the evangelical faith have been largely generated, transmitted and maintained by youthwork. Because this youthwork has been focused on one section of society, the result has been that the subculture of English evangelicalism has been limited to this group.

If, then, evangelicals are to be successful in reaching out to other groups in society, they have to learn to contextualize not simply the methods of outreach, but the whole shape of evangelical spirituality and church life. Reaching the unchurched is a radical task involving imagination, innovation and risk. There is a sense in which the current expressions of evangelical spirituality need to be unlearned in order that they may be re-expressed within new social and cultural contexts. As youthwork has been the key to the development of evangelical subculture in the past, it is also the key to its future. We need to understand where we have come from if we are ever to get a grip on where we should be going. Furthermore, as young people have been the key to the development of evangelical culture and identity in the past, they are very likely to be so in the future. If this is the case, then the study of youthwork and youth culture can no longer remain marginal to theological enquiry, research and teaching. Youth ministry and the study of popular culture need to be drawn into the centre of teaching at theological colleges, instead of being treated as one-off sessions or ignored altogether.

Paradoxically, while youthwork is largely overlooked in theological colleges, it is still the case that many evangelical ordinands and clergy continue to regard their training on camps and houseparties as the most useful and formative part of their preparation for ministry. The result of this, however, is that such training is largely unreflective and lacks the broad examination associated with other aspects of the Church's life. If it is right to say that youthwork is one of the key areas which has made evangelicalism what it is, and if youthwork also contributes to the tribal affiliations which make up the current scene, how can we exclude it from serious theological reflection? Alongside this, the re-alization that youthwork might be at the heart of the isolation of evangelicalism within one social group should convince us that theological examination of the work is an urgent necessity. Youthwork is not an optional extra for evangelical theological education. It is central.

Chapter 2

The 'Grand Strategy'

Between the wars, according to Bebbington, evangelicals hit upon a 'grand strategy' which was designed to secure the future for them.[1] He quoted Bishop Taylor Smith's comment: 'Concentrate on young people, they will bring you in the greatest dividends.' Smith saw youthwork as the means whereby evangelicals might reply to the onslaught of liberalism. To win a student for Christ in IVF circles was to win a 'keyman'. Theological dispute was seen as a distraction from the vital task of winning the next generation for Christ.[2]

It was this vision which inspired a new wave of evangelical leaders to invest time and energy in youthwork. With the inspiration of pioneer evangelical organizations behind them, they were to apply the lessons they had learned in churches up and down the country, and to a wider social mix of young people. The history of youth fellowship work in England is therefore largely the story of a movement downwards, as successive leaders attempted to adapt approaches developed in work amongst the upper middle classes to those further down the social scale. The confidence with which this enterprise was embarked upon was dimmed only by the slow realization that a faith contextualized within the culture of the upper middle classes does not travel well.[3]

As evangelical youthwork began to be successful in reaching beyond the predominantly public school and Oxbridge context from which it was born, it slowly began to change. Work among the more academic 'grammar school types' demanded new ways of running meetings and reading the

Bible and new styles of leadership. Evangelicals engaged in youthwork were to look for inspiration to the world of education and the new thinking which was entering schools. Through SU and other groups, teachers and educationalists were to begin to adapt existing practice to young people in the state schools.[4]

These changes in youthwork began to shape the culture of evangelicalism itself, and they help to explain how the evangelical movement in the 1990s has come to be a broader and more diverse movement. As attention shifted to work among young people who were outside the relatively privileged social groups attracted by existing work, it became evident that there were limits on evangelistic activity. Young people from what were known as secondary modern schools presented a challenge which eventually proved to be a bridge too far. The key to understanding this failure of the evangelical church to reach lower-, middle- and working-class young people lies, in part, in the evolution of the youth fellowship.

The Creation of the Youth Fellowship

The youth fellowship is by no means an exclusively evangelical invention. During the early part of this century there was a widespread move within the Church to establish groups for young people. The youth fellowship evolved from a growing feeling that young people beyond Sunday school age, that is around ten, and in an Anglican context following Confirmation, should be gathered together to continue their Christian education. This would be 'education not given at high pressure over a short period (as in a Confirmation class), but continuously over years as part of the normal routine of the adolescent's life'.[5] The youth fellowship, according to Taylor, would attract young people where the older style Bible classes and Communicants' Guilds broke down.

The youth fellowship was to be for those young people who already attended church, the religiously committed, as opposed to the youth club, which was for the mass of unattached young people.[6] The meetings would bring together those young people over the age of fourteen who had been confirmed and were too old for Sunday school or Bible classes. Pioneers in developing church-based youth fellowships were a group called the Anglican Young People's Association (AYPA – now known as Anglican Youth).

AYPA was originally started in Canada by Canon Brown who was Rector of St James' Church in Paris, Ontario at the turn of the century.[7] The work spread to Britain in the 1930s under the leadership of a Canadian theological student, and grew rapidly in wartime Britain. In 1939 there were around thirty-six branches and by 1948 this had grown to 300.[8] The AYPA was based on four main principles: worship, work, fellowship and edification. Members were also encouraged to take part in church life by worshipping there each Sunday. 'Work' was to be expressed both in their regular employment and in parish affairs: 'Generally speaking the branch will try to be the handmaid of the parish priest'.[9] 'Fellowship' was to be an all-embracing approach to every aspect of life, while 'edification' was primarily worked out through what was termed 'Corporate Mental Action' (CMA). Each meeting of the branch would be organized according to the principles of CMA. There were five parts to every meeting: 'Prepare, picture, ponder, pray and promise'. AYPA's sophisticated programme for doctrinal instruction, *Unto a Full Grown Man*, details meeting plans which follow this five-point pattern in some detail, including suggestions for hymns and prayers. *Unto a Full Grown Man* is extremely comprehensive and it runs to ten volumes which deal with every major doctrine and biblical theme, as well as aspects of morality and the Church's year.[10] AYPA were very serious about instruction in the faith:

> The aim of Corporate Mental Action is to enable young Christians whatever may be their work in the world or place in society, to come as members of one living and active Church, to think together, talk together and pray together about Christian dogma and its application to daily life.[11]

The AYPA was to be deeply influential on Anglican youthwork. During the 1930s and 40s and on into the 1950s, many parishes of a high and broad church tradition were to run fellowship groups along the lines advocated by the Association. C. H. Plummer writing in 1948 sees the youth fellowship as the gathering place for the 'inner group of young people in the parish'.[12] In 1955 The Church of England Youth Council (CEYC) published its report *The Church and Young People*, which stressed the value of youth fellowship work. However, it also pointed out that they were to be found mainly in the suburbs and in the cities.[13] In rural areas the CEYC considered the approach to be a little 'intellectual for the rustic mind'.[14]

Youth fellowships were not without their critics, especially among those Christians who were advocating a partnership with the State in the establishment of what came to be called 'the youth service'. Plummer, reviewing Taylor's *Youth Fellowship Work* in the CEYC journal *The Review*, points out that 'The book was written for a particular constituency and therefore must have but a limited value for those who are not of that constituency.'[15] There was a body of opinion which was concerned that the youth fellowship approach would not reach what was termed 'the 99', that is those outside the Church.[16] Despite these reservations, in Anglican circles youth fellowship work, and in particular, the AYPA, continued to have an influential role even into the 1960s.[17]

Pathfinders and the Young Churchmen's Fellowship: The Early Years

Evangelical churches were also active in youthwork between the wars. Most churches would have had some form of Bible class for young people over the age of ten or eleven who had left Sunday school.[18] The Bible class tradition had been continued by organizations such as Crusaders and Covenanters.[19] Many churches continued to run Bible classes even into the 1960s,[20] but it was in 1935 that the first 'Pathfinder Group' was formed by Herbert Taylor, a young curate from Emmanuel, Tolworth.[21] Taylor's innovation was to build on the traditions associated with Bible classes, and in particular Crusaders, and integrate them into the life of a parish church.

Pathfinders

Herbert Taylor wanted to find a lively and attractive follow-on to Sunday school for the children from the new estate which surrounded his church:

> He sensed that God was speaking to him about the youngsters in his church. It was of the utmost importance to provide a group which would present Christ in a way appropriate to their age group, and that would give them a sense of belonging to the wider family of the Church.[22]

Possibly influenced by Crusaders, Herbert Taylor devised a simple lapel badge based on a shield containing a St Andrew's cross. The work grew extremely quickly and soon there were two groups, one for older young people and one for the younger group. Alongside the groups a club was started and sports activities were introduced. Pathfinders began to spread beyond the parish. At first this happened informally when friends visited the church and took the idea back to their own churches. Around twenty groups started in this way between 1935 and 1953, mainly in the South of England.[23]

Pathfinders was to be formally made a national movement when Canon Tom Livermore suggested that the collection of groups linked with Hebert Taylor join together under the Church Society. This they did in the 1950s and Richard Bowdler, who was Tom Livermore's curate, became the first full-time secretary. Pathfinders, which catered for young people aged between ten and fifteen, fitted neatly into the

Church Society, because it dealt with the age group just below that targeted by the society's other youth organization, the Young Churchmen's Fellowship.

The Young Churchmen's Fellowship

In 1930 a small group of young evangelicals met to discuss the possibility of starting a movement for 'young churchmen'. This new movement was to 'join together young evangelicals to educate the youth of the Church of England in the maintenance of the Church's doctrine as expressed in the 39 Articles and to seek closer co-operation with Christians of other denominations'.[24] Under the chairmanship of the Revd Hugh Gough, the group began to work out a shape for this new organization. Links were soon established with the Crusader Union and the IVF became the source of a doctrinal basis. An official link was soon made with the National Church League, the evangelical organization which later became the Church Society.[25]

The committee decided that a public meeting should be held and letters were sent to the presidents of CICCU, the London Inter-Faculty Christian Union (LIFCU) and the Oxford Inter-Collegiate Christian Union (OICCU).[26] Advertisements were also placed in Crusader and CSSM magazines. On 25 June 1931, 200 people gathered at Church House for the launch of what was at first termed the Young Churchmen's Movement ('Movement' was subsequently replaced by 'Fellowship'). At this first meeting ninety-seven people are reported to have signed up immediately and plans were soon in place to run a series of lunchtime services at St Stephen's, Wallbrook. Activities in the first few years included a weekend conference, promotional meetings in Oxford, Liverpool and Cambridge, and a mission in Felixstowe led by the President of CICCU, R. J. Cobb, at which many young people came to faith. The minutes of the YCM record that 'young people learnt that in these days we need not be ashamed of the Gospel of Christ'.[27] Following the mission a number of Bible classes were established for young people who had responded to Christ.

In the early days the YCM was primarily an organization to which individual 'Churchmen' belonged. Despite the name it was made clear right from the start that women were to be admitted into, 'full membership of the movement without any restrictions'.[28] Given the success of the London mid-week lunchtime meetings, it is clear that most of the members would have been in their first jobs in the City or in the professions. In 1934, however, it was decided that 'associates' from young people's fellowships might be allowed to join, in groups of not less than ten, for a subscription charge of 6d. The first group to join under this arrangement was from Christ Church, Beckenham, closely followed by the young people's fellowship from Chorley in Lancashire, who had seventy-five members.[29] Within a couple of years the needs of young people's fellowships in the parishes were increasingly occupying the minds of the committee. In 1935 a syllabus for groups was drawn up and a book entitled *Youth: A Challenge* was to be circulated round affiliated parishes. As part of affiliation the movement offered to supply a speaker for meetings and use of the library, and a study circle was started.

Reaching Out with the Youth Fellowship

After the Second World War evangelical youthwork had established a pattern: Bible classes or Pathfinders for those aged between ten and fourteen, and a youth fellowship for the fourteen-plus group. Each age range might also have associated with it some form of youth club which would attract both the committed and the uncommitted. By the 1950s this pattern was being reproduced in parishes around the country by a generation of young evangelical clergy, many of whom had themselves been deeply influenced by evangelical youthwork.

The initiative came first from the Pathfinders, where

summer camps became a focus for growth. The first Pathfinder camp, which was held at Shanklin, Isle of Wight,
came about when Keith Weston, then curate at Emmanuel,
Northwood, invited Herbert Taylor to be commandant at a
camp. Hebert Taylor wrote back to him saying, 'Yes as long
as it's a Pathfinder camp'.[30] Pathfinder camps were to be
greatly influenced by those already being run for public
school boys. The following is an extract from the publicity
brochure for the 'Pathfinder Camp for Boys at Teignmouth'
in 1954, led by Herbert Taylor. Among his officers on the
camp was a young Mr M. A. Baughen who we are told acted
as 'subby'.

> We shall have a full staff of experienced officers in Camp,
> many of them University Students. Boys will sleep in
> Bell Tents with their Tent Officers, and there will be
> two marquees, one for meals and the other for Games,
> Sing-Songs and Prayers. The food will be in the hands of
> competent ladies, and the supply will be good and plenti-
> ful. There will be a Canteen with those extras boys enjoy,
> and a Camp Bank, where all valuables may be put. The
> health of the boys will be under the care of the Camp
> Medical Officer who will be in touch with the local
> Doctor.

> The Day will be spent in Games, Bathing and Outings,
> and there will be freedom of choice with fitting supervis-
> ion. Particular care will be taken over bathing and no boy
> will be allowed to bathe without an Officer present. There
> will be a Camp rag 'newspaper', compiled by Officers and
> boys, and Sing-Songs for all who desire to take part in
> them.

> It is a Christian Camp and so Prayers will be held daily,
> and Services on Sundays, that through these and the
> example and conversation of the Officers, the boys may
> be helped to find the Lord Jesus Christ as their Saviour
> and Friend, and the Secret of true Christian character.
> We shall endeavour to put the Christian Faith across in a

way that boys can understand and appreciate, and we shall set ourselves to answer boys' natural questions on this important matter.

H. C. TAYLOR Commandant, Christ Church Vicarage, Orpington, Kent.[31]

Richard Bowdler, who was himself a graduate of Bash camps, was key to the invigorating activity within Pathfinders in the 1950s and 60s. Soon a series of annual rallies was started and a four-year teaching syllabus for the groups was designed. Under Bowdler's leadership a number of Bash campers began to get involved with Pathfinders and later with the YCF, including Michael Green, Timothy Hoare and Kenneth Habershon.

The YCF began to grow and develop as increasing numbers of Pathfinders moved into the older age bracket. Bowdler saw the importance of there being a vibrant follow-up to Pathfinders and so he encouraged first Timothy Hoare and then Kenneth Habershon to become full-time secretaries.[32] In the 1950s YCF held two or three annual camps and houseparties, and the number of camps began to grow steadily. In 1966 the Limpsfield houseparty was started by Habershon. The style of this work built on lessons learned at Iwerne Minster, and the houseparties went from strength to strength. As the work grew, new houseparties were started by Andrew Cornes and Don Humphries among many others.

The key to the growth of YCF, however, was the work in parishes around the country. Each parish would have had a slightly different emphasis.[33] Central to parish work was the establishing and maintaining of a committed core or nucleus within the youth fellowship. The camps complemented the efforts of curates and lay people in churches all around the country by providing a spiritual highlight once or twice a year for key young people. The camps were also important because they served as the chief means whereby leaders were trained to work with young people. In this way YCF camps and houseparties provided the opportunity for young evangelical Christians to gain their first taste of leadership. There can have been very few Anglican evangelical leaders who were curates or students between the mid-1960s and 1980s who did not sharpen their skills by helping at a CYFA or Pathfinder Venture. In this way a whole host of leaders arose from this ministry including Michael Baughen, Michael Saward, Gavin Reid, George Hoffman, John Goldingay, Richard Bewes, David Huggett, Garth Hewitt, David Gillett and many others. It is a tribute to the strength of this tradition that the present leadership at CYFA can trace their ministry back through a network of camps and houseparties to Limpsfield and through Limpsfield and Kenneth Habershon to Eric Nash.[34]

The Inter-School Christian Fellowship

The development of parish-based youthwork was part of a wider attempt by evangelicals to reach beyond their traditional upper middle-class constituency. Evangelical Christians were well aware of the class-specific nature of many of the existing models of youthwork. In the 1950s CSSM joined together with IVF and Crusaders to inaugurate the 'Inter-School Christian Fellowship' (ISCF).[35] It was the clear intention of this group to extend the successful ministry in public schools into the state school sector.

The chosen method of working was to encourage the setting-up of a Christian Union in every school. Christian groups, many run by Christian teachers, were already starting to spring up in state schools. The aim of this initiative was to encourge this development, but there was also a concern to apply lessons learned in the universities to a school setting. The key to this thinking was that groups, as far as possible, should be pupil-run. The 'Inter-School Christian Fellowship' could therefore be seen as a junior branch of the 'Inter-Varsity Fellowship'.[36] In the early days the work was pioneered by two full-time secretaries, one of whom was Branse Burbridge, a well-known World War II fighter pilot. ISCF laid emphasis on 'balanced Christian character and practical Christian living'[37] and the initiative soon spread through many schools in the country.

Following the lead of other evangelical youth organizations, ISCF also began to run its own holidays and camps. 'Interschool holidays', as they were known, were extremely well attended. Adapting to the needs of young people from state schools, new kinds of adventure activities as well as craft and study holidays were added to the traditional houseparty model. But, whatever the activity, as Sylvester notes,

> . . . it helped to forge the young people and their leaders into a unified group where it was natural to speak of the way Christ could meet man's deepest needs. The activities were not seen as 'bait' to attract young people to camp so that they could hear the gospel, but as an essential part of the process of building relationships, through which Christ could be shared.[38]

In the early days some interschool camps were to hang on to a more exclusive policy and made it clear that young people who attended secondary modern schools were not accepted. The 'Inter-School Cambrian Camp' brochure for 1955, for instance, carries the following notice: 'Boys Eligible: Those aged 13½ years and over who in June are at Public, Private or Secondary Grammar Schools'.[39] These attitudes, it must be stressed, were far from typical in ISCF.

One of the key factors in the spread of school-based Christian Unions was the influx of evangelicals who had trained as teachers.[40] In the postwar period, Christian colleges began to concentrate their efforts on teacher training and in particular on the development of religious education. It was these young Christian teachers, many of whom would have been involved in college-based Christian groups, who were to set up CUs in their schools. In connection with the rise in numbers of Christian teachers, a number of evangelical groups associated with schools were to emerge, and eventually the Christian Education Fellowship, the Teachers' Prayer Bond, and ISCF together set up the Association of Christian Teachers (ACT).

With the basic pattern of youthwork established by the 1960s evangelical clergy were set to turn their sights towards outreach. The key question was how to spread the message of Christ among young people of a variety of backgrounds. The 1944 Education Act instituted a two-tier secondary school system throughout England and Wales. At the age of eleven pupils would take the 'eleven-plus' exam. The results of this test would determine whether a pupil was to go on to a secondary modern or a grammar school. According to Arthur Marwick, 'The route to better jobs and to higher education was through the grammar schools; the secondary modern school was the route to the traditional working-class occupations.'[41] By the mid-1960s evangelicals were beginning to address the problem of how to evangelize young people who were attending secondary modern schools.

In the secondary modern schools of the day a number of Christian groups had been established. It was found that in a less academic context the groups were best run by teachers, and so there was a shift away from the pupil-led approach which seemed to operate most successfully among sixth-formers and in the grammar schools. In 1959 Michael Eastman was employed to provide on-going support and networking for the groups already established in secondary modern schools.[42] He was particularly influenced by current educational thinking, drawing on Richard Hoggart's *The Uses of Literacy*[43] and the new ideas in religious education associated with Loukes and Goldman.[44] As well as offering support for already established groups, Eastman was given the task of finding the best ways of working in this new environment: 'I was encouraged to try to pioneer new approaches. At first we tried to adapt what existed. I soon realised that this was not possible.'[45]

The new ideas generated by Eastman and others were to be formative in the development of evangelical work with young people but they were also to lead to significant controversy within SU.

Those behind initiatives within the state school sector, who often shared a background in teaching, were concerned that the faith should be seen in less elitist terms. Many of these new leaders came to Christian work with a degree of suspicion or even antipathy for private education.[46] Evangelical youthwork, as it travelled into the grammar schools and secondary moderns, was gradually changing. In adapting evangelical youthwork to a new social context workers were starting to innovate and adopt new methods of working. The slightly more egalitarian feel of the state school groups led to conflict within SU between ISCF and the more traditional VPS. ISCF, faced with a different clientele, were much more inclined to follow the educational thinking current in the state school system which encouraged open discussion. As Sylvester points out, 'The climate of thought was different, too, as the more traditional teaching methods in the public schools meant that boys were more ready to sit and listen. Some VPS staff thought that the 'open-ended' discussion-type Bible study of the ISCF was too vague to be effective.'[47]

This controversy, which to a large extent still remains within SU, points to the way that mission among young people was again starting to shape evangelical faith in quite fundamental ways. Despite Sylvester's tendency to minimize the nature of the disagreement, the fissure revealed in this discussion is a familiar one as it continues on into the current debate between Open Evangelicals and Proclamation Trust and the more recent emergence of Reform. What is particularly revealing in these discussions within SU is that they indicate how the different shades of opinion within evangelicalism are closely connected to the emergence, and enduring character, of particular youth ministries.

The perception of faith as primarily conceptual, and conveyed by authoritative teaching from the Bible, was reinforced by the context within which VPS ministry had evolved. But what was starting to emerge from those working in state schools was a shared and more experiential approach to Christian truth. For both of these groups within SU there was a concern to maintain a thoroughly evangelical approach to the Bible and faith. The cultural contexts in which they were doing this, however, were starting to have an impact on what evangelical faith looked like. In the current atmosphere of conflict and discussion within the evangelical constituency there needs to be some reflection on the way in which different emphases within the movement have evolved from mission in particular social contexts. To ignore the centrality of youthwork to this discussion is to miss the crucial role which it has played in creating the various theological expressions and party allegiances which characterize our present situation.

The Thinking Behind the Strategy

By the 1960s evangelical youthwork was starting to define itself and lay down a framework for future development. In 1965 three books were published outlining the evangelical approach to youth work: *Towards Tomorrow's Church* by David Watson, *Christian Youth Groups* by Michael Saward and Michael Eastman, and *Old Faith, Young World* by David Winter. What emerges from these is a remarkably clear and uniform vision of the way forward for evangelical youthwork.

All three publications are keen to define church-based work as being distinct from secular youth clubs. Winter makes it clear that while it is possible to follow a Christian course in a local authority project, in a club in a church setting it is important to maintain a strong and committed group of church-going young people:

> The only effective answer is the Christian nucleus: the members, young people themselves, who are committed Christians and share the leader's vision for the work. If the nucleus is a substantial size – say, a third or half membership – and consistent in its witness, the leader's task is made much more simple. Christian standards should not

have to be imposed from above, but should grow naturally from within the membership.[48]

David Watson is also clear that the key to success is the committed nucleus of Christians. In his parish in St Mark's, Gillingham a pattern of a youth fellowship on Sunday evenings in one of the leaders' homes, and a week-night club in the church hall was established. The club was seen as a place where the Christian young people could evangelize their peers:

> It is no good trying to take on a large and pagan club, and then infuse a little bit of Christianity into it. Any club leader will tell you that this simply does not work. By this I do not wish to suggest for a moment that Christians have no place in a local youth club which is professedly 'secular'. Of course not! . . . But for an effective setting for evangelism within a church-run organisation, a Christian nucleus is virtually essential.[49]

The nucleus, according to Watson, would affect the whole atmosphere of the club so that outsiders would 'at once sense warmth, love, life'.

Michael Eastman and Michael Saward are forthright in their assessment that Christian youthwork in the mid-1960s was divided into two groups. The first group had lost their nerve and the second had found theirs. The former seemed to have 'lost confidence in the power of the historic gospel to transform young lives' and because of this they never mention religion. The latter 'appears to be gaining in confidence in the belief that only a clear and simple proclamation of the call to costly discipleship will produce the calibre of Christians able to stand up to the secularization and materialism of modern society.'[50] It would seem that this second group represented the attitude of many evangelicals who were developing a passion for youthwork at the time. The authors, however, are also of the belief that there is a place for evangelical Christians to be involved in Local Education Authority youthwork. Such people, however, should be well trained and sent out as missionaries into secular clubs.

Through the work of Frontier Youth Trust (FYT) Eastman was to pursue these ideas in much greater depth.[51]

Given the efforts which had gone into the reorganization of LEA-sponsored youthwork in the postwar period there was a need for the Church to look to nurture its own young people. The Church 'must also offer to its own young people a new kind of Christian youth work – a call to disciplined living, to costly fellowship, to active evangelism, to training in the Lord's service. This must be the prime task of the Christian youth group in the future.'[52] There was little to be gained from a group which was overrun by 'an undisciplined crowd': 'There is only one way and that is to build up a nucleus of converted Christian members who will set the whole tone of the group.'[53]

Evangelicals in the mid-1960s, it seems, were generally of one mind concerning youthwork. The local church should focus its attention on establishing a group for the committed since there was a far better chance of helping and winning towards Christian discipleship boys and girls with prior association of some kind with the Church.[54] Regular outreach at a local level would involve running a club or some other activity (coffee bars were much in vogue). This would perhaps be supplemented by joining with other groups for rallies, or evangelistic campaigns. The foundation of all this work remained the commitment to building a strong nucleus group attached to the local church. There were, however, limitations to this strategy.

These three youthwork books published in 1965 consider the problems that certain young people can prove to be.[55] David Watson gives a good deal of consideration to those young people who were in 'gangs'.[56] Saward and Eastman divide young people into three main groups, pointing out that most young people could be seen as being 'average'; they focus particular attention on the two extreme ends of the spectrum: 'the bright group' and 'the dull group'. The dull group, we are told, are semi-literate and incapable of sustained discussion because they rarely have the facts at their disposal. In noting that these young people will primarily think in concrete terms the authors point out that this poses serious problems for protestant religion where a conceptual presentation of the faith has been regarded as the norm.[57] Despite some reservations we must have with the terms, the spirit of these observations was well ahead of its time and is just as relevant in our current context.

The Primacy of the Youth Fellowship

As evangelical youthwork emerged out of the 1960s the youth fellowship had become the basic pattern in churches and schools up and down the country. Present-day youth ministry owes a great debt to the generation of clergy and teachers who gave so much to reaching young people for Christ. The establishment of church youth programmes and school-based Christian groups was to add considerable momentum to the growth of evangelical churches. Leaders were being trained at camps and houseparties and by lead-ing school CUs. These young people were to generate through their activities many of the cultural aspects which we see in contemporary evangelicalism. Through SU and other groups a greater sophistication in educational theory and practice gradually spread beyond youthwork to many areas of evangelical church life, including discussion-based home groups, Sunday school material, and resources for worship.[58] In all these it was the growth in youthwork which led to an explosion in creativity and the numerical growth which characterizes the current scene.

The legacy of this remarkable period, however, has with-in it limitations which have a direct impact on the ability of the Church to reach out to a wide variety of young people in present-day society. The problems were associated with the importance that was placed upon the youth fellowship. The consensus was fairly clear that the way forward lay in developing a strong core of committed Christians who would then reach out to their friends and attract them into the group. The problem was that even in the 1960s some young people did not seem to fit easily into these groups.

Reaching the 'secondary modern type' was seen as particularly problematic. Efforts were made to address this issue,
but in the main the evangelical church tended to concentrate
on those groups with whom it was most successful. Over the
years this tendency has become even more marked. The
problem is that like tends to attract like. There are limits to
the variety of young people who can be contained within one
youthwork programme. When outreach relies on Christian
young people attracting their friends, there are many young
people who for one reason or another fall outside these
social contacts and are untouched by the gospel. These
problems to a great extent remain with us today. The task of
youth ministry in the next few years is not only to address
the needs of Christian young people and those who socially
fit the mix within our existing youth fellowships, but also to
devote considerable effort to finding new ways to reach
those beyond the fringes of the Church.

These questions are far from being new or original. Those
within the youthwork world soon realized that their methods
of work were leaving significant sections of the population
untouched by the gospel. Over the last thirty years a
number of youthworkers have therefore devoted themselves
to working on what they call 'the frontiers'. SU was again to
lead the way in this new movement of urban mission and it
is to this story that we turn in the next chapter.

Chapter 3

Pushing the Frontiers

In the late 1950s a generation of evangelicals turned their attention to youthwork in urban areas. If the youth fellowship was mainly for the 'grammar school' type, the 'open' youth club was the method favoured for reaching the secondary modern young person. 'Open' youthwork was so named because it was meant to be open to those young people who did not attend church. It was also seen as being 'open' because it did not place any conditions on attendance. Reaching out to young people in the inner cities, and on the estates which were increasingly to ring urban development, was to prove costly and deeply challenging. The story of frontier youthwork, as it became known, is characterized by Christian fortitude and sacrifice, often in tough and uncompromising situations. From the commitment and faithful service of these youth leaders a significant tradition of evangelical mission and social engagement in urban contexts emerged.[1]

Urban mission amongst young people has, more often than not, found itself marginalized within the evangelical churches. While at the level of national consultations and international conferences evangelicals have embraced a more holistic approach to social care, local churches have largely abandoned the youth club as a practical approach to outreach. Evangelical theology has been broadened by contact with urban mission, but at the level of practice this work has often been ignored by mainstream evangelicalism. As the youth fellowship has grown, the youth club has declined. The story of frontier youthwork is therefore far from being a

success story. The work of frontier youth leaders is probably
best seen as being the prophetic conscience of the Church.

Urban mission has a long history stretching back to the
university and public school settlement and club initiatives
of the last century. In the 1960s a new generation of evangelical leaders were drawn to places such as the Cambridge
University Mission in Bermondsey and Shrewsbury House
in Liverpool. Others started projects of their own. A fresh
concern for urban mission was being born and at the heart
of this was the Mayflower Family Centre in Canning Town.
The work of David Sheppard, George Burton and others in
the Mayflower team influenced many in the evangelical
wing of the Church to follow their lead into work among
young people in urban areas. The Mayflower also had a
major influence on the growth of the Frontier Youth Trust.[2]
The evolution of the work in Canning Town has been
extremely well documented by those most closely involved.
This chapter uses their material as a case study of the
evolution of evangelical urban youthwork over the last thirty
years. It also illustrates more general observations on the
significance and limitations of this tradition of youthwork.[3]

The Mayflower and the Stirring of a Tradition

In 1958 David Sheppard moved to the Mayflower. At St
Mary's, Islington, where he had previously been a curate,
Sheppard had seen how ineffectual the Bible class or youth
fellowship approach to youthwork had proved to be with
inner city young people. What was needed was a new way
of working. His vision was of Christian people committed
to living long term in the inner cities, and thereby providing
a place which could act as neutral ground, or a bridge, where
friendship and relationships could develop.[4] Central to the
plan to reach out to young people was the development of a
youth club:

> Many think of youngsters' needs primarily in terms of
> providing facilities and activities for them. Boys' clubs

and youth clubs were born in days of poverty and it was natural to think this way then. But today in Britain the need is not to 'keep them off the streets': my own belief is that what youngsters want most from adults is unjudging friendship . . . To bring Christian impact into a club, we need a good number of helpers who have real faith, and want to share it. They are ready to turn up faithfully, and out of the large numbers in the club to offer friendship to a handful of young people. . . a club is built round friendships, and with some youngsters these can only be made literally by 'sitting where they sit', or standing where they stand.[5]

It was George Burton who pioneered this relational style of youth club work at the Mayflower. Glasgow-born, he was appointed in 1958 to work alongside David Sheppard in the Mayflower's youth clubs after a rich and varied life of international travel and service. From the very start the pattern of Christian outreach and emphasis on relationships was clear. When Burton arrived at the Mayflower for his first club night there were only fifteen young people in the building. The annual fair was at a local park so Burton took Jean Lodge Patch, a senior helper, and set out to contact the young people at the fair. They spent the evening wandering around the stalls and sideshows chatting to the young people they met.[6] From this point on the work began to grow and soon the clubs were bursting at the seams.

David Sheppard as team leader set clear objectives for the work. Chief among these was the development of an 'indigenous' church with local Christian leaders.[7] Building up a church of committed believers in Canning Town was seen by Burton to be analogous to the missionary work of the Church overseas:

No matter how well the missionary masters the language and customs of those around him, he remains a foreigner and the message he brings is open to rejection as being part and parcel of an alien culture. But build up national Christians and they will be in a far better position to present the gospel to their own people in a meaningful way.[8]

The realization that in Canning Town there needed to be an indigenous church was not simply a comment on who attended the church. It also meant that the church should reflect the culture of the local area. In setting up an indigenous church as one of the aims of the work Sheppard was building into the work of the Mayflower a critique of the middle-class culture, a culture which he shared. To encourage the growth of an indigenous church was therefore to involve a large measure of self-understanding and even criticism. George Burton was the leader of the team in this respect.

Burton was clear that for many working-class people the Church was alien because it was associated with being 'posh, snobbish and educated'.[9] David Sheppard paid tribute to the way that Burton challenged the assumption that many middle-class values were seen as necessarily Christian: 'Why should we assume that people from a non-reading background could not become thoughtful deeply committed Christians ?'[10] As the work began to grow, it became more apparent how culturally specific the evangelical faith had become. When Burton took a group of young people from Canning Town to the evangelical conference centre run by John Bickersteth at Ashburnham, things started to go wrong. He wrote to David Sheppard in frustration:

> I feel that I must get things off my chest. Ashburnham is a wonderful place but it is only suited for the good boy. John Bickersteth could not have been more co-operative and I know that I am looking for the impossible from other Christians when I take the East End teenagers out camping. I find that I am up against a code of behaviour that is expected from the grammar school and above type. If I spent my time watching that the tent pegs did not get broken and the boys cleaned behind their ears and cleaned their teeth, did not eat sweets before their main dish, and concentrated on teaching them to respect other people's property and was continually apologising for

their noisy behaviour and the unseemly mannerisms and teaching them to say 'thank you' and 'very sorry' and getting them to fit into a pattern of behaviour that middle class Christians have laid down, then I would not be doing the job that Christ has called me to . . .[11]

The aim, however, was not just to criticize the middle-class culture of the Church but also to encourage working-class values and behaviours. Significant efforts were made to affirm the local Canning Town culture rather than judge it: key phrases were 'unjudging friendship' and 'accepting people as they are'.[12] In tackling the issue of culture the team moved beyond the ephemera of behaviour expected of a Christian by a predominantly middle-class Church, which was seen as a stumbling-block to young people from the inner cities.

Sheppard and Burton soon realized that the very language in which the faith was expressed needed to be re-examined. On one occasion together they worked through a pile of Christian literature scoring out the words which they felt people in Canning Town would fail to understand. In the end they were left with very few words at all.[13]

Despite the problems Burton was eventually able to establish a small group of Christian young people known as the 'Sunday Club'. As well as attending meetings to discuss the faith, members of the group were encouraged to exercise leadership roles in the club work. There was a concern to try to keep them as a group where faith might have a chance to grow within their own culture, although some people in the church at the Mayflower felt that the group was isolated. It was through this work that Burton began to see local Canning Town young people take on leadership in Christian ministry. His ministry and the success of the Sunday Club was an example of the ideals of evangelical youthwork of this period. But where Burton succeeded, however, others found the going getting tougher and tougher.

The Frontier Youth Trust

The Mayflower was one of 'the crucibles in which has been forged new approaches to Christian youthwork'.[14] But it was soon found that in places all around the country evangelicals were being drawn to give their lives to young people in urban areas. They included people like Andrew Piersnee, who was warden at the Cambridge University Mission in the 1950s and later moved on to pioneer the Oxford and Kilburn Club, or George Venables who founded the Home Croft Youth Club, and Maurice Smith who started the Knights Association of Youth Clubs.[15]

These and other leaders were to meet together in a series of conferences under the title 'Youth Clubs as a Sphere of Christian Service'.[16] Around twenty people attended the first gathering in 1955 and numbers rose steadily until by 1963 over 200 youth leaders came together.[17] Following the first conference a newsletter was produced which went under the title of 'The Fellowship of Christian Youth Club Workers'. Youth club leaders from the Mayflower, the Cambridge University Mission, All Souls Club House and the Oxford and Kilburn Club, the Knights Association of Youth Clubs the Greenhouse and Elizabeth Reid Club and others began to meet in London on a regular basis.[18] In 1964, the Frontier Youth Trust for Christian Club Work was set up, and in 1966 a provisional partnership with Scripture Union was entered into and formalized in 1969. David Sheppard was the first Secretary of FYT and the offices were originally based in the Mayflower Centre. Michael Eastman, who was brought to faith through Gidea Park Crusader class, was appointed as the first full-time Secretary and development worker in 1967.[19]

Urban ministry was pioneered by people firmly rooted within the evangelical culture who were charged with the task of reaching out beyond the frontiers of the Church. Some of the leaders in the early days of Frontier Youth Trust were former Bash campers, who included, along with David Sheppard, Philip Thompson who was the first Chair of

FYT and John Stott who chaired the trustees of the new organization. For these and the others involved, urban mission was clearly seen as an effort to move beyond the social groups usually attracted by the evangelical constituency, hence the use of the term 'frontier': 'Frontier is the unexplored beyond the point we have reached'.[20]

Such outreach demanded new methods of working, brought about new partnerships and led to the development of a distinctive theology. These three factors, while fuelling frontier work itself, also moved those who continued in the work further from the mainstream of evangelical subculture.

Frontier Methods

From the start FYT was clear that there were many and various ways of reaching out to young people.[21] New ways of working had to come about because the existing approaches to youthwork were not reaching significant groups of young people: 'Many areas and young people are not touched by any method, especially in the industrial centres in Britain and abroad so that alongside existing forms of Christian youth work, there is room for new experiments and methods.'[22]

In 1974 Eddie Neale travelled around the country visiting frontier youthwork projects, including a youth club in St Helens, a festival for Jesus in London, work with young people queuing for the cinema in Bishop's Stortford, a theatre company in Liverpool, a bus project in Welwyn Garden City, and community work with groups in Soho. The variety of the work is testimony to the inventiveness of those engaged in frontier mission. Evangelicals experimented with coffee bars, drop-in centres and work outside a fixed club or centre which was known as 'detached' youthwork,[23] but in the main churches saw frontier work primarily in terms of youth club work. This in part comes from the emphasis placed on club work by those working on the frontiers.

The original title for FYT was 'The Frontier Trust for Christian Club Work'.[24] The first publication put out by SU after FYT joined them, *Christians in the Youth Service*, devotes many of its pages to encouraging churches to set up youth clubs. It does warn, however, that 'the youth club should not be seen as a new gimmick for filling the pews, or the choir, or for putting the churchyard in order.'[25] The youth club was being seen as a fundamental strategy for reaching young people in an urban context. Roger Sainsbury, while he was at Shrewsbury House in Liverpool, wrote of the value of club work:

> I feel a large number of working class young people today think that the Church will not accept them. 'I can't go to Church because I swear like a trooper', I've heard more than one say. I believe a Christian Open Youth Club can show that the Body of Christ, the Church, does care and will accept them.[26]

The FYT guide to setting up a club, *Making a Start*, published in the 1970s, appears to go a little further in claiming God's guidance in the development of the youth club approach. The authors make their commitment very clear: '. . . we believe the instinct for open club work was a right one – indeed a God-given one. Our contention is that in the appropriate situation, open club work is the method ideally suited to approaching young people.'[27]

It was common for churches in the 1960s and 70s to experiment with running youth clubs as a method of reaching out to young people. David Watson's *Towards Tomorrow's Church*[28] was written to encourage churches to run such a club alongside a youth fellowship. It seems clear that despite a variety of approaches to youthwork the open youth club was the model which was generally advocated for reaching young people not touched by the youth fellowship.

The problem was that in a good many cases churches which started youth clubs were soon attracting young people who they found difficult to handle. By the 1970s young people appeared to be less willing to submit to the rules needed to run a club. *Making a Start* suggests that before a club is opened the youth leaders and church officials make a tour of the building and the authors give a list of hints on the issues which should be raised with the church. They include:

> Point out to Church leaders that the only kind of No Entry sign that youngsters understand is a locked and bolted door. If there are rooms or cupboards that are not to be touched insist that they are properly locked.
>
> Pianos are a nightmare. They must be locked and covered.
>
> Plastic plumbing is hopeless – if it exists, get it boxed in.
>
> In a more modern building there may be a flat roof. It will not be designed for walking on.[29]

Such a list seems to relate more to keeping dangerous animals than to a Christian youth club. Can it be any wonder that many churches found the prospect of the youth club less than inviting? For those who had entered into it ill prepared there were a good many painful memories. 'The attitude of many churches is simply "Don't mention open clubs here – we've had all that and we don't want any more."'[30] According to Eastman, 'The multiple use of premises may well have been at the root of the demise of more open youthwork than any other cause. Damage to buildings still ranks high as the reason for not taking this on.'[31] By the 1980s even the well resourced and professionally staffed Mayflower Centre was experiencing problems with the increasingly disturbed and violent behaviour of many young people.

The violence and struggle that characterized Pip Wilson's description of the work in his book *Gutter Feelings*[32] was eventually to prove too much. In a youthwork report written towards the end of his time at the Mayflower, Wilson reveals some of his concern for the future of the work: 'For the first time I have thought that it is becoming impossible to run a club in Canning Town. . . The kids are so aggressive and explosive that even I – twenty years a youth worker and ten years in Canning Town – cannot handle these hard, tough teenagers.'[33]

Problems with the open club as a method of working with young people were felt not just by the churches but by the youth service in general. In the 1980s and 90s the number of young people attending youth clubs has dropped dramatically.[34] Open youthwork, be it of the youth club or drop-in coffee bar type, was starting to be seen as a problem and evangelistically unsuccessful by many evangelical churches. In contrast, youth fellowship work was proving to be a fruitful method of outreach, albeit with those young people who did well at school and fitted more easily into prevailing Church subculture. Perceived problems with the existing methods of open youthwork meant that the mainstream evangelical churches tended to invest much more heavily in the youth fellowship as their only method of youthwork. The effect of this was slowly to polarize the traditions of youthwork within evangelicalism. While those reaching out on the frontiers continued to give themselves in ministry in tough places, often seeing little reward, those working in churches, many of which were located in the suburbs, regarded the youth fellowship as the only viable method of youthwork. The authors of *Making a Start* seem to support this analysis when they point out that:

> There is now, therefore, a powerful body of opinion, apparently with right very much on their side, who see the youth fellowship, with the possible addition of a closed club, as the only way forward in parish-based youth work. Church open clubs are anathema. They would consider this to be almost self-evident.[35]

Partnerships on the Frontier

From the very start those working on the frontiers of the Church saw that there was a need to draw on the experience, professionalism, and resources of the Local Education Authority – (LEA) funded youth service. *Christians in the Youth Service* encourages churches to apply for grants from LEAs to help fund part-time or full-time workers.[36] The youth service was recommended as a career and Christians were encouraged to share in the post-Albemarle world where 'considerable thought and effort have been given to the . . . proper professional training and status' of the youth leader.[37]

Linking evangelical youthwork so closely to the youth service was to affect significantly the impact of those ministering on the frontiers. The most visible result of partnership with LEAs was seen in the increasingly professional and well-staffed projects run by churches. In the 1980s the Mayflower was able to employ seven full-time youthworkers who supported a team of thirty-five volunteer and part-time workers. By the end of the decade, however, the criteria used by LEAs to fund projects shifted and a number of evangelical projects found that their funding was under threat or cut entirely.[38] Perhaps more significant than the unreliability of funding was the extent to which the work itself was to be affected by the secular values of the youth service.

Along with funding from LEAs came the demand for 'professionally' recognized training.[39] Training for a secular youthwork qualification, however, was not the same as training to be an evangelist, or indeed a missionary, in an urban context. Education inevitably shapes people, and youthwork courses were a crucial factor in 'forming' the values and practice of those who passed through them. As youthwork courses moved further away from the heritage which they shared with the evangelical church, those working on the frontiers were finding themselves allied to a tradition of youthwork which was less and less sympathetic to a committed Christian perspective. Peter Stow recounts how the secular youthwork course he followed, which was connected to a Christian college, did little to help him apply his faith to his work: 'College had broken down all my assumptions, and put nothing in their place.'[40]

The negative effects of 'professional' youthwork training were possibly less significant than the fact that the endorsement of such training tended to squeeze out training for mission. For while FYT has been clear that mission theology lies at the heart of its philosophy,[41] a commitment to the

importance of professionally recognized training has perhaps meant that young evangelical Christians wishing to be
trained have not benefited from extensive study of the theology of mission which work in frontier situations requires.
As early as 1965 people such as George Burton were uneasy
with a perceived lack of desire on the part of those within
FYT to 'save souls'. By the 1990s Watherston was more
openly critical: 'At a theological level, in the face of the lack
of response to the gospel, an urban theology had developed
in FYT which seemed to down play the need for repentance
and the validity of conversion.'[42]

This comment is something of a cheap shot at evangelical
youthworkers who were struggling to make sense of the
urban reality they were encountering. Nevertheless it is
questionable to what extent youthworkers trained within a
secular framework were adequately prepared for what remains
one of the more challenging areas of mission theology. When
Pip Wilson says that in the 1980s the programmes at the
Mayflower run under the philosophy of social education
had a 'golden thread of explicitly Christian principle' running through them, there are significant questions as to how
this perspective is held in tension with a clear commitment
to evangelism.[43] This is not to suggest that Wilson or others
in the team necessarily abandoned their evangelical stance.
The reality is that work on the frontiers involves relationships and commitments which are less clear cut and more
challenging to the evangelical subculture than those faced
by youthworkers running youth fellowships. The youthwork
scene has, along with the wider society, gone pluralist and
secularist,[44] and it is precisely for this reason that many
Christian youthworkers have found its training and professional ethos to be less than helpful to an evangelical commitment. One youthworker quoted at length in FYT literature
clearly found the links between his newfound skills as a
frontier youthworker and the expectations of the evangelical
church difficult to reconcile:

> I got a bit confused at first, because I used to think of my
> youth work as evangelism, and got very discouraged when

there were no immediate results. Now I am happier about it. I can see that my youth work is the same as any other job, that it is worth doing in itself.[45]

The work which the youthworker is describing was in many respects exemplary. The question really is one of identity. Is urban mission like any other job? Is this secular youthwork rather than Christian theology speaking? According to Eastman the professional youthworker is really no different from the Christian doctor or engineer.[46] From one perspective this view has a good deal to commend it, but it has also to be said that such attitudes undermine a commitment to missiology as much as they support it. It is one thing to be as professional a youthworker as possible and operate essentially a secular and largely non-evangelistic youth project. Such a person may well seek to maintain a witness and even see young people come to faith. I would maintain that it is quite another thing self-consciously and incarnationally to enter into a community as a mission agent of Christ. Within FYT circles this distinction has not been widely understood and consequently the impact of secular professional youthwork has been down played. Evangelical commitment which embraces secular frameworks has in my view led to dualism and possibly elements of liberalism. In seeking significant partnerships outside the Church and in particular in embracing secular models of training, those working on the frontiers have significantly increased their distance from the mainstream churches.

A Theology for the Frontiers

The experience at the Mayflower and elsewhere led frontier workers to question the 'middle-class nature of the Church'. What began to evolve from those within FYT was a distinctive missionary theology which sought to help those working beyond the boundaries of the Church. As Pip Wilson recorded during his early days in youthwork, he felt that the Church did not understand him. FYT at this time was a crucial support in offering a theology that was relevant.[47] The inspiration for this theology was coming from people such as Chris Sugden, who suggested that the Bible should be read from the 'underside' at the FYT National Event in 1983, Andrew Kirk who reflected on liberation theology, and the founder of the Sojourners Jim Wallis. But it was Jim Punton who more than anyone else articulated the theological mind of frontier youthworkers.[48] There is a sense of streams coming together as evangelicals from around the world began to work out a theology for urban mission. Michael Eastman recalls that in the 1960s his first contact with FYT made him feel he was among friends. Together the group began to explore the class captivity of the gospel: 'We didn't have a language for it then. We were regarded as rocking the boat.'[49] This is not the place for an extensive treatment of frontier theology, but highlights from it show how far thinking has progressed in this area.

Central to evangelical youthwork in urban contexts has been a realization that a long-term presence in a community is the starting-point for ministry.[50] This theology of presence has been seen in terms of 'incarnation':

> The essence of mission as it relates particularly to these young people is that of 'incarnation'. The approach is that of 'going' with an emphasis on 'identification with' which allows a sharing in the lives of those to whom the one on mission is sent.[51]

Incarnation was not just about presence; it was also about the manner in which relationships were built with young people. According to Pip Wilson, 'Incarnation in the youth club, among young people is presence without oppression. That is what we strive to live out and the result, we have come to realise, is not the message. The medium is the message.'[52]

Roger Sainsbury also saw that involvement in the lives of young people was the essential basis for evangelism. Relationships were the way that Christian youthworkers earned the right to speak of Christ.[53] Incarnational language

was foundational to frontier theology but it was the linkages
between presence, the Kingdom of God and biblical concepts
of 'Shalom' made by Jim Punton and others which gave
shape to the vision and hopes of many evangelicals working
in urban contexts. Frontier work, according to Eastman, was
inspired by a reading of the Gospels where Jesus was the
Prince of Shalom:

> . . . the mission of Jesus included heralding the reign of
> God; demonstrating it; bearing signs to it in healing, in
> exposing and opposing the non-shalom of poverty, injus-
> tice, exploitation, racism, and idolatry of every kind; in
> identification with oppressed and powerless; in loving,
> sacrificial service; in disciplining men and women with
> his new community of love and brotherhood with its life
> in the Spirit of total worship and mission.[54]

Such a theology was fundamental in helping evangelical
Christians to journey into urban mission. The increasing
sophistication in developing a theology of mission, however,
also needed to be complemented by the development of a
theology which arose from young people in urban contexts.
The former is a theology of mission, the second is a local
and contextual theology which is created by young people
themselves.[55]

The original vision of David Sheppard and the early
pioneers in FYT was the growth of indigenous churches.
Seeing young people come to faith and then to read the
Bible from the 'underside' was clearly the desire and aim of
frontier work. Unfortunately this enterprise proved extremely
difficult to achieve. In the first place many people found it
hard to evangelize in urban contexts. Veteran FYT staff
member Arkle Bell is fairly blunt in his appraisal of the
work when he points out that 'We have seen little success
this century in making the Gospel relevant to working class
culture.'[56] Another veteran FYT worker Terry Dunnell sees
the failure of the Church to evangelize young people as part
of a much wider failure of the Church to reach the English
working classes.[57]

Where projects were successful in bringing young people
to faith people found themselves wrestling with the problem
of the Church. John Benington's controversial study *Culture,
Class and Christian Beliefs*[58] arose from his own experience of
seeing three young people from working-class backgrounds
come to faith and then slip away. He concluded that it was
the Church which was to blame for the young people losing
their faith – 'the Christianity which they met, rather than
the Christ they met has failed.'[59]

Michael Eastman raised the question of the Church as
early as 1976. In summing up the various contributions for
the FYT publication *Inside Out*, he says that one of the key
questions arising from frontier ministry among young people is 'So what for the Church?'[60] Despite the fact that the
1974 FYT conference, meeting at Westhill College, recognized that 'Frontier work should result in indigenous
churches', and that 'FYT has a responsibility to foster and
serve such churches',[61] by 1988 Michael Eastman was asking
the very same question again.[62] What answers we have to
this question from those within the frontier tradition of
youthwork are at present partial.

Conclusion

Those called to work on the frontiers have been a prophetic
voice within the Church. The patterns of ministry and the
distinctive theology to which they have given voice have
served to shape evangelicalism. To work on the frontiers is
always to court marginalization. Out of sight is out of mind.
There is also something unrelentingly bleak about frontier
youthwork. Pip Wilson sums up his years at the Mayflower
by saying: 'I would never say that the youthwork at the
Mayflower was successful, only that it survived against all
odds in demonstrating the Kingdom of God in Canning
Town.'[63]

This sort of statement carries a great deal of authority and
it is very impressive, but is it any wonder that the evangelical
churches tended to retreat to places where they could see a

richer harvest? Evangelicals will invest heavily in urban ministry only if they can be sure that young people will really come to faith. In our current context the key to this would seem to be the question of planting indigenous churches. While the story of those who have given themselves in frontier mission among young people is inspiring and instructive, there is little indication that the answers to the problems and opportunities of young people in the Church will come from this quarter.

Chapter 4

The Jesus Movement and the Subculture

In 1976 Gavin Reid, then evangelistic secretary of CPAS, introduced a musical event for youth fellowships with the remark, 'Let's have a feeling of wrapped aroundness'.[1] Change, it seems, was certainly in the air in evangelical circles and much of it was brought about by young people who were 'turning on to Jesus' and adopting the style and language of the Jesus Movement from the USA. Bebbington is clear that in the 1960s and early 70s a cultural revolution was taking place among evangelicals. So impressed was he by this change that he was willing to assert that 'The gulf that had once yawned between the church and the world had virtually disappeared.'[2] What narrowed this gap was the Jesus Movement, for it was through the Jesus Movement that aspects of popular youth culture were to merge with evangelicalism. The creative energy which was brought about as young people discovered an exciting 'hip' form of Christianity led to widespread changes as Christian young people, through music, festivals, art, magazines, theatre, worship and community life, generated the evangelical subculture which we live with today.

The Jesus Movement

The Jesus Movement has its origins in the hippie youth subculture of the United States. Enroth, Ericson and Peters in their survey of movement were uncertain as to the exact origins of what they call the 'Jesus people', but around 1967 a number of different Christian ministries in the USA began to develop in parallel ways. One of these was the coffee bar ministry in the heart of the hippie district of Haight-Ashbury, San Francisco. A group of people rented a storefront and used it simply to talk with the street people about Jesus and the Bible. This outreach work was named the Living Room. As the group grew they rented a small two-storey home in Navoto, California where a commune was established which was known as the House of Acts.[3] Similar patterns of community living, informal gatherings and an emphasis on evangelism were repeated in group after group.

Outreach work to the young hippie drop-outs on the streets was to be a major characteristic of this movement. The late 1960s was a period of great experimentation and social unrest for young people in the USA. Thirty years on, the age of Timothy Leary, Vietnam, civil rights and Woodstock can sometimes appear as a golden age of freedom and self-expression. Images of teenagers facing armed national guardsmen outside the Pentagon and placing flowers in their rifles are very moving, but many young people were extremely damaged by their experiences in the 60s:

> Life on the streets is not all flowers and love anymore. Kids are flipping out; they are ending up in psychiatric wards or committing suicide. Young girls are going insane as they give themselves away in free love. Babies are born in public rest-rooms. 'Do your thing' sounded groovy once, but it has horrible effects. There are vegetables walking around who once were strong men, and women.[4]

The new religious movement was born out of these experiences. In California groups of hippie Christians were going out onto the streets talking about Jesus. These young people had felt lost, without any meaning in their life, but Jesus had met them and made them whole. They were on the streets with a zeal to rescue their fellow hippies who were hooked on drugs or lost and confused in some other way. Theirs was a ministry of love offering hope to anyone

who would listen. As the euphoria of the counterculture
began to blow itself out individual young people were left
still asking many of their original questions. 'I'm trying to
get my head together', said one young man.[5] The anxiety and
confusion left in the wake of the hippie era led many young
people to turn to the Christian faith.

Most of the young people involved in the counterculture
who dropped out in the 60s were from comfortable, middle-
class homes.[6] Police picking people off the streets in Berkeley
were surprised at how young and 'nice' the young people
they were dealing with were:

> Adults are amazed when they see these kids. They are not
> hoodlums or the derelicts that city policemen used to
> know. Many of them are well educated, soft spoken,
> fresh-faced kids – guys still trying to grow a beard, girls
> who left home where they had their own room and tele-
> phone. In Berkeley, 50 per cent of the runaways who are
> under eighteen come from families with an income above
> ten thousand dollars per year, and over 80 per cent of
> them are white.[7]

Middle-class young people found in the Jesus Movement
both a moderation and a legitimation of their countercul-
tural lifestyles and values.[8] A Jesus person could keep their
'alternative' dress and music whilst embracing what was
in essence old-time conservative evangelical religion.[9] The
Jesus revolution was a radicalization of the Christian faith,
but it was also at the same time a significant retreat from
the challenge to middle-class society and values seen within
the counterculture. Palms was clear that 'Anti-establishment
slogans don't rid the young people of all the drives and
feelings that they have because they are products of the
American culture and establishment.' Young people brought
up in middle-class families essentially shared middle-class
values and were therefore still a part of 'the system'.[10] The
conservative evangelical faith that made up the Jesus revolution was a refuge for confused and bruised young people
disillusioned with the hippie myth.

The Jesus Movement was to generate a new breed of Christian leader, and most notable among these was Arthur Blessitt, the 'Minister of Sunset Strip'. Blessitt arrived in Hollywood in 1965 and after a period of sidewalk evangelism he opened 'His Place', a gospel nightclub. The story of his ministry on Sunset Strip, then the centre of the Los Angeles sex industry, is told in dramatic detail by Blessitt himself in *Turned on to Jesus*.[11] 'His Place' became the means by which young people caught up in the drugs scene encountered the Christian faith, according to the authors of *The Story of the Jesus People*:

> It became the place to go. It was in. Hundreds trooped through our door each evening ... The toilet service became one of our His Place traditions. Whenever a doper gives his heart to Christ, we move him straight to the john. Once I counted eighteen bodies squeezed into our little bathroom. 'I don't need this anymore. I'm high on the Lord,' the typical convert declares. He pulls out his cache of grass, reds, speed, or acid and drops it into the bowl.[12]

Popularized by people like Blessitt the movement quickly began to replicate aspects of the current youth culture. The 'Jesus Revolution' was a style of consumption complete with psychedelic posters, badges and bumper stickers. Popular youth culture was mixed with evangelicalism to create a hip religion with its own language proclaiming 'Smile, God Loves You', 'Honk if you love Jesus', 'Have a nice forever' and 'God's speed doesn't kill'.[13] In Berkeley, the centre of much student unrest, Jack Sparks, who was once associated with Campus Crusade for Christ established the Christian World Liberation Front (CWLF). The CWLF developed a ministry among street people in Berkeley and students on the University of California campus there. In July 1969 Sparks, and the group which he gathered around him, began to publish an underground newspaper called *Right On*.[14] Along with the newspaper there were numerous other publications including a translation of the letters of the New

Testament called *Letters to Street Christians*. The following is 1 John 2.14ff in street language:

> Dig it! God has laid a heavy love on us! He calls us His children and we are! The world system doesn't recognise that we're his children because it doesn't know him. Right on brothers and sisters we are God's children even though we're a long way from being what he's going to make us. Don't get hooked on the ego-tripping and the world system. Anybody who loves that system, doesn't really love God . . . (Dig it! This whole plastic bag is exactly what Jesus liberated us from.)[15]

Hip language appealed to young people who were alienated by their past experiences of the straight church. This new Jesus type of faith was in their style, their language, but in most other respects (apart from the emphasis on communal living) it was not very revolutionary at all. In fact the CWLF set out to oppose the politically radical Berkeley Liberation Movement.

The Jesus Movement was far from being a radical theology of 'liberation' growing from the new youth counter-culture. Leaders like Blessitt and Sparks generally ensured that the idealism of the young was privatized and turned inwards. The lack of a political agenda was quite striking and yet hardly surprising when it is recognized that the Christianity which was embraced by the mainstream members of the Jesus Movement, despite its hip presentation, was really just old-style revivalism. Within a very few years most Jesus people groups had either merged into mainline churches in the USA or had formed their own highly conservative house churches.[16]

From the very earliest days a small number of mainline churches in the States were able to adopt the new 'hip style'. In 1969 in Southern California a small group of Christians with their minister Chuck Smith started to build a church building which was called Calvary Chapel. By 1971 over one thousand young people were worshipping in the church every week. Enroth, Ericson and Peters describe the

Sunday worship as a mixture between a 1950s Youth For Christ rally and a rock festival. The church was packed with young people from the wealthy middle-class homes of Orange County.[17] Many of these young people had adopted hippie-style long hair, beads and psychedelic shirts. Calvary Chapel also became famous for its open air baptism ceremonies which took place in the sea. Each month hundreds of young people would be drawn together for an informal service and to be plunged under the waves. Communal houses were established to help those who were converted from off the streets. These 'houses' were also used for outreach into the local community by having an open-door policy. Key to the growth of a youth-orientated ministry at Calvary Chapel was the then youth minister Lonee Frisbee. Enroth records that Frisbee was particularly interested in the manifestation of charismatic gifts, although this was not shared by all of the ministry team. The charismatic influence of Calvary Chapel continued and it was from this church that John Wimber left to start his Vineyard fellowship.

The Jesus Movement, much like the counterculture it mimicked, spawned its own commercial industries. Consumer items such as posters, badges, stickers and even a 'Jesus wristwatch' became commonplace.[18] Christians also produced their own versions of the popular media, so that along with the underground newspapers such as *Right On* or the very popular *Hollywood Free Press* there were Christian radio stations and Jesus festivals. Well-established evangelical organizations soon adopted the style of the Jesus people. The IVF sponsored a multimedia presentation of the Christian message called 'Twenty One Hundred' in which rock music, slides and lighting effects were used to communicate the gospel to students.[19] The American Bible Society produced *The New Testament in Today's English Version* (published in Britain as *Good News for Modern Man*). The Jesus Movement also spawned its own version of rock music. Larry Norman, the most famous performer of the Jesus Movement, started to sing 'Jesus songs' at Hollywood Presbyterian

Church's 'Salt Company'. Norman's music was credible in
its rock style and yet concerned to spell out the gospel in its
lyrics. Some would say that he invented 'Jesus Rock Music'.[20]

The Jesus revolution was very much a charismatic movement. Ruben Ortega, who made a detailed study of Jesus
people in California, concluded that of those he interviewed
85 to 89 per cent were associated in one way or another with
Pentecostalism. Most had a firm belief in the gifts of the
Holy Spirit and many had spoken in tongues.[21] Palms notes
that 'For many teachers of the Jesus kids, the emphasis on
speaking in tongues is as strong as the emphasis on the new
birth.' Enroth, Ericson and Peters point out that setting
themselves alongside the Great Awakening of the eighteenth
century the Jesus People saw themselves as participating in
a genuine movement of the Spirit.[22]

The Jesus Movement in Britain

The Jesus revolution in Britain was primarily a matter of
style. While some people were deeply affected by the new
movement and it has had lasting effects on the Christian
youth scene (such as the Greenbelt festival), there was little
or no 'Jesus Movement' among British young people. It was
primarily churches and Christian groups during the 1970s
who adopted the characteristics of the American movement
in an attempt to win young people to Christ. While in the
USA a generation of young people felt the need for meaning and religious identity coming out of the chaos of the
1960s counterculture, there is little evidence of a similar mass
movement in Britain. Instead, church groups were able to
adopt a much more contemporary style and pop and rock
music found their way into the regular worship of the
Church. The Jesus Movement also stimulated the growth of
festivals, magazines and record companies. Although all of
these new initiatives were outside the official Church structures, they continued to be to a greater or lesser extent
linked to the establishment.

The effect of the Jesus Movement was to breathe new life

into the Church based on the appropriation of aspects of
youth culture. On the whole this was inspired by the
American examples exported to this country by the likes of
Blessitt and Larry Norman. The long-term impact of this
new style of 'Jesus' Christianity on the culture of the evangelical church is crucial to any understanding of present-day
youthwork.

The Festival of Light

The Jesus Movement became news in Britain in 1971 with
the visit of Arthur Blessitt who hit the headlines in London
by appearing on television carrying a massive wooden cross.[23]
Blessitt's visit to London coincided with the Festival of Light
and his address at the rally in Trafalgar Square became the
high point of the festival with many coming forward for
counselling after accepting Christ into their lives.[24] The
Festival of Light grew from the experience of a missionary
called Peter Hill who on his return to Britain was appalled
by the amount of erotic and pornographic material that was
available in books and films. The festival, which followed
the lighting of beacons all over Britain, was supported by
individuals such as Lord Longford, Mary Whitehouse and
Malcolm Muggeridge. Thirty thousand people gathered in
Trafalgar Square while at the parallel gathering in Hyde
Park eighty thousand were present to attend a service of
dedication.[25] The youth-orientated Jesus Movement was at
the heart of the development of the festival. As Flo Dobbie's
account of the festival puts it,

IT'S IN THE AIR! IT'S NEWS!

Thousands of young people are gathering in London's
parks, on California's beaches, in conference halls, domes,
tents: what are they talking about? JESUS! A revolution
is on the move, worldwide, with a new battle cry, 'Jesus is
coming!'[26]

The influence of the Jesus Movement in Britain was
again seen at the 1972 follow-up to the Festival of Light,

held in Hyde Park, when a number of Christian pop musicians were involved in the 'Jesus Festival'. Similar events were held on a smaller scale all over the country.[27]

The link between the Jesus Movement and the Festival of Light placed this new movement firmly within right-wing conservative Christianity in Britain. Leech points out that, coming so close to the *Oz* trial and the problems surrounding the publication of *The Little Red School Book*, the Festival of Light was perceived by most young people within the counterculture in Britain to be an attempt by the establishment to assert their right to determine how people led their lives.

> The aim of the organisers was to fight 'Moral Pollution', which in other words means a religious minority trying once more to dictate society's more wayward sexual habits. If the Festival had wished to increase these fears, they could hardly have done better than to include Lord Longford, Malcolm Muggeridge and Mary Whitehouse among their widely publicised supporters! All three were anathema to the counter-culture.[28]

The Festival of Light, however, was one of the main ways in which the Jesus Movement from the USA was given exposure in Britain. Blessitt and Larry Norman were given a major stage in this country through the festival, with the result that many young evangelical Christians were deeply affected by this new brand of hip Christianity. The 'style' of the Jesus Movement was widely copied by teenagers and young adults within the Church. The Jesus revolution therefore was not so much rooted in a general movement of God's Spirit among young people outside the Church, as promoted to young people who were already within the fold. The link with the evangelical establishment meant that although it was in many ways a radical departure for the Church, the Jesus revolution in Britain remained conservative and therefore safe.

The festival was significant, however, in the boost it gave to the spread of the charismatic movement in Britain. In the aftermath of the early festivals and through association with workers linked to Blessitt, an Anglican clergyman, Peter Philip, ran an open house drop-in ministry for young people involved in the counterculture. He and his wife had both been baptised in the Spirit. This new experience was incorporated into what Neale describes as an 'openly charismatic' youth ministry:[29]

> We try to really praise the Lord. Not just standing up and mouthing a hymn, but really praising him. We try to share our problems and joys, our lives together, so that we are fully open with each other . . . not just plastic problems either . . . We are trying to learn how to pray so that we expect God to work . . . praying so that we expect healing to happen.[30]

The festival was to stimulate charismatics in a wide variety of church contexts. Walker sees the Festival of Light as playing an important role in the spread of the new charismatic 'restoration movement'. It was in the massed gatherings in Trafalgar Square and around the country that isolated groups began to recognize each other as fellow travellers on the same road:

> Singing and speaking in tongues, free-wheeling worship, fingers pointed high to the Jesus who is king, and cries of 'hallelujah' and 'amen' became a feature of the mass demonstrations. Charismatics were soon able to seek each other out as the Pentecostal signals were self evident for all to see. And now house church groups found (perhaps for the first time) just how many of them there were . . . The Festival of Light did not give birth to Restoration, but it did confirm for many that 'something' was emerging.[31]

Music Gospel Outreach

In the 1960s a gospel music scene developed in Britain. Outreach to young people through Christian coffee bars

was becoming an increasingly popular evangelistic strategy.
Seeing them as being halfway between the Church and the
secular world, Christians would use these events as a means
of attracting young people from outside the Church into the
youth fellowship. Christian folk groups and eventually rock
bands emerged offering entertainment with a message.
Young people in the 60s were willing to come and hear a live
musical act and the churches saw that music was a way of
drawing outsiders in.

'Music Gospel Outreach' (MGO) was started by Pete
Meadows, David Payne, Geoff Shearn and John Webb in
the mid-1960s as a vehicle for helping Christian musicians.
Meadows recalls the important role that it had in spreading
Christian music. 'MGO was there to train and equip those
using music to share their faith.'[32] Through publications and
training conferences a group of Christian musicians were
encouraged to use music not only as artistic expression, but
also as a means for outreach and evangelism. MGO sponsored concerts and events which predated the arrival of the
American Jesus Movement in Britain, but the influence of
Larry Norman and others from the States was soon evident.
Inspired and encouraged by developments in America during the early 1970s, MGO continued to organize Jesus
music concerts. They also set up their own record company
to promote British Christian musicians. Artists on the
MGO-sponsored 'Key' record label included Graham
Kendrick, Malcolm and Alwyn and Judy MacKenzie. In
January 1973 the 'Start the Year with Jesus' concerts at the
Royal Albert Hall drew 10,500 people. MGO was committed to evangelistic events which would draw young people
to hear the good news about Jesus. One radical move,
designed to encourage outreach, was the idea of selling
tickets for concerts in sets of four – two for Christians and
two for non-Christians.[33]

In 1972 MGO published *Songs for Jesus,* a small songbook
containing seventeen new-style Christian songs. Alongside
material by American Jesus musicians Larry Norman and
Randy Stonehill, there were songs by the new British artists,

Malcolm and Alwyn, Parchment, Graham Kendrick and Judy MacKenzie. The book has a home-made feel to it with the music being handwritten by Judy MacKenzie. These songs were introduced by her as 'thank you songs for those who live Jesus style'.[34] Although the songs were meant to be used by groups to sing together, much like choruses, the book is really the published music from a collection of Christian albums. MacKenzie says that they are recorded in the 'easiest keys for guitar work', but to learn the songs the musician is directed to listen to the 'relative records'. The feel of the Jesus Movement in Britain is well represented in this songbook. Malcolm and Alwyn in 'Set the World on Fire' place the movement in a historical context. Reference is made to Luther's disagreements with the priests of his day, Wesley travelling by horse to preach the gospel, and William Booth's Salvation Army bands. All of these we are told have set the world on fire. Now come the Jesus people who sing and give their characteristic sign of a single finger pointing to the sky.

Graham Kendrick, who later had a significant role as a worship leader and songwriter, was also prominent in the early years of the Jesus Movement in Britain. Kendrick's material featured in the MGO collection but the most notable British contribution was made by the Liverpool-based folk group Parchment whose 'Light up the Fire' was adopted as the unofficial anthem of the Festival of Light. The song was eventually released as a single on the secular label Pye and many Christian hopes were resting on the rise of this song in the national charts. The feeling was that if the song got into the 'top 20' then an appearance on the influential *Top of the Pops* would be assured. An informal Christian campaign was launched to boost the sales of this single. The MGO-sponsored *Buzz* magazine took up the challenge and urged its young readers to buy the single: 'You can help by going out and buying the single – NOW if you haven't heard it yet, you won't be disappointed we promise you.'[35]

In the event the single peaked at number thirty in the charts and all the efforts seemed to be in vain. The B side of

'Light up the Fire' was a song written by Judy MacKenzie called 'Let there be Light'. The song, also published in *Songs for Jesus*, seems to sum up the atmosphere of the mainstream Jesus Movement in 1970s Britain. 'Let There be Light' tells of dreams which didn't come true in the counterculture and a confusion which leads people to wish for light in the land and in their lives.

Evidently evangelicals on this side of the Atlantic also saw the 1960s as being a chaotic time. Jesus was therefore being presented as the answer to the troubles and stresses of the world. Young people who sought freedom in drugs and the sexual revolution were being invited to turn to Christ who could offer 'peace for the body and peace for the mind'. Not every group of Christians in 1972 influenced by the Jesus Movement found the Festival of Light or the sentiments expressed by Parchment to be to their particular liking. Alongside the mainstream MGO and *Buzz* there was *The Catonsville Roadrunner*, a more critical and radical publication. *Roadrunner* was deeply critical of the festival, saying that there was 'Not much Light at the Festival'.[36] The event was described by the magazine as thirty thousand people singing trite choruses and waving little flags saying that 'Jesus was the solution'. For *Roadrunner* the festival was simply evidence that Christians were right wing and sexually repressed. Such attitudes, it should be stressed, particularly within the evangelical world were comparatively rare.

Buzz magazine began its life as a publication for the new generation of British Christians who were interested in the emerging evangelical subculture. It contained advertisements for the latest Christian music and events, and reviews of Christian albums, films and books. While *Buzz*, on occasion, felt able to challenge certain evangelical Christian attitudes, most notably on pop and rock music, on the whole it was a mainstream magazine which promoted Christian products. Meadows sees *Buzz* as being influential on the British Christian scene in that it dealt with issues to do with contemporary culture from a Christian perspective. The magazine looked bright and had a *Daily Mail* style. At one point sales reached 30,000, making *Buzz* the largest selling Christian news publication.[37] The existence of *Buzz* was evidence of a steadily growing Christian youth subculture. The magazine was the chief means by which Christian artists and record companies could advertise their products. The emergence of Christian consumer items and cultural products provided the writers with a rich source for comment and controversy. As the secular music press was to pop music, *Buzz* was to the Christian subculture. As Christians sought to express their faith in the forms of modern media, *Buzz* was able to comment on, critique and promote these activities. In general, evangelicals created their own separate companies to develop their products. Distinctively Christian companies were formed to make and distribute Christian records, books and films and to promote Christian tours and events. The products of the evangelical subculture were manufactured by Christian industry and sold in a Christian market. This market was primarily young people.

By the 1980s *Buzz* was able to fill two or three pages each month advertising Christian events around the country. These ranged from national tours by artists such as Adrian Snell to the Riding Lights Theatre Company. Such artists were appearing in medium-sized venues, but small events in church halls were also part of the scene. *Buzz* played a full part in creating a demand for Christian consumer items, but the magazine also reflected the demand that there was for Jesus music.

As *Buzz* transformed into the more adult-orientated *Alpha*, the mantle has been taken up by Tony Cummings. Cummings, a former editor of *Buzz*, now edits the magazine *Cross Rhythms* which has a strong focus on Christian music. The development of the evangelical subculture can be clearly seen in Cummings' editorial in the first edition of the magazine:

> With tens of thousands of believers currently buying all forms of music there's obviously a big need in the Christian community for an authoritatively written, culturally

aware magazine which is both a comprehensive source of information and is a platform to deal with the dozens of issues raised by the rapid growth of the Christian music scene.[38]

Cummings and his partners now run their own successful radio show and Christian music festival. Their latest *Christian Music Directory* has well over 500 entries.

Those who started MGO and *Buzz* built a strong and enduring presence within British evangelicalism. Their *Alpha* magazine is a widely read evangelical monthly magazine; Spring Harvest is one of the largest annual gatherings of evangelical Christians in Britain; *Youthwork* magazine is the major Christian monthly publication focusing on youthwork,[39] and Brainstormers is one of the largest training weekends for Christian youthworkers. All of these have had a tremendous impact on present-day styles of worship, theology and ministry in the evangelical constituency and they have all evolved from the early ministry of MGO.

Spree 73

The Jesus Movement encouraged the tendency within evangelicalism towards festivals and large events as a means of encouraging young people in the faith. One of the largest of these was 'Spree 73'. Spree was a five-day event held in Earls Court in London with a final rally to hear Billy Graham in Wembley Stadium. Some 12,000 people came from all over the country to this event and the numbers swelled to 18,000–20,000 for the Saturday gathering at Wembley. The overall objective was to provide young people with training for evangelism. The mornings were spent in teaching sessions and the afternoons were given over to house-to-house and street evangelism. The evenings saw an inspirational mix of worship and teaching. Jasper records that Spree was an 'insiders' affair' with delegates wearing plastic armbands. This was one way to identify any visitor or anarchist who 'slipped in unawares and disrupted otherwise peaceful homely times'.[40] At the Wembley event the rather sparse crowd, as well as listening to Billy Graham preach, was entertained by Christian artists such as Cliff Richard and Johnny Cash. The gospel choir 'Choralerna' sang the theme tune, 'Let's Join Together'. Secular journalist Nick Kent of the *New Musical Express* was predictably not impressed by the event.

> Be sure to go out and buy the record [of 'Let's Join Together'] at your local record store to commemorate this 'joyous event' pleads the M.C. But it's somehow all too late. I've already found my way to the exit and stagger out, my sneer sagging with boredom. God bless 'em all, but when you're taking names, you can cancel my subscription to the resurrection. O.K. ?[41]

For the organizers the size of the gathering at Spree was to be a symbol of how the Christian faith could bring about change. Since the 1970s evangelicals had staged large events as a means of stimulating young people to turn to Christ. While it is clear that for many young Christians such gatherings were to be important landmarks in their Christian journey, for people such as Nick Kent they failed to impress. It could be argued that the persistence of these large events, however well meaning, has in effect only served to isolate Christian young people in an increasingly distinctive and attractive Christian subculture.

Lonesome Stone

In July 1973 a group called the Jesus Family, originating in the USA, staged the musical *Lonesome Stone* at the Rainbow Theatre. The Jesus Family was started in Milwaukee out of a small group from an old hippie commune. The group was led by Jim Palosaari, who with his wife Sue had fled involvement in the hippie scene in Haight Ashbury and the Berkeley riots and eventually found Christ at an old style revival meeting near the Canadian border. The group made their way to Britain and met up with the Christian businessman

Kenneth Frampton. Frampton helped to fund the outreach work in which Palosaari and these young hippie Christians were engaged. Very soon a communal house was established in Bromley and another followed in Tulse Hill.[42] *Lonesome Stone* was a much publicised Christian response to the other religious musicals of the time, *Godspell* and *Jesus Christ Superstar*. The publicity for the event announced:

> First time in a secular theatre – what *Jesus Christ Superstar* and *Godspell* failed to present. *Lonesome Stone*, a story of what Jesus is doing now, by his Spirit, in thousands of lives. This is a multi-media production of the Jesus Generation portrayed in music, film and drama. A glimpse into the history of this modern day phenomenon that is sweeping the world. This is the story and music of the Jesus Revolution told by people living in it.[43]

The plan was to stage a headline-stealing event which would sweep hundreds of young people off the streets. The musical featured the rock band Sheep and the members of cast were part of the Jesus Family. Jasper points out that the musical, although attracting a great deal of attention in the media, failed to live up to its billing. The production, he says, was 'disorganized' and 'amateur' and for these reasons received a good deal of criticism from the secular and the religious press. *Buzz* was particularly forthright in its views on the event.[44] Apart from the artistic demerits of *Lonesome Stone*, the production also received criticism for its portrayal of the Christian faith as an answer to the problems faced by young people in the 1970s. The message of the musical portrayed young people as being in the midst of a dark 'atomic age' surrounded by 'materialism, sex, new gurus, astrology and mind expanding and bending drugs'.[45] It was questionable to what extent views which were so rooted in the excesses of American west coast hippie culture could speak relevantly to British young people in the 1970s. In the event most of those influenced were Christian young people from the churches who saw a new hip freedom with a Christian edge to it which could liven up their local church situation. The experiences of these young people from the USA may well have been a long way from the average youth group member's life, but they were attractive in the way they dressed and talked, as well as in the music they played. *Lonesome Stone* may not have led to a mass conversion of secular young people, but did offer evangelical young people an attractive vision of a youth-orientated Christianity.

Lonesome Stone and the Jesus Family were to act as an important stimulus to the development of a Christian sub-culture among British young people. Through their communal lifestyle and regular visits to different parts of Britain the Jesus Family began to draw together a number of British musicians who were also seeking to minister through Christian rock music. Nick Stone recalls how his folk group, known as Capel House, went to live in Bromley with the Jesus Family and started to join in with the evangelistic activities. Capel House, which also included key figures in the development of Greenbelt festival Steve and Ruth Shaw and Martin Evans, shared a communal hippie lifestyle. While they were living in Suffolk they came to faith in Christ. Joining the Jesus Family for a while they were to be able to express their Christian commitment through full-time ministry. The Jesus Family made a big impression on the group, as Stone recalls:

> They were a Church on their own. They were into discipleship and dedication to Jesus. Here were people living it out. As individuals they were not worried about clothes, food or where they were living. This was an opportunity to minister. It was a complete lifestyle – Bible studies, prayer meetings and witnessing on the streets.[46]

Living in community had its problems. Stone was aware that the ideals of the group were often in tension with the personalities of people, many of whom had been through a good deal of problems in their lives. Therefore personal conflict often marred community life.

At the same time Frampton was also supporting a young musician called Dave Reece. Reece's band the Mighty Flyers rehearsed in Frampton's warehouse in Bromley and they also began to be involved in evangelistic work with the Jesus Family. In 1973 the musical *Lonesome Stone* was on tour round Britain. The idea was that the Jesus Family would always work alongside existing churches in the towns and cities they visited. Efforts were made to contact local ministers and clergy in advance to gain their support and when the group left it was hoped that new Christians would find a home in the supporting churches. Late in the year they went to Manchester. Nick Stone, who had now joined the Mighty Flyers, along with the other members of the band moved to Manchester to set up a visit of the Jesus Family. The group worked with local churches who would stage evangelistic concerts. Within a short time a network of Bible study groups was established for young Christians who had responded to Christ through their ministry. Communities were set up, often in houses provided by local Anglican churches who had accommodation vacant during clergy interregnums. Stone recalls that at first churches were suspicious of the hippie clothes and communal living of the Jesus Family, but many recognized the need for outreach to young people. The Jesus Family during this period were able to reach out to young people in the hippie subculture who the churches would otherwise fail to attract. The group in Manchester kept the name Jesus Family and continued to exist for the next ten years or so, running their own Sunday worship meetings. By the mid 1980s, however, numbers had dwindled, and the Manchester-based Jesus Family merged with a local ecumenical project.[47]

Greenbelt

In 1973 *Lonesome Stone* was on tour in Suffolk. James Holloway, the son of a Baptist minister, who also played in a blues band All Things New went to see *Lonesome Stone* at Mildenhall Airbase and he shared a vision for a Christian arts festival with Jim Palosaari. Find yourself a field 'then you've got yourself a festival,' encouraged Palosaari.[48] Thus the Greenbelt festival was born which found its first rural welcome at Prospect Farm, Charsfield, in 1974. The venture was also financed by Kenneth Frampton's Deo Gloria Trust. A team of people were gathered together to organize the festival including Peter Holmes from Deo Gloria, Jonathan Cooke, manager of All Things New, and Lindy Farrow (later Cooke). The festival was centred on activities from one main stage. In between the folk and rock acts were Christian speakers, among them the evangelist Eric Delve and charismatic leader Jean Darnell. There was a performance of *Lonesome Stone* with the Jesus Family turning up in force with their brightly painted double-decker bus. The influential charismatic musical *Come Together* was performed on the Sunday with a service of 'Breaking of Bread'. Rock bands were well to the fore with the British bands the Mighty Flyers, All Things New, and After the Fire performing alongside the brass-orientated rock sound of the US-based Liberation Suite.

While the numbers were a long way down on the 10,000 people predicted, Greenbelt was immediately heralded as a success. After the event Peter Holmes commented to a local newspaper that what had happened at Prospect Farm 'was the beginning of a young people's church'. This was an overstatement, but the first Greenbelt effectively put Christian rock music on the map. Veteran Greenbelter Stone recalls that up until 1974 the mainstream Christian acts sponsored by MGO and others were mainly folk-orientated. The significance of Greenbelt was that it gave a platform to new Christian rock bands like the Mighty Flyers and After the Fire.[49] Most acts, however, felt that they had to say something about their faith in Christ from the stage to explain what they were about. Although *Lonesome Stone* was in effect an evangelistic event, the musical also included a number of cover versions of secular rock songs like the hippie anthem 'Are you going to San Francisco?'. In this way Christians were opened up to seeing secular music as being of value, although not all the bands were this sympathetic to secular music: 'There was an idea that if you were Christians then all your songs had to be about Jesus. The only way to redeem secular music was to put Christian words to it.'[50]

Over the years Greenbelt became a forum for exploring the relationship between Christianity and culture. The 1975 festival saw the development of a whole series of seminars on artistic topics, from arts and crafts to architecture. By 1977 there were over thirty-five hours of seminars: John Gladwin was exploring 'Christ the creator', while Graham Kendrick was talking about leading worship. Greenbelt was to become a gathering place for evangelicals who wished to look beyond the boundaries of mainstream church life. Just as on stage bands explored rock music, in the seminar tents people like the late Jim Punton were to open the eyes of many to a radical and social understanding of the faith. Meanwhile the debate about the role of Christian music continued to run (as perhaps it still does to some extent). There were those who saw Christian music as primarily a tool for evangelism, and others who were more concerned to see Christians expressing themselves on a variety of topics through their artistic activities. Cooke was at pains to portray Greenbelt as pushing the frontiers of evangelical thought:

> It's God's world: he gave it to us and we have to explore all possibilities, biblically, practically and mentally. In a sense Greenbelt has always lived dangerously, we don't want to send people away with a nice safe package. If they go away slightly confused I wouldn't regard that as a failure if we are getting people to think.[51]

Getting people to think over the last twenty years or so has been very much part of Greenbelt's concern. Graham Cray, who was for a time chairman of the executive committee, was encouraged by the 1981 festival because the speakers were beginning to talk about issues of '. . . radical discipleship and Christian involvement in society. Structural and political things were covered as well as the individual's walk with God.' Malcolm Doney considers that there has, from time to time, been a clash within Greenbelt between the charismatic and the intellectual traditions represented at the festival. Graham Cray in his leadership was one of the few people able to model how these two could be brought together.[52]

It is perhaps because of these traditions that Greenbelt has continued to be an important meeting place for Christians from both within and outside the evangelical tradition. The festival has acted as a place where ideas are cross-fertilized and new perspectives spread more widely. Perhaps above all Greenbelt has been a place where people meet who might never have done so had the festival not existed. The informal networking that takes place at Greenbelt every year has had a deeply significant role in the creation of what some might call 'open evangelicals'.[53] The fact that Greenbelt can embrace such a wide variety of opinion and create a space where ideas are discussed enthusiastically and critically has been of crucial importance for the Church. In particular in the area of faith and culture Greenbelt has pioneered new understandings. In recent years the festival has played an important role in encouraging the spread of worship which marries contemporary culture and the Christian faith. It was at Greenbelt in 1988 that the majority of the Christian community first came into contact with the pioneering worship of the Sheffield-based 'Nine O'clock Service' (NOS).[54] Within a couple of years Greenbelt was hosting groups from Oxford and from Glasgow who were also experimenting with worship for young people. In 1992 Graham Cray led a seminar in London on the topic at the Greenhouse where over a hundred people had travelled from around the country to discuss new forms of worship based on contemporary youth culture. When problems emerged concerning NOS Greenbelt was one of the key gathering points where those involved in new worship services could meet and talk.

By 1983 Greenbelt, which had now moved to Knebworth, was playing host to around 30,000 people.[55] It was clear that the numbers coming to the festival represented a substantial market for Christian musicians and artists. Greenbelt in fact had always had an aspect of commercial enterprise about it. Nick Stone remembers that the Jesus Family who ran a bookstall in Manchester took a selection of books along to the 1974 festival. In one weekend this small bookstall sold more books than they had cleared in a whole year's trading in Manchester. Within a very short time groups such as Scripture Union, Traidcraft, Word Records and others were starting to realize the commercial potential of Greenbelt. It became very important for Christian record companies for their artists to perform at the festival. A good slot on the main stage was often accompanied by the release of a new album and a certain amount of promotion and advertising. Greenbelt itself has not been above this commercial side of the festival, investing heavily in their own Greenbelt shop where the punter could buy Greenbelt T-shirts, sweatshirts, baseball caps, in fact almost anything the Greenbelt logo could be printed on. Some of those involved in running Greenbelt in the earliest days had a clear commercial interest in what happened at the festival. Jonathan Cooke, for instance, was not only festival organizer, but also the manager of several acts featured prominently on the main stage.

For many young people used to the youth fellowship at their local church, a visit to Greenbelt was a baptism into a new and dynamic Christian subculture. Young people were to find at Greenbelt heroes in the Christian rock and pop world to follow. They became avid fans of bands such as Fat and Frantic and 'Phil and John'. Older Christians might catch up on the latest thinking in the seminars but as the festival got bigger and bigger members of youth groups were drawn into more impersonal relationships with Christian artists. Greenbelt can be seen in this way as fostering the evangelical subculture, despite its stated aims as expressed by Cooke. At times one could almost feel that what was being preached in the seminar programme was being subverted by the big-name acts on the main stage. The roles of radical disciple and fan fit uncomfortably with one another, the one being committed and active, and the other equally committed but essentially passive. The one demands creativity and imagination, the other asks only for consumption. The commercial pressures in a festival the size of Greenbelt are inevitable. Christian artists, however well meaning, need to make a living and to do this they need to sell their music.

The Jesus Movement and Evangelical Subculture

The impact of the Jesus revolution on youthwork in England has been tremendous. The emergence of specifically targeted Christian records, festivals and magazines has meant that Christian young people have been given the chance to buy into this new hip culture. As these young people have grown up events and products have moved with them. The net result has been that changes brought about by and for young people have now passed into the mainstream life of the majority of evangelical churches in this country.

This chapter started with Bebbington's view that for the first time in this period the barriers between evangelicalism and the world had come down. This is only partly true. While the new generation of evangelicals were delighting in the appropriation of youth-orientated media and events, their activity tended to take place outside the flow of the wider youth culture. Separate record companies, publishing houses and organizations tended to concentrate their efforts on producing a distinctive subculture for Christian young people. The net result was that young people were to experience evangelical youthwork as the invitation to consume specifically Christian products as alternatives to those marketed in the secular world.[56] Barriers between the world and the Church were coming down in that evangelicals were learning to operate in ways that mimicked the dynamics of youth culture. Evangelicalism can therefore accurately be described as a subculture because it has chosen to operate in a similar manner to other youth subcultures.

The creation of separate marketplaces, festivals and publishers led very quickly to increasing isolation within the evangelical subculture. It was youthwork and young people which were again the driving force in these developments.

The subsequent history of evangelical youthwork is, therefore, to a large extent the story of the development and influence of this subculture. The next two sections of this book show how the subculture generated by youthwork has impacted the wider evangelical community, first by looking at the developments in worship, and second by looking at the need to keep young people safe.

PART II

Youthwork and Worship

Chapter 5

Songs for Each Generation

Evangelical faith has always been expressed in song as much as in words. It is well known that hymn-singing is one of the distinctive features of the movement,[1] but perhaps it is less well known that work amongst young people has been the context for the development of evangelical choruses and songs more recently. Songs which were sung by young people at camps, beach missions, festivals and houseparties have become regular features of church life. It has often been evangelical young people who have created the styles of music and worship which have then been adopted by the rest of the evangelical constituency. The most pervasive, if not distinctive, aspect of evangelical worship, the 'chorus', was invented for work with young people and children. CSSM was famous for singing and in particular for its chorus book. The chorus came about because simple catchy songs were needed to teach to children at the special services and beach missions. Some of these choruses were chosen from popular hymns, as the name suggests: CSSM workers would leave out the more complex verses of a well-known hymn and simply use the shorter refrain. Other choruses were written specially. The tradition of producing chorus books for use with young people which was started by CSSM has continued, and in recent years there has been an explosion in the publication of songs for use in worship.

Since the war evangelicalism has experienced an extraordinary renaissance.[2] This remarkable growth and renewed vigour has been characterized by the ability of evangelicalism to adapt to cultural change. In Tidball's words, 'evangelicalism is a living movement, always adapting to the culture which it inhabits and changing as the culture changes.'[3]

Youthwork is one of the arenas within which evangelicalism has come to an accommodation with changes in modern culture. In the intimate relationships created in youth groups and especially on camps and at festivals, successive generations of evangelical youthworkers have sought to present the faith in attractive and relevant ways to young people. Such activities were inevitably to shape the culture of evangelical religion and have resulted in changes in the cultural 'atmosphere'. The songs which have formed such an important part of church worship offer an important insight into the changing face of a subculture.

The Songs We Sing

Over the last thirty years there have been three collections of songs which have been particularly popular both for use in youthwork and for use in church: *Youth Praise* (1966), *Sound of Living Waters* (1974) and *Songs of Fellowship* (1981). Each of these song collections, and the revisions and subsequent volumes which they spawned, have served the Christian community for roughly one decade.[4] Each of these songbooks speaks with a distinctive voice which seems to capture the spirit of the decade during which they were most commonly used. To read the lyrics, or indeed to sing your way through each of them in turn, is an enlightening and somewhat disconcerting experience. The songbooks appear to come from such different worlds. This is so much the case that to move from one to the other is almost like visiting another country (particularly when contrasting *Youth Praise* with *Songs of Fellowship*). The books are obviously products of distinctive traditions within evanglicalism but they also indicate the broad flow of mainstream evangelical church life.

Songbooks are theological but they are not systematic theology. Songs reflect doctrine but they are not doctrinal statements. The form of a popular song is much less exact, less rigorous in composition than that which would be expected in the theological seminar or an academic essay. There are therefore limits to the extent to which analysis of a group of songs can be taken as indicative of a particular movement within the Church. But it is also true to say that songs somehow take us to the heart of people's beliefs. Songs move us deeply. Part of the reason for this is that they have the ability to marry the rational and the emotional. Words set to music touch us in a multitude of ways. Singing is powerful because it is a deeply personal experience to use our own bodies to make music. Singing also has an important function for groups who wish to worship. To sing a song with others is to feel a sense of unity, so that we are able to say that we are 'joined together in song'.

To explore the songs which evangelicals have sung is to enter the world of 'popular religion' as opposed to official religion. It is a characteristic of protestantism that hymns and songs, and before that metrical psalms, have been the main place where the congregation played an active part in worship.[5] Choruses and hymns are the people's praise and it is no wonder that they have come to play such a crucial role in evangelical worship. They have a special power for us, and one of the reasons for this is that they are able to evoke memories. Songs remind us of people or events. Individual songs can build up associations for us which over time give them a deeply personal meaning. In this way songs, while not being formal theology, can very often lead us into more profound moments of encounter with God. In this sense they can be seen as indicators of a popular theology; that is, one which by association builds up around the symbolic language, musical feel and style of songs used in worship.

The popular theology which can be glimpsed in the study of Christian choruses and songs is not only personal; it is also collective. The symbolic language of each of these song-books was, for a time, shared by thousands of Christians in evangelical churches across the country. The successive popularity of the books is not only evidence of the importance of these songs for evangelical people, but it also points to changes within the popular theology of evangelicalism. Recurring themes and key phrases breathe through the songbooks and give each one a unique voice. The particular emphases in *Youth Praise, Sound of Living Waters* and *Songs of Fellowship* are of interest because they show how certain aspects of the biblical story and particular forms of symbolic expression rang true at different points during this period. The songbooks each represent a shared symbolic world which large numbers of evangelical Christians held in common. It is possible to see a gradual shift of theological perspective, particularly when the earliest material in *Youth Praise* is contrasted with the later work in *Songs of Fellowship*.

To look at the significance of worship songs in this way is to enter into the subcultural world of evangelical religion. The songbooks lead directly to the web of interests, activities and relationships which make up the evangelical world. The songs are written by people who themselves were part of a community of belief, and offer a picture of a group of people sharing a view of the faith. The songs also find their place in the wider market of evangelicalism: these books were commercial products offered for sale. The subculture has this commercial aspect, but there is also a sense in which the values and perspectives of these songs were also marketed. The theological progression seen in the songbooks is important because over the last thirty years large numbers of evangelical people have travelled a similar path. The songs were in part the cause of this, but they also simply indicate the changes which were taking place.

Youth Praise

The Historical Setting of 'Youth Praise'

The 1960s saw a new generation of evangelical clergy beginning to transform the life of the Church of England.[6] Through John Stott's revival of the Eclectics Society for young evangelical clergy in 1955[7] and through the renewed emphasis on biblical theology fostered by the UCCF[8] an articulate and confident group of young clergy were nurtured and began to emerge onto the scene. These young leaders within the Church were to make their mark at the National Evangelical Anglican Conference (NEAC) at Keele in 1967 where one commentator noted that 'Youth and ability were to the fore among the bright, thrusting and unsquashable men and women who gave this congress an unmistakable glitter.'[9] Keele was a decisive turning-point where on a number of issues evangelical Anglicans resolved to come out from the 'ghetto'.[10]

The impact of younger evangelical leaders at Keele was just one indication of changes taking place in parishes throughout the country. Bebbington refers to the 'new wave' of young evangelical Anglican clergy who burst out of the traditional evangelical parishes and as they did so they began to adopt a broader range of liturgical practices. One of the major factors in bringing about change was the need to develop worship which was relevant to young people.[11] It was these clergy who had themselves been brought to faith and nurtured within the traditions of evangelical youth-work, who now began to devote their time and energy to running youthwork in parishes around the country (see Chapter 2). Work with young people quickly led to the development of new resources for worship and in particular songs and songbooks. Michael Saward records that 'In the early 1960s a number of us who were curates with large youth groups set about producing our own local song and chorus books.'[12]

One of these young curates was Michael Baughen, who while he was at Hyson Green published a collection of songs for use with young people entitled *Zing Sing*. When he moved on to Reigate he was writing his own material which was published as *Zing Sing 5*. This book, according to Baughen, 'went round the place like wildfire'.[13] Baughen, with help from Richard Bewes, was the editor of the new collection of songs *Youth Praise* which was published in 1966 by Falcon Books for the Church Pastoral Aid Society.

Youth Praise was specifically designed for the new youth fellowships that had sprung up in most evangelical churches in
the postwar period. The book's introduction makes its aim
very clear: 'This book has been compiled to try to meet the
evident need for a composite youth music book in Christian
youth groups of many kinds.'[14]

From its initial success further books were soon to follow,
and in 1969 a companion volume was published. *Youth Praise
2* included a number of metrical psalms. The success of
these triggered off a four-year project which resulted in the
publication of *Psalm Praise* (1973). Until the introduction of
Sound of Living Waters in 1974 these three books were the
staple diet of Christian youth groups, and indeed of many
churches. Baughen (now Bishop of Chester) and Bewes were
both prominent evangelical Anglicans who were to occupy
key appointments at All Souls, Langham Place. Those
involved in bringing the material together in the early stages
included many of the most influential and prominent figures in the development of Anglican evangelicalism over the
last thirty years: Michael Botting, Kenneth Habershon,
Gavin Reid, David Watson and Norman Warren, with
encouragement being given by John Stott and Timothy
Dudley-Smith.[15] *Youth Praise* therefore gives a vital insight
into the character of the renaissance among evangelicals.

In *Youth Praise* we find the sentiments that the new wave
of young evangelical clergy wanted to see passed on to
young Christians. The songs display the values, attitudes
and theological perspectives of evangelicalism in the 1960s.
Youth Praise places itself within the context of 'teaching'
young people about the faith. The songs were meant to be
sung, according to the book's introduction, 'purposefully
rather than just for the sake of singing'.[16] To this end they
are grouped under a series of titles which indicate either a
particular theme (such as 'God's Invitation') or a way of using
the songs in youthwork ('At the Beginning of the Meeting').
The songs are there for instruction as well as fun; they are,
as the compilers put it, 'musical entertainment with a religious flavour'.[17] A close study of the material in *Youth Praise*

reveals some of the assumptions about the Christian life and
the experience of God which evangelical Christians held in
common during this period.

One of the key values which comes through in the words,
music and packaging of *Youth Praise* is that the Christian
faith can be presented in a lively and modern style. This
message is made clear from the front cover which uses 'blob-
like' 1960s lettering for the title. *Youth Praise* was distinctive
because it managed to incorporate aspects of contemporary
youth culture into worship. According to Bebbington the
book was 'a collection of modern choruses designed to appeal
to the burgeoning pop culture'.[18] Baughen and Bewes saw
themselves as providing 'words and tunes, in adequate number and variety, to allow contemporary expression of youth
praise and prayer and worship'.[19] There are a variety of musical styles found within *Youth Praise*, but it is the way that
contemporary styles of folk, and even rock, music are used
which gave the book its distinctive feel. Significant contributions were made by gospel groups such as The Venturers,
who arranged 'Can it be true?' (YP 36) and wrote the
twelve-bar blues number 'Jesus is the Saviour' (YP 61) and
The Followers who wrote the music to 'The King of Love'
(YP 63). Alongside folk and rock inspired tunes there are
traditional hymns which have been given contemporary
tunes, and spirituals and songs such as 'Gone! Gone!' (YP
49) or 'He lives' (YP 52) which have echos of popular
musicals of the time. In the words of the cover blurb, 'Here
are songs for all moods and for all tastes – all youthful and
all full of the exciting certainty of Christian belief'.[20]

The Symbolic World of 'Youth Praise'

Youth Praise is characterized by the repetition of a number
of themes so that the lyrics of the songs, when taken
together, paint a distinctive picture of the Christian faith
which reflects a particular symbolic world.

Jesus is most real at the moment of conversion

Religious experience is deeply engrained within the thought of *Youth Praise*, and most intensely focused on the moment of conversion. We are told in no uncertain terms in 'If you want joy' (YP 72) that we must allow Jesus to come into our hearts. The message of the repetitive lyric is reinforced by the rolling and and somewhat insistent effect of the rhythm which has three rather than four beats to each bar. The total effect of tune and words in YP 72 is to impress the message on the singer, yet there is also a slight sense of superficiality in the repetition of the word 'joy'. One wonders if this is really an accurate description of the Christian faith. There is an almost adolescent feel to the optimism of the song. The 'joy' of conversion in *Youth Praise* is a totally life-changing event which pervades the whole of a person's life. In 'Life is wonderful now' (YP 46) Jesus changes everything and gives total happiness, so conversion is the key to a marvellous and wonderful, joy-filled life. Again there is something of a simplification going on here. While Christian conversion is profound and of no small significance, 'Life is wonderful now' has got to be, at least to some extent, a somewhat rose-tinted view of Christian discipleship. It is the effect of words and music together which gives a hint of jolly superficiality to the song. The tune bounces along and we seem to set off on the Christian journey with apparently not a care in the world.

The concentration on the moment of conversion in *Youth Praise* leads to a state where distress is replaced by happiness. This impression is, to some extent, balanced by the use of the road and following Jesus as a metaphor for the Christian life as in 'When the road is rough' (YP 96) which gives some impression that life as a Christian can be tough and demanding. The passive ease of the conversion experience is a contrast to the tough life of discipleship. Conversion is most often referred to as opening up and 'letting Jesus in'. The place where Jesus 'comes in' is generally the heart. Jesus is depicted as patiently waiting, knocking on the

closed door of our heart (YP 73); to let him in is to experience fellowship with the divine (YP 68), but it is also to
experience a sense of release and freedom from what is often
seen as a bad and sinful past. YP 58 talks of a life which is
full of sin when Jesus find us. We feel that we are filled with
'misery and woe'. In this state Jesus embraces us in his loving arms and leads us on the path ahead. Conversion seen in
these terms is more often than not an internal experience or
a sense of release. There is again something adolescent in
the way this is expressed. In part this is deliberate as in 'Jesus
is the Saviour' (YP 61) which uses the teenage language of
feeling 'alone and blue'. When we are in this state Jesus, we
are assured, can 'pull us through'. In these and other ways
the song accurately expresses some of the anxieties which
characterize adolescence in terms which young people of
the day would have readily identified with. Jesus is confidently presented as the answer to common teenage feelings of
loneliness and depression.

The emphasis on conversion reminds the singer of those
who have not as yet responded to the claims of Christ. *Youth
Praise* is a book of celebration and worship but it always
keeps at least one eye on those who do not believe and who
might be persuaded to join in. Such is the emphasis on
conversion that a whole section is devoted to 'testimony'
and another is labelled 'challenge'. This invitation to the
uncommitted is born out of a confidence in the Christian
experience, even if at times it is delivered a little heavy-
handedly. 'Make up your mind' (YP 76) offers a basic and
uncompromising choice between the narrow path and the
broad. We are told in no uncertain terms that now is the
time to come to a decision and make up our minds. We
either go Jesus' way or we go our own. On the one side
there may be a large and attractive crowd, but on the other
there is a small band of followers of Christ. To join this
latter group will be costly and demanding; people may even
shun you but Jesus offers so much more. To receive the
power and liberty of Christ you have first to make up your
mind.

Focus on the death of Christ

With the moment of conversion being regarded as 'where the action is' in a spiritual sense, it is no surprise that the death of Christ features above any other event in his life in these songs. 'Calvary', 'tree', 'me' and 'free' trip off the tongue regularly in *Youth Praise*. The words seem made for each other, but this repetition highlights how very important these ideas were not only to the compilers but also to those who sang the songs. Young people through lyrics were encouraged to remind themselves continually of the death of Christ. 'Lord of the cross' (YP 11) presents the Passion as an event which sets our hearts on fire and makes us sing with gladness of the love of Christ. In this and in many of the other songs young people are urged to find in the events of the crucifixion a source of comfort in times of trouble. Days may well be filled with 'sorrow and care' and loneliness may be an ever-present problem but for those who believe, 'Burdens are lifted at Calvary' (YP 104). The authors are clear that the death of Christ should be seen as an atonement for sins, but this leads on to a sense of wonder at the generosity of God in bestowing such riches. Forgiveness is followed by gratitude and it is this which motivates us to a life of dedicated service. Because we have been set free by Jesus' death we are now moved to follow along the way (YP 42). 'I'll be a friend to Jesus' (YP 109) makes it clear that the trial and sufferings of Christ change us. The lyric dwells on how Jesus was deserted by his friends when he was on the cross and challenges the singer to be a friend to Jesus in the present.

The life of Christ

Youth Praise is from beginning to end a Jesus book. References to the earthly life of Christ fill almost every page. From the lyrics it would be possible to construct in some detail the events recorded in the Gospels. The songs dwell at length on the life of Jesus, from his humanity and birth

(YP 89), his miracles (YP 80) and his ministry (YP 89), to the story of his Passion, death and resurrection (YP 10). Jesus is also commonly referred to as King or Lord, but in a good many songs this title is balanced by reference to the nature of the incarnation (YP 9).

As with the death of Christ the songs frequently draw the singer into the life of Christ as a source of inspiration and wonder. Contemplation of the events of the gospel are offered as a major source of praise, worship, and thanksgiving. 'Can it be true?' (YP 36) offers a moving portrait of Jesus who walked the earth and shared in work, joy, and pain with his friends. Out of his great love for the world, the song says, he left his own world to be with us but ultimately he met a shameful and friendless death.

When we hear this story we are left marvelling and asking if it can really be true. In this way *Youth Praise*, while affirming the lordship of Christ, never loses sight of the humanity of Jesus. The emphasis on the suffering and struggle of Jesus' ministry is always there, but through it new life can come, and the worshipper is in turn asked to be a friend to Jesus who was so badly treated.

Following Christ

The most common metaphor in *Youth Praise* for the Christian life is that of a journey or a road. People need to choose between the right and wrong way (YP 76), for there is only one way to heaven and 'you'd better be on that road'. 'I want to walk' (YP 121) makes it plain that being on the move with Jesus involves complete surrender of body and soul. A walk with Jesus should be sought after as a daily thing (YP 101). The road may well turn out to be 'rough and steep', but the answer is to 'fix your eyes upon Jesus' (YP 96). Jesus is a leader who will guide you through darkness because indeed he is the way (YP 97). Following Jesus is a matter of denying self (YP 81) but also of being willing to take on a life of prayer, Bible reading and witness (YP 121). Reading the word shows us the way (YP 121). The Bible is referred to throughout *Youth Praise* as the authoritative source of guidance in the Christian life. It is important to feed on the word daily, to begin the day with Jesus and then to walk the way with him (YP 88).

The Christian life and the world

Ever concrete and down to earth, *Youth Praise* made it clear to young people what the Christian life was about. Bible reading, daily prayer and a life of service for God were all reinforced through the medium of song. There is a whole section devoted to Bible reading and prayer. The willingness to spell out the behaviour which is expected of a believer in such clear terms is an indication of the book's commitment to a practical expression of the Christian faith lived out in daily life.

In *Youth Praise* Jesus is often seen as a friend. As a friend he is special and unique because he is faithful as well as being 'strong and true' (YP 58). He offers care and assurance, but at the same time we are told that he will lead us in the way we ought to go. The friendship of Jesus is powerfully expressed as an internal experience which makes the believer 'feel better', but there is also a sense of mission and engagement with the ordinary things of life. YP 13 offers thanks for every new morning, forgiveness and the Spirit's power, as well as for 'leisure and employment'. This breadth of reference to life outside spiritual matters shows at least an inclination to value life beyond the evangelical ghetto. There is also a concern for the poor and underprivileged. YP 89 directly links events in the life of Christ which show him suffering injustice and poverty with the situation of the present-day homeless and oppressed. Christian mission is, however, more often seen in terms of witness and evangelism and primarily this is carried out by preaching the message.

Sound of Living Waters

The Historical Setting of 'Sound of Living Waters'

During the 1970s and 80s relatively few evangelical churches remained unaffected by charismatic renewal. The new openness to the Spirit was characterized by a freedom in praise, prayer and thanksgiving. This style of worship, and in particular the songs of renewal, spread widely throughout the Church.[21] The publication of *Sound of Living Waters* in 1974 was a key factor in popularizing the charismatic movement.[22] Renewal within the Church, however, was linked to the wider cultural changes in society brought about by young people in the counterculture. While significantly linked to youth culture and taken up by Christian young people around the country, the charismatic movement was to carry within it a conservative ethos which was itself a reaction to the youth culture of the 1960s.

The charismatic movement was moulded most powerfully by its context. In both the United States and Britain young people were embracing hippie style and behaviour in increasing numbers. Charismatic renewal 'created a Christian version of the counterculture'.[23] It is in the discovery of a new freedom of expression in worship that parallels between the movement and youth culture are seen most clearly. Michael Harper, one of the early leaders of the movement in Britain, places great emphasis on the liberty brought about by renewal in the Spirit: 'One of the clearest marks of a true outpouring of the Spirit is the free and spontaneous worship which those affected offer to God sometimes for hours on end.'[24]

Spontaneity was woven into the fabric of worship so that there was a sense of waiting on God for his leading. Space was created in services and meetings so that a variety of people could contribute to worship in an unstructured way.[25] It was music, and especially the songs sung by the Fisherfolk and later published in *Sound of Living Waters*, which led the way in bringing about liturgical change. As Tom Walker, when he was Vicar of St John's, Harborne, in Birmingham puts it:

> . . . with the introduction of Fisherfolk type choruses, the whole meeting suddenly came alive and there was a new freedom of expression. The accompaniment of the singing just happened without prior arrangement at all so that hand clapping, the use of tambourines, guitar and other instruments gradually were introduced as an expression of every member participation.[26]

Charismatic worship was the place where evangelicals tapped into the wider youth culture and started to 'express themselves'. In prayer and song people were encouraged to lay bare their feelings for God. Expression was not only limited to singing; the body also suddenly became important in worship. Hands were raised in prayer and praise, and congregations began to embrace each other with 'hugs and hugging'.[27] Dance as performance and communal dancing began to be part of services and there was a new emphasis on the visual arts, with the creation of banners with bright and stylistic decoration which were hung in churches.[28] According to the report *The Charismatic Movement in the Church of England*, renewal was regarded by some as a form of Christian existentialism whose attitudes could be summed up as a feeling that 'Above all God is alive and well, and meeting with us, teaching us, leading us – NOW!'[29]

In particular God was leading people to express themselves by writing songs and music to be used in worship. 'A creative talent has been unleashed, and all and sundry now write their praises and their prayers to be sung as new songs.'[30] The new songs enabled worship to be structured much less formally than had previously been the case. The relative simplicity of the music made it possible for anyone in the worship meeting to start singing; the musicians would then have to 'catch up' and start playing along. Songs could be punctuated by extemporary prayers or prophecy and at times lead into a communal singing in tongues. Bebbington views the renewal movement as 'a Christian version of "doing your own thing", a principle near to the heart of the expressive revolution.'[31]

Young people were very responsive to the new emphasis on experience of God which was growing in the Church. Faith Lees, who was one of the founders of a charismatic community based at Post Green, records how 3,000 young people attended their first arts seminar in 1972.[32] At the festival they were entertained by Judy MacKenzie, Gordon Giltrap and Stewart Henderson as well as receiving teaching from Jean Darnell. Post Green, much like Greenbelt, was to become a melting-pot where the Jesus Movement, the charismatic movement and later issues of simple lifestyle and involvement in urban ministry were to mingle together.[33] From the very start young people were at the forefront of the renewal in the Church. Harper saw this as one of the more significant features of the early days of the movement.[34] Tom Walker records how, after spending the weekend with David Watson and young people from St Mark's, Gillingham (one of the first Anglican parishes to be touched by renewal), he and his wife were led into an experience of the Holy Spirit.[35]

It was a book about youthwork which was a major factor in the spread of the charismatic movement in Britain. *The Cross and the Switchblade*, which was later made into a film, told the story of the Pentecostal pastor David Wilkerson who reached out to teenage gangs in New York. As part of a gripping story of relationship-based outreach to some of the toughest young people in American society, Wilkerson explains how 'baptism in the Spirit' could turn lives around and even free young people from heroin addiction.[36] The book was widely read by British evangelicals and in the 1960s it was an important source of inspiration for those thinking about baptism and the gifts of the Spirit. It was also one of the main books distributed by the Fountain Trust, the organization set up by Michael Harper to spread charismatic renewal within traditional denominations in Britain.[37]

It was through the ministry of David Wilkerson that the

Episcopal priest Graham Pulkingham (whose wife was one of the editors of *Sound of Living Waters*) received baptism in the Spirit. When Pulkingham took up his appointment as Vicar of the Church of the Redeemer in inner-city Houston, Texas, he was immediately struck by the deep social and spiritual needs of the young people in his area. His first move was to open up the church building to some of these young people, but he felt powerless to help them. In *Gathered for Power* he tells how he sought out Wilkerson in New York and eventually came into a new experience of the Spirit.[38] Back in the parish in Houston a community of people renewed in the Spirit began to grow. People became committed to moving back into the inner-city area round the church and a series of programmes to help the poor in the local community was initiated. The result of renewal was a transformed church which was 'charismatic in ministry, corporate in life and leadership, sacrificial in loving service and eucharistic to its core – a flavour not possible until the parish and the community had become one'.[39]

'Sound of Living Waters' and Renewal

In the early 1970s Pulkingham came to Britain, first touring with the music group the Fisherfolk[40] and later establishing the Community of the Celebration, which was eventually to link with the group at Post Green.[41] Graham's wife Betty was the creative force behind the evolution of the worship at the Church of the Redeemer. With her background in choral music it was soon recognized that worship was a 'charism' given to Betty.[42] Under her guidance an approach to music evolved which embraced a variety of musical styles, and was also devoted to charismatic worship. This type of worship was much appreciated in England. Graham Pulkingham, and in particular the Fisherfolk, significantly influenced the ministry of David and Anne Watson at St Michael le Belfrey in York. Anne was inspired by the shared community life of the church in Houston and in time a number of community houses were also established in

York.[43] David was perhaps more enamoured with the songs of the Fisherfolk:

> Through the marvellous ministry of the Fisherfolk we learned the combination of dignity and joy, depth and simplicity, quality and gentleness, spiritual sensitivity and artistic skill. Countless people today are hurting, often because of the pain of broken relationships; but through gentleness of worship the Spirit of God can touch and heal those inner wounds.[44]

It is in this description of the worship led by the group from the Church of the Redeemer that we start to see the paradox of charismatic renewal in England. It is strange that a movement which at heart is a response to a need for experience and self-expression should be so mild and reasonable. In part this is explained by the origins of those who were first affected within the Church. Those from the mainstream denominations who were attracted to charismatic renewal were from solidly upper middle-class professional backgrounds; Michael Harper was curate at All Souls, Langham Place, David Watson and David MacInnes were both products of Bash camps, while Tom and Faith Lees were titled gentry. They shared a clear desire to seek God in new ways but on the whole this was done to the accompaniment of the reassuringly conservative *Sound of Living Waters*.

Subtitled 'Songs of Renewal', the book was edited by Betty Pulkingham and Jeanne Harper and published in 1974. In 1977 a further volume was added called *Fresh Sounds*, published shortly after the widespread success of the musical *Come Together* which was promoted in the UK by Jean Darnell.[45] *Sound of Living Waters* included 'Holy, holy' (SLW 19) which was made popular by *Come Together* but alongside it there was a remarkably broad range of music. Traditional hymns are well represented, as are older gospel songs. Mixed in with these there are new compositions, many of them written or arranged by those directly involved in the renewal movement. Behind the choice of songs, however, there is a clear attempt to persuade. Older hymns are generally included because they share a symbolic vocabulary with the charismatic movement. In the words of the foreword these songs and hymns have a proven 'usefulness in worship':

> The ocean is deep and wide and so also is the musical scope of this book; it is not confined to youth or content with the old. Simply turn the page and it will transport you from Handel to the sound of rock in 'Godspell'. We believe the mixture of sounds reflects the wideness of God's mercy – like the wideness of the sea.[46]

The results of this attempt to embrace a wide range of musical styles within charismatic worship were very significant. The use of great hymns of praise like 'Praise to the Lord' (SLW 11) or 'Amazing grace' (SLW 5) or even 'Morning has broken' (SLW 9) gave a reassuring stability to a new and essentially innovative movement within the Church. *Sound of Living Waters* claims the musical middle ground but paradoxically it also introduces quite startling changes in the Church. While Betty Pulkingham and Jeanne Harper saw their book as having a 'unity characterised by gentleness and peaceful praise', others saw more fundamental developments taking place. Bebbington is clear about the impact of renewal on the Church: 'In the more flexible 60s and 70s the charismatic movement dissolved the familiar contours of church services wherever it appeared.'[47] Such changes were mainly brought about in informal ways. People caught renewal not so much by theological discussion but through sharing in worship. Renewal, therefore, was to a large extent a movement in popular theology. The musically conservative nature of *Sound of Living Waters* was in no way incidental to the spread of renewal at this popular level.

The second effect of the eclectic nature of *Sound of Living Waters* was that it reinforced the community aspects of the new movement. *Youth Praise*, while being fairly mainstream, is self-consciously opening up a dialogue with wider youth culture. *Sound of Living Waters*, while widely used by young people and youth groups, sees itself in the context of the whole community of the Church. It is 'folk art' rather than 'pop culture' which characterizes the ethos of the book. The editors self-consciously present the songs as the result of a work of the Spirit in the Church. The Church, which is often referred to as 'the body of Christ', is seen as diverse and yet unified, a place where everyone has something creative to offer. The introduction informs us that along with established composers 'a secretary called Sylvia, a young college student called Diane, and four-year-old David, son of one of the editors' have all contributed. According to Gunstone it is this participatory, folk art, aspect of charismatic worship which is most distinctive: 'To join in folk arts you do not have to be an expert; you just do your best and provided it is tolerable, it is accepted that it expresses you and is therefore welcomed in with all that others contribute.'[48]

It is this aspect of renewal, along with a theology of the body of Christ, which sets off a centripetal movement within the Church. Folk art assumes a common folk culture. It is precisely this communal aspect of modern life which was coming under strain in post-1960s Britain. Popular culture, and in particular youth culture, is characterized by alternative centres of identity formation and construction.[49] The development of a more 'folk' feel to worship and church life was a reaction to the movement within the wider culture. Christian people felt the lack of any genuine communal identity and so began to manufacture their own. This development set the Church on a course of cultural creation which was separate from the diverse and pluralistic popular culture in society at large. The result was a renewed and engaging Christian subculture. This was essentially a romantic enterprise which was to reinforce the dislocation of the evangelical churches from mainstream popular culture.[50] The attempt to recreate community through fostering Christian folk art was attractive, but also dangerous. The cultural productivity in the Church very soon became disconnected from any reference point in the wider culture. In the shallow pools and sunny backwaters of the churches the evangelical subculture quickly grew. 'Community' and 'folk

art' combined to offer a comforting and convenient escape
from the harsh realities which characterized the pluralistic
urban communities within which many churches were set.
Sound of Living Waters takes aspects of the counterculture
and domesticates it. It was a religion for ex-hippies who
now had children and straight jobs.

During the 1970s and 80s charismatic renewal was to
make a profound impact on evangelicalism in this country.
Not surprisingly the movement was seen as being very controversial and by no means all evangelicals were to follow its
lead.[51] At the NEAC in Keele in 1967 the movement was
hardly mentioned. By the 1977 gathering in Nottingham,
charismatics were very much to the fore, with David Watson
as one of the main speakers and the worship conducted in a
charismatic style similar to that found at Fountain Trust
conferences.[52] *Sound of Living Waters* illustrates these changes
within the evangelical churches. The images and symbols
used in the songs take us to the heart of a movement which
was at its most profound and also at its most influential as
it worshipped.

The Symbolic World of 'Sound of Living Waters'

Sound of Living Waters is characterized by an atmosphere of
thanksgiving and praise. The subtitles under which the songs
are arranged give a feel for a community which is committed to worship. The sections include: 'Hallelujah! . . . Songs
of Praise and Thanksgiving', 'Kneel and Adore . . . Songs
of Worship' and 'Suffer – Reign . . . Songs of Faith and
Victory'. Worship is clearly seen as deep and demanding,
but it is also an activity with which most people can engage.

Sound of Living Waters is concerned to include people
and make worship as accessible as possible. While relatively
complex hymns are included, the overall tenor of the book
is simplicity. Many of the songs use very few words. SLW
25 is called 'Alleluia', and the first verse is simply the title
repeated eight times. Similar instructions are given for
SLW 57 where the lyric for verse one is simply the word

Jesus repeated five times. Both these songs were arranged by Betty Pulkingham and they were characteristic of a growing trend in charismatic worship. The simplification of song lyrics enabled people to do without songbooks, so arms could be raised in praise or eyes closed in prayer. Simplification of the lyrics of the songs allowed more freedom and expression in the worship. At times the community values of *Sound of Living Waters* mean that it comes close to songs round the camp-fire – it includes 'Go tell it on the mountain' (SLW 121) and 'Kum ba yah' (SLW 42).

It was not just the lyrics which were more accessible. The music was arranged for guitar and in such a way that musicians with relatively little experience could accompany them. *Youth Praise*, while including guitar chords, is essentially written for the piano. The average guitarist in a youth group would find the guitar chords used in *Youth Praise* demanding, to say the least.[53] In *Sound of Living Waters* the arrangements for songs, and even in some cases the hymns, rarely demand more than a basic competence from the guitarist. As a result the material was widely used in churches and youth fellowships, and was ideal for the new 'music groups' which were slowly emerging in churches up and down the country.

Children were very much to the fore in *Sound of Living Waters*. Some of the songs were written by children and the book contains a number of very good children's songs, including 'The butterfly song' (SLW 106) with lines asking the singer to imagine that they are a 'fuzzy-wuzzy bear' thanking God for their 'fuzzy-wuzzy hair'. According to *Sound of Living Waters* to be like a child is essential to developing an attitude of worship. The section devoted to children's songs has the title 'Come as Children . . . Songs for Children of All Ages'. At times the book appears to set out deliberately to develop child-like, and some might say childish, behaviour among those who worship, as in 'The joy of the Lord' (SLW 83), where the chorus repeats 'ha' thirty times in succession. *Sound of Living Waters* may get the balance wrong at times, but this is brought about by a sincere desire to encourage worship which embraces the child in each of us. In the music edition the section entitled 'Become . . . Songs of Wholeness and Maturity' has a picture of a tiny child taking its first steps towards a male figure who is crouching down with outstretched arms. Wholeness and maturity are achieved as we develop within us the simplicity and the trust which characterize childhood.

Songs used in worship carry significant meanings and the 'songs of renewal' are certainly no exception to this rule. *Sound of Living Waters* has a rich pattern of Christian symbol and 'theology' but it is the combination of repeated themes which gives the book a distinctive voice and emphasis.

Jesus is most real when we gather together to praise him

Conversion as a one-off experience is rarely, if ever, mentioned in *Sound of Living Waters*. Experience of God is generally seen less as a past event and more as an on-going reality which continues on a day-to-day basis. Songs which might refer to a moment of conversion are often written in such a way that the experience of God can also be seen as happening on a more continuous basis. When 'Jesus, Jesus, wonderful Lord' (SLW 32) speaks of Jesus touching us and making us whole, this could be taken by different people in different ways. For one person the line might speak of conversion while for another it could be another experience of God's blessing.

Conversion in *Youth Praise* is essentially an individual encounter with God. In *Sound of Living Waters* experience of God is much more of a corporate matter. *Sound of Living Waters* is a 'we' book. In general the songs talk about a moment when we encounter God together as in 'Son of God' (SLW 21) and 'I will sing, I will sing' (SLW 7) where worship is referred to as 'coming before the Lord'. Coming before God is a continuing theme which builds the sense of a corporate activity within which we meet God together.

Thus it is when we 'gather together' that God reveals himself in power and glory. Togetherness leads to a confidence in meeting with God and so the song 'We see the Lord' (SLW 23) can talk of meeting God together in the temple. For those involved in renewal God's presence was an ongoing and significant experience in the Christian life, but this experience is most clearly focused in the act of worship itself. It is when we join together to praise him that God visits us in this way. The effect of this is that it pulls the attention of Christian people into being together in (most commonly) church services or church-based meetings. Individually we may decide to offer our lives to God (SLW 19) but we do this alongside others in worship.

When we give ourselves in worship we meet God. Thus awe and reverence characterize worship, because God is really here with us (SLW 22). The presence of God and indeed the Christian life are both centred on 'the body of Christ'. The singer is urged to delight in the fellowship of believers, as in the Fisherfolk song arranged by Betty Pulkingham, 'We really want to thank you, Lord' (SLW 69), where the body of believers is seen as a gift and a place were we 'live and move in the love of Christ'. Being with each other is therefore the context within which we most profoundly experience God.

One of the subsections in the book is entitled 'Songs of the Kingdom . . . The Body of Christ'. The close association of the gathered community of believers and God's powerful activity runs through the whole of the book. When Christians come together for praise and worship wonderful signs of God's presence take place. We are 'set free for service'. Within the Christian fellowship people care for each other with 'tenderness' and it is through this pastoral support, and in the context of praise, that we experience healing. 'The body song' (SLW 111) adapts 1 Corinthians 12.14–26 and applies the idea of belonging together in Christ to our present-day life within the Church. We each belong to the other because God has made the body and it is he who keeps it together. By gathering in worship and by life within 'the body' we see that the Kingdom is 'among us' (SLW 61). Within this fellowship of believers we are urged to love one another because this is God's new commandment to us (SLW 66, 70).

Jesus then and Jesus now

More often than not songs are addressed to, or speak about, Jesus. Events from the historical life of Christ are spread throughout the book. These range from a full account of the Passion and resurrection in 'The canticle of the gift' (SLW 2), to a record of the nativity in 'Calypso carol' (SLW 118). The humanity of Christ and his earthly ministry are also regularly used as a focus for reflection and praise, but the emphasis is generally on the way that Jesus touches and changes people's lives (SLW 32). SLW 49, 'Here comes Jesus', links the event in the gospels where Jesus walks on the water and calms the storm to the present experience of believers. As Jesus lifted Peter out of the water so today he will 'lift you up and he'll help you to stand'. 'The foot wash-ing song' (SLW 125) recounts how at the last supper Jesus washed his disciples' feet. Followers of Christ are urged to serve one another by also washing each other's feet.

Sound of Living Waters manages to keep clear links between the suffering human aspect of Jesus and the triumph of the risen Lord. Both the humanity and the divinity of Christ are balanced in the songs. 'The canticle of the gift' (SLW 2) manages to retell the story of Christ including his birth to Mary and his death on the cross, as well as referring to Christ the Lord and King enthroned in heaven. Each of these perspectives on the gospel is seen as a wonderful gift and therefore a matter for praise and rejoicing. The same Jesus who lived, died and rose again is also welcomed as a friend. As Paul Mazak (aged four) puts it, 'Jesus is a friend of mine, praise him' (SLW 114). Love for Jesus and love for other people as well as ourselves is recommended by another four- year-old who wrote 'We love the Lord' (SLW 112).

The Holy Spirit

While *Sound of Living Waters*, much like *Youth Praise*, is mainly a 'Jesus' book, many of the songs also refer to the Holy Spirit. In some a trinitarian theme is followed, as in 'Holy, holy' (SLW 19). In other songs a more traditional concluding verse gives a trinitarian flavour to the worship (SLW 12). It is the Spirit which is seen as the aspect of the Godhead who is 'active' in the present. The Spirit will 'fall afresh' on us (SLW 28). It is the Spirit who will 'fill our hearts anew' (SLW 19); the descending Spirit imparts 'gracious powers' (SLW 33). Charismatic gifts have their origin in the activity of the Spirit (SLW 77). The activity of the Spirit is continually referred to as something 'new' or 'fresh'. There is therefore a sense that God is doing something 'among us' now which is special and exciting. This fresh activity of God is linked directly with the events in the Acts of the Apostles, as in 'Silver and gold' (SLW 50). This song tells the story of Peter and John and the man who was healed and started 'walking and leaping and praising God'. Now is a special time and we should not be afraid, as 'Fear not! rejoice and be glad' (SLW 59) says; God has done great things by pouring out his Spirit on everyone who confesses the name of Christ. When the Spirit comes he brings teaching (SLW 41), healing (SLW 50), and repentance. The effect of an encounter with God is often described as a 'touch' but this is always gentle (SLW 32). The work of God could also be extremely powerful and even disturbing. The quiet and meditative tones of 'Spirit of the living God' (SLW 29) remind us of the energy of God which breaks us, moulds us and fills us.

Living waters

Water is a powerful and characteristic image for the Holy Spirit in many of the songs. 'The Holy Ghost Medley' (SLW 77) tells of the water that Christ gave to the woman in John's Gospel. Just like that woman the water we receive will not only satisfy us, it will also be source of spiritual enrichment for others. We drink in the water which comes in generous supply and this, in turn, wells up within us and begins to overflow. Water is a symbol of the Spirit's life and power renewing the Church and bringing others to Jesus. Those outside the Church therefore are often seen as 'thirsty' and they are invited to drink from the living waters (SLW 88). Such images are open-ended and inclusive. They generally leave room for the believer to place himself or herself as the 'thirsty' one. In this way Christians are also urged to thirst continually for God and drink at his wells. But these waters need to flow into the desert and set the captives free (SLW 91). Constant spiritual renewal results in a sense of mission both to those inside the body and also to those outside (SLW 93).

There is a sense that what God by his Spirit inspired Jesus to do, the Church should also be doing. Mission and involvement is lived out primarily within the life of the body, but occasionally this spills over into the surrounding community. The Church is a vessel which through its praise and life together receives the living water from God. As the people are filled they overflow into mission and outreach. God fills the Church to such an extent that it is out of excessive 'fullness' and filling that we reach out to others (SLW 131). Jesus gives us the water and it springs up within us and flows out, so when we drink at the springs of living water we find that our soul is satisfied (SLW 77). When the Spirit falls on people they will be deeply affected by the experience, but they will need to return continually to be filled afresh (SLW 29).

Apocalyptic

The pouring out of the Spirit is seen as a mark of the last times when old men shall dream dreams and young men shall prophesy. The fig tree is budding and the vine is bearing fruit; this is not a time for fear because the Lord has done a great thing by pouring out his Spirit on all 'mankind'

(SLW 59). Scattered throughout *Sound of Living Waters*, but by no means universally prevalent, there are apocalyptic images and symbols. Jesus is spoken of as 'the Lamb' (SLW 34) and as the one who mounts in triumph riding on the clouds (SLW 79). Believers are seen as a royal priesthood to whom God has come (SLW 95). These images are sometimes combined with Israeli folk tunes which were often used as the accompaniment to dancing. The Jewish roots of many of these songs, often drawn from the Psalms, lend a strange and exotic flavour to lyrics which refer to Aaron's beard, Hermon's dew and Zion (SLW 98). While *Sound of Living Waters* has only a faint tinge of this Jewish apocalyptic imagery, in *Songs of Fellowship* it was to become the staple diet.

Songs of Fellowship

The 1980s was the era of large Christian festivals. Greenbelt, Spring Harvest and Dales and Downs Bible Weeks all emerged during the decade as major influences on the Church. It was through the popularity of Christian festivals that the style of worship and music which had once characterized only youthwork became the norm in churches up and down the land.

Perhaps the most highly regarded worship leader and songwriter from this period is Graham Kendrick. Although Kendrick was to become prominent after the publication of book one of *Songs of Fellowship*, his career illustrates the move from work primarily aimed at young people to music which was to be used in worship with people of all ages. In the early 1970s, along with Clive Calver, Kendrick toured the country as a travelling evangelist and musician. His band would play in coffee bars which aimed to draw young people off the streets to hear the Christian message. In 1976 he became musical director for British Youth for Christ and when Spring Harvest was started in 1978 by BYFC and *Buzz* magazine he was the natural person to lead worship at the event. His role at the festival encouraged him to write songs and his own skills as a worship leader began to grow. By 1983 the worship aspect of his ministry had developed to such an extent that he ceased to perform at concerts. Through the platform of Spring Harvest, Graham Kendrick and other songwriters were to spread worship songs throughout the evangelical (and other) churches in Britain.[54] The *Songs of Fellowship* series, published by Kingsway Publications, was to make much of this material more widely available.

Songs of Fellowship also has its roots in the spread of what Walker calls 'restorationist' new churches during the 1980s. Identified as a separate strand of Pentecostalism outside the main denominations, these independent and much more radical churches were growing in Britain throughout the 1970s.[55] In the 1980s they burst onto the scene and through festivals such as the Dales Bible Week their influence was to spread widely both within and outside the main denominations. Worship was the chief means by which the ideas associated with restorationism were to spread:

> The Dales, not surprisingly . . . became the shop window for Restoration teaching and worship. Its music has had far-reaching effects outside its own circle. All the Pentecostal denominations, and many Baptist and charismatic mainstream churches can be found singing 'songs of the kingdom' that originated at the Dales.[56]

At the start of the 1980s the charismatic renewal in the mainstream churches appeared to have been largely domesticated and absorbed. In the late 1970s the Fountain Trust decided to close itself down and despite the establishment of denominational charismatic groups many within the mainline churches began to look towards the new restorationist churches for inspiration.[57]

Songs of Fellowship Book 1 represents a significant new departure in the symbolic language used by evangelical Christians in postwar Britain. The distinctive nature of the language and theology represented by the songs owes much of its inspiration to the radical charismatic vision of the restorationist churches. Published in 1981, the book was quickly adopted by Christian groups and churches. Two more volumes of songs and one of more traditional hymns were added and in 1985 the combined edition soon established itself as one of the most commonly used songbooks in evangelical churches. Though widely used, *Songs of Fellowship* is clear that it represents a new development in worship amongst God's people. The cover information speaks of the book as 'reflecting the onward move of God's Spirit among his people . . .'. Despite an evident connection with the new life in the British churches, the lack of named compilers or editors lends a certain facelessness to the *Songs of Fellowship* series. The combination of songbooks, words editions and various worship records and tapes gives a corporate business atmosphere. With no Michael Baughen or Betty Pulkingham to greet us warmly we are left with Kingsway Publications who assure us that they will continue to publish 'a developing series of worship aids'.[58]

Musically the book is a retreat from an attempt to associate Christian worship with teenage style. *Songs of Fellowship* rarely, if ever, ventures into forms of music associated with youth culture. The style is generally that of middle-of-the-road adult-orientated soft rock music, although at times the songs seem to adopt a kind of quasi-classical musical voice. 'I hear the sound of rustling' (SF 48) sounds like a military march, 'I love you Lord' (SF 49) has a classical lilt in its melody, while 'Jesus we enthrone You' (SF 86) feels almost anthemic and royal in style. The directions in the music edition regularly indicate that songs are to be sung 'majestically' or 'with majesty' (SF 71, 101, 132, 14). Occasionally songs are to be sung 'triumphantly' (SF 32, 36, 41, 80) or 'worshipfully' (SF 6, 87, 109, 99). *Songs of Fellowship* is always more like easy-listening than classical music, but the general direction of the musical style is away from genres easily recognizable outside the Christian community. In this sense *Songs of Fellowship* does a U-turn away from the direction

taken by *Youth Praise*. It is a musical cul-de-sac where Christians are inventing a style of their own which is less and less
accessible to those outside the Christian Church.

The Symbolic World of 'Songs of Fellowship'

Jesus enthroned on his people's praise

Songs of Fellowship has no reference to the life of Jesus,
except his death and resurrection. It would be impossible to
reconstruct the gospel story from this songbook. There is
little or no reference to the incarnation, nor to Christ's ministry of teaching and healing. The events of the passion are
told only in relation to their present-day effect on our lives.
In fact one song suggests that the historical facts about
Christ are a distraction from his experiential reality; 'Jesus,
come closer to me now' (SF 67) speaks of needing to see
Jesus now, 'no more just words and facts about a man who
lived long ago'.

The earthly life of Jesus has be subsumed in the concentration upon the risen Lord who reigns from on high. *Songs
of Fellowship* concentrates on the Jesus who has risen from
the dead and who is Lord (SF 36). As Lord his name is
higher than any other (SF 37), but he is also 'our King' (SF
17). In worship and through singing we are able to express
our love for the one who is Lord and King. 'I love you Lord'
(SF 49) has both an intimacy in the lyrics, where the King
is asked to 'take joy' in the 'sweet sound' of the voice of the
singer while there is a 'regal' note in the melody. The direction is that it should be sung 'with feeling'. The Christian
encounters Jesus the King as he or she joins in worship,
because praise creates a throne for the Lord. 'Lord Jesus, we
enthrone you' (SF 86) tells of the worshippers building a
throne of worship where Jesus can come and take his place.
The message of the song is reinforced by the stately character of the melody lines. It is a royal Jesus on the throne who
is 'clothed in righteousness' and a holy God who is worthy

of honour and praise. Jesus from this lofty position is the one who has a name which is high over all (SF 26). That the Lord reigns is a matter for rejoicing. The singer is asked to be glad and to 'give the glory to him' (SF 30). Jesus who is over all holds the key to salvation; 'No man could break him down' and he 'breaks all chains to redeem us' (SF 35). The heavenly Lord, however, is also able to come and touch people in a personal way (SF 60).

Jesus brings new life to the believer; indeed it could be said that it is no longer we who live, but Christ who lives in us (SF 56). Jesus inspires a 'sweet' fellowship between believers (SF 23). The songs ask us to sing of Jesus as lovely, gentle, pure and kind. Yet this picture of Jesus is not so romanticized that we lose sight of his death on the cross (SF 68). Although the death of Christ is referred to as painful (SF 71), the cross is rarely, if ever, seen as a place of profound suffering and struggle. The forgiveness of Christ is to be celebrated with a good deal of expression and exuberance. Forgiveness inspires hand-clapping and dancing (SF 44). It is a Jesus who has touched our lives who is to be constantly thanked and praised (SF 116) because he is such a friend (SF 117). This Jesus is the one who is 'changing me', he is 'The Son of righteousness' (*sic*) who rises over me (SF 70).

A strange olden-day world

Songs of Fellowship has old-fashioned phrases and words throughout. Many of these originate from the Authorised Version of the Bible. Words such as 'magnify', 'acclaim' and 'ascribe' are often used for our praise of God. Many of the songs use the 'thee' and 'thou' forms of the older transla-tions. At times it is hard to see why songwriters of the 1980s would consciously choose to express themselves in these archaic terms. There is, however, a romantic nostalgia in the language which by drawing on Old Testament terminology seems to hark back to a time in the past when things were 'alright'. In general this time is described as when the temple still stood and God came to meet his people. Being in the temple, however, also refers very much to the present experience of Christians. To meet God in the house of the Lord it is necessary to go through a process of change. This is often seen as the refiner's fire which makes us pure as gold (SF 70). Worshippers 'enter his gates' (SF 62), they 'stand by night in the house of the Lord', and lift up their hands in the holy place (SF 16). There is mysticism in the intimate encounter with God which takes place in the temple; there believers enter within the veil to look upon God's face (SF 155).

Believers are seen as the people of God, a royal priesthood set aside to worship him as a 'holy nation' (SF 14). The chosen people are also symbolized in the use of the connected image of 'Zion', the city of God. We are born within the gates of Zion and God will 'establish her' (SF 12). God is building the walls of the city of Zion and the workers are asked to rest from their labours for a while to dance round the walls and see what God is doing; the labourers are the stones in this wall (SF 17). God is building a temple made without hands and a city without walls. This city is enclosed by fire and built out of living stones (SF 98). There is a close identification between the people of God and the Kingdom of God. So much is this the case that 'I want to sing about Jesus' (SF 60) describes the people of the Kingdom as holy, washed and free.

The Father offers safety

It is a recurring theme that believers find safety and security in God. Believers are able to shelter in the temple (SF 145). The city motif and the image of the temple generally imply some escape from a hostile outside world. This place is a refuge where people can feel secure in a dangerous world where thousands may fall around us (SF 145). So good is it to be in the temple that there is often desire to stay there for ever (SF 33). Alongside the temple as a place of refuge and safety God is also described as a rock who offers shelter.

'Hear my cry, O Lord' ('In the shelter of His wings') (SF 33) speaks of the safety which we find under God's wings. To be near to God is to be not only secure but confident (SF 119). Security and safety are occasionally seen as leading to following or serving (SF 57). But the general tone of the songs implies that 'out there' among the enemies and the nations it is a tough and alien environment and it is far better to be 'inside in the temple'.

Connected with the theme of safety and security is an emphasis on God as a caring and loving Father. 'Abba Father' (SF 1) encourages us to join our will to that of God. Our Father then holds us in such a way that our hearts never go cold. God is often seen as a loving Father who takes away the cares and worries of his children. In the shadow of his wings problems seem to vanish and we feel secure. In some cases the security found in a loving Father verges on over-dependency as in 'Father, I place into your hands' (SF 21).

The stress on God as Father is matched by the continual use of 'man', 'men' and 'mankind' in a good number of the songs. Very rarely do songs attempt to include women by the use of, say, 'brothers and sisters'. The repeated use of male imagery makes *Songs of Fellowship* a fiercely masculine book and masculinity is joined closely to a view of family. Under God the Father we now have a new family and in God's family we have security (SF 144). In this family we are all one, God is the father of us all and we are all his chosen sons (SF 150). By dwelling together in this united family all men know about the work he has done (SF 150). This is a Father who has a big open heart and we are simply asked to 'just hold onto his hand' (SF 143).

Triumph over the nations

The vision of the mission of the people of God in *Songs of Fellowship* is primarily that of an apocalyptic battle. Surrounding the holy people are 'the nations'. The nations will eventually come to the Lord at Mount Zion (SF 91) and it is there that they will offer praise to God. The nations are 'thirsty' (SF 13) and in need of healing (SF 48). Light comes through the reflected praise and love of Zion and this Light acts in such a way that the nations 'fear his holy name' (SF 123). Alongside the nations a recurring metaphor is that of 'the land'. The people of God are prepared by him to 'move through this land' by his Spirit (SF 25). Often employing military metaphors drawn from the Old Testament, the songs tell believers to march upon the land. 'We are God's own army' (SF 142) speaks of us as an army, brothers together. As a body we claim the land which God has set before us. When this happens God's glory will spread throughout the earth and the nations will acknowledge Christ as Lord.

The continual use of 'the nations' and 'the land' has the effect of distancing those outside the Christian Church. It is hard to see the connection between our next-door neighbours or the people we work with and and the alien feel which arises from the use of the term 'the nations'. In this context Christian mission and witness becomes closely connected with victory and triumph. The nations will see believers 'justified' and held as a royal diadem in the hand of God (SF 125). The land is there to be taken and a new city is to be built upon it. This new city will be the new Jerusalem, 'God's dwelling place with men' (SF 126). This present time is seen in 'I hear the sound of rustling' (SF 48) as a moment when a slumbering Church is rising from its knees. The old dry bones are coming to life because the day of Jesus is drawing near. What is emerging is an army dedicated to God but also committed to war. We are commissioned by God and when they hear of what is coming the devils will flee before the perfect work which Jesus has begun. This new Church will be 'a people of power' who will, under the Spirit's inspiration, move through the land (SF 25). The symbolism of *Songs of Fellowship* leaves little room for concrete references to how believers are to live out the Christian faith in their daily lives.

'Youth Praise', 'Sound of Living Waters' and 'Songs of Fellowship': The Message of the Books

The analysis of the songs which evangelicals have sung over the last thirty years shows a developing mind set. In the key areas of Christian experience, the importance of the earthly life of Christ and Christian mission, significant changes are evident. These changes chart the flow of popular theology within the subculture. They also indicate how forces set in train within youthwork have been adapted and developed as time has gone on. Many of these developments, if this analysis is right, are cause for concern and reflection. For the purposes of this study the songbooks indicate a crucial move from an inclusive approach to youth culture and secular culture towards a greater exclusivity.

Youth Praise is clearly concerned to engage in a dialogue with youth culture. There is an openness to the unchurched and a concrete feel about the need for outreach and the social implications of mission. *Sound of Living Waters* begins what could be described as a centripetal movement towards increased involvement within the Church. The feeling that it was important to gather together and be 'filled' has isolated Christians within their own activities and subculture. Joy in the fellowship of the body of the Church predominated and active engagement with the unchurched became increasingly marginalized. In *Songs of Fellowship* an apocalyptic alarm begins to enter the vocabulary of the songs. The people of God gather together for refuge, escaping into the comforting arms of their Father. Following Christ has been turned into an encounter in the temple, safe from prying eyes. The vulnerable and human Jesus has been replaced by a reigning Lord who sends his army to march on the land and triumph over the nations.

If the language of songs has at least a partial correlation with the theology and spirituality of the people who sing them then this picture has deep implications for the Christian Church. The developments reflected in the language of these songbooks hold the clue to the character of Christian youthwork. In particular, the current need to create safe places for Christian young people to retreat from the world is seen as corresponding to a general sense of alarm about the secular world which is felt widely among evangelicals. These issues are the focus of Part III, which will explore in more depth the links between the concern of Christian parents for the safety of their children and the continued development of the evangelical subculture. The next chapter, however, examines a complementary movement based on the rise of family as a metaphor for the Church.

Chapter 6

Family Church

In the last fifty years or so there have been significant changes in emphasis within evangelicalism towards the 'family' as the basic building block of the Church. In the evangelical mind church and family have become intimately interlinked. The growth in 'family services' and all-age worship has tended to focus attention on the church as 'family'. As a result the worship of the local church has become much more centralized. The rhetoric of the 'family service' and 'all-age worship' generally has within it a powerful conviction that everyone connected to the church should attend one service. In many evangelical parishes these ideas have also been reinforced by a renewed commitment to more regular Communion services.

New thinking concerning the worship of the whole Church has had a significant impact on the development of youthwork. The youth fellowship is crucially affected by the church of which it is part. In the first instance, whatever happens in the youthwork, the most basic reality that forms the bedrock of Christian experience for many young people will be church attendance with parents. Second, most youth fellowships have at their core young people whose parents go to the local church. Of course youth fellowship will, to some extent, be a separate group but its fundamental reference point will generally be the church to which it is attached. Young people therefore are seen, in the majority of churches, as part of the family and their attendance is often overtly encouraged and almost certainly hoped for. In the youth fellowship a certain distance is allowed, but underlying this will be a general pressure towards what is seen as the centre of the church's life: the main service on a Sunday.

The clear priority given to attendance at one service has led to tensions in Christian youthwork. Young people have often wanted to design and take part in services which reflect their own culture. The 'youth service' has been in existence for many years, perhaps fuelled by people's experience of worshipping in more informal and relaxed ways at house-parties and at festivals. The response of the evangelical church in many places has been to incorporate elements of this style of worship into its own life. This is how evangelicalism has been able to renew itself in the postwar era. Innovation which happens at youth events outside the local congregation in time find a place in the ongoing worship of the church. It is the centralizing tendencies which arise in part from the emphasis on 'family' in the church which make this kind of adaptation possible. In recent years there has been a burst of experimentation in the area of youth culture and worship.[1] The centralizing inclination of the churches is being challenged by the desire of young people and young adults to create new and innovative styles of worship within their own age groups and culture. The church as 'family' forms an essential backdrop to these developments. When we ask the question 'Should there be a youth congregation?' we are brought face to face with the question of family.

Family Matters

The family has come to play an increasingly important role in evangelical thinking in recent years. This has grown from a sense of alarm at changes within the wider society. For many people, and not just Christians, there is a feeling that current trends are a threat to the family. In the face of, among other things, rising divorce rates, teenage pregnancy, lone parent families, cohabitation before marriage and a growing awareness of sexual and physical abuse, people are extremely concerned. According to the Anglican report on the family, *Something to Celebrate*, there is a temptation to look back to a golden age of 'moral certainty and family stability, where roles and rules were clear and everybody knew his or her own place'.[2]

The concentration on the family is understandable because for many of us it remains an extraordinarily important institution:

> The idea of the family has a powerful grip on people's imaginations and represents something over and above their actual experience. The family is invested with significance because it expresses, perhaps more purely than any other idea, a sense of collective well being.[3]

In a fast-changing and unpredictable environment, families provide a 'haven and a retreat'.[4] For many people families are looked to as places of strength, stability and security in what seems an extremely frightening world.[5] For evangelicals this perception is acutely the case. Families are seen not simply as the primary environment within which the faith is taught; they act as an important symbol within the subculture. According to *Something to Celebrate*, for evangelicals 'the family matters as a symbol of social stability and moral virtue. It is a divinely ordained guard against the ambiguities, individuation and experimentation of the modern world which has lost its way morally and religiously.'[6]

For evangelicals the family is also seen as referring to the Church. This theological interpretation of the family offers a good deal to a wounded and damaged society. The evangelical *New Dictionary of Christian Ethics and Pastoral Theology* sees the Scriptures as offering a series of healthy family roles which can 'change the damaged patterns of behaviour frequently passed on from one generation to the next'.[7] The church also acting as a family can provide role models which bring about change through relationships: 'Adoption into God's family can provide the psychic energy to change – as individuals know that they are accepted into that family, that they belong to it and that they experience God's power.'[8] In such a view the family, both in its literal and its ecclesial sense, becomes increasingly central to the thinking of the local church. For many evangelical clergy, lay people, parents and youthworkers the family has become an important concept which is increasingly central to their whole understanding of Christian spirituality and mission. The widespread desire for a feeling of being family with one another has therefore shaped a good deal of contemporary evangelical church life.

The Family and Worship

The Church as a caring family brought together to worship God has exercised a considerable influence on the Anglican Church today:

> Imagine a church congregation in which men and women, girls and boys, young and old, share together to worship God, to learn from one another about their faith, to pray together about their mutual concerns and joys, to serve those in the community who are outside the church. Whenever possible, the members are not separated into groups according to age or sex but are together. At times, of course there are activities for parents and very young children, a club for lively junior age children, a group for adolescents and study sessions for adults. But the first instinct of this church is to say 'What can we all do?'[9]

This is the vision which has been behind a number of more recent developments in family-orientated worship. The roots of this emphasis are to be found in three very different traditions, but each has played an important part in shaping the sensibilities of current evangelicalism.

Family Church

In the 1920s and 30s Herbert Hamilton, a Congregational minister, began to reflect on the links between Sunday school and the worshipping life of the Church. As Children's and Youth Secretary of the Congregational Church he toured the country often taking as his theme the need to 'bridge the gulf' or of 'trying to join school and Church together'.[10] The influential Hadow Report of 1931 raised questions in his mind concerning the nature and place of Christian education. He became convinced that education needed to be a co-operative activity, and that it should take place in the context of a community. He therefore began to encourage Sunday schools and churches to cease being two separate organizations and through the institution of services for young people and the setting up of a system of churchgoers acting as pastoral 'friends' for young people, vital connections started to be made. It was Hamilton who first introduced onto the Sunday school scene concepts of 'junior church', 'children in church' and 'family church'.[11] One of his colleagues, Hodgeson, sums up Hamilton's approach to work with young people in the church:

> Family Church starts by assuming one Church which includes the last baptised (or dedicated) baby and the oldest saint in one living fellowship of mutual, loving and caring relationships. It assumes a membership that cares for its children not merely as prospective church members but as individuals; a spiritual home which includes both nursery and drawing room, and in which – as in any home worthy of the name – the children are as much at home in the drawing room as they are in the nursery; and the grown ups are often found down on the carpet sharing the children's interests intelligently, sympathetically and constructively. It is the Church – i.e. the living, personal relationships that are a Church – which educates a child for Churchmanship.[12]

Appointed Principal of Westhill College, Birmingham in 1945, Hamilton was able to exercise an important influence on the shape of education in a church context. Over the next twenty years all the major denominations, to some extent or another, were to adopt his ideas.[13] The Anglican report *Towards the Conversion of England* recognized problems in separate Sunday school education and identified the parish church as the basic unit for outreach to both young and old.[14] It was these ideas which were to predominate in the evangelical revival in postwar Britain. The development of closer links between the education of children and the teaching pattern of the wider Church eventually led to the evolution of integrated and progessive programmes of teaching which are common in churches today, such as the Scripture Union 'Salt Programme' for all-age teaching and adult worship.

Parish and People

On the catholic side of the Church of England crucial developments were to take place in the 1930s. Central to this was the work of Fr A. G. Herbert of the Society of the Sacred Mission. Much influenced by the continental 'liturgical movement' Herbert began to spread the idea that the Communion service should become the main service in the Anglican Church. In 1937 he initiated and edited a book called *The Parish Communion* which brought together essays from a number of the key thinkers on worship and liturgy within the Church. In his own essay Herbert's starting-point for considering the development of the parish Communion is the work of Christ and the nature of the Church:

> The movement for the establishing of the Parish Communion must not be side tracked . . . it is, in fact, part of the Liturgical Movement which is going on in our day in every part of Christendom, and which is fundamentally a movement of return to the sacraments and the liturgy, as the sacramental expression of our redemption through Christ and the nature of the Church as the mystical body.[15]

From these basic theological convictions came the emergence of the 'parish Communion' within the catholic tradition of the Church. In 1949 the movement 'Parish and People' was established and throughout the 50s it experienced considerable growth and exercised widespread influence both within and outside the catholic tradition of the Church.[16] Among evangelicals the renewed emphasis on weekly Communion, advocated by 'Parish and People' was seen as very suspect. At the 1961 Islington Conference concerns were raised and warning given on the spread of sacramental practices. By the time of Keele, however, it was noticeable that many of those present supported more regular Communion. It was felt that although evangelicals tended to have high regard for Communion, according to Hylson-Smith 'They had rather let the sacrament be pushed to the outer fringes of Church life and the ministry of the word had become divorced from it.'[17] The conference went so far as to include in its pronouncement a controversial suggestion that evangelicals should 'work towards weekly communion as the central corporate service of the Church'.[18]

There was therefore a significant shift in evangelical Anglican practice towards more regular Communion, and whilst the 1977 NEAC gathering backtracked a little on the Keele resolution, change was widespread.[19] In many places it was the influence of the charismatic movement which brought a significant loosening in evangelical attitudes along with a general climate of liturgical experimentation.[20] The efforts of Colin Buchanan and other evangelical leaders heralded a less rigid approach.[21]

The Family Service

In the early 1960s a number of evangelicals were experimenting with less formal styles of worship. One of these pioneers was Michael Botting who whilst he was at St Matthew's, Fulham, began to devise his own 'family services'.[22] The idea was to develop a service which could act as a bridge to families and children on the fringes of the church and be an occasion when children and parents could worship together.[23] The development of these services soon spread with the use of simple liturgical forms incorporating quizzes, choruses, audio-visual aids and of course the all-important overhead projector.

Botting gathered together a group of eclectics and under

the auspices of CPAS a family service book was published in 1967. Saward points out that this was the first prayer book in the Church of England which consistently used the 'you' form of address as opposed to the more traditional 'thou'.[24] A number of those prominent in this work were also innovators in the area of youthwork, and the vast majority of the songs included in the original book were drawn from *Youth Praise*. A series of resources and teaching material from CPAS were to follow and eventually a comprehensive service book, which included versions of the ASB Communion service, was published in 1986 under the title *Christian Family Worship* edited by Michael Perry. The spread of family services was to have a considerable impact on the worship of many local churches. The Anglican report *Patterns for Worship* saw the developments as 'reflecting an enormous amount of creative energy and the kind of God-centred worship that is resulting in a considerable growth of new Christians'.[25] Archbishop Carey writing in the foreword to the new edition of Botting's *Teaching the Family* praised the family service by saying that it 'provides just the right basic biblical teaching that those on the fringe of the Church require'.[26]

Children at the Centre

The growth in family services, parish Communions, and the family church/Christian education movement, are indications of a widespread shift in the Church's life. Increasingly it is seen as integral that children are a part of the whole Church in worship. In all sections of the Church, including evangelicalism, this has become a core value. As Perham puts it, 'The norm from which the parish needs to begin is that children should be present by right at the worship of the parochial family.'[27] In some places children have been allowed to take Communion.[28] In others children come forward with the adults to receive a blessing when Communion is administered. These initiatives indicate a widespread move to demonstrate in a symbolic way that children are a part of the congregation and members of the 'family of faith'.[29] Such developments, however, have not been without their problems and controversies. The Anglican report *Children in the Way* makes it clear that the exclusion of children from Communion prior to Confirmation, which is still the Church of England's practice, is a major stumbling block to valuing them as full members of the Church.[30] The 1995 Council of Churches for Britain and Ireland report is entitled *Unfinished Business* because of the feeling that there is much still to be done in the inclusion of children within the life of the Church.[31] Debate within the Church has also been critical of the emphasis on 'family' over the last thirty years.

Unfinished Business points out that, given the widespread changes in society, the emphasis on family in the Church's life has tended to be regarded by many as an exclusive endorsement of the nuclear family. This impression has served to alienate those who do not fit into the neat mould of this ideal.[32] A similar point is made in *Something to Celebrate:*

> When we speak of the 'family of the Church', we are trying to express the intimacy of personal relationship with God our 'heavenly father' and with our 'brothers' and 'sisters' in Christ which belonging to the Church makes possible. But in so doing, we are sometimes in danger of making the natural family the dominant model for church relationships. This idea can be reinforced liturgically if too much prominence is given to 'family services', where the impression can be given – however unintentionally – that the church is there solely for the benefit of parents and children in nuclear families.[33]

The concentration upon the Church as family worshipping together has also tended to isolate those attending who might be seen as fringe members. Hastings points out that the renewed emphasis on the Communion service as the main act of worship in many churches has meant that those on the periphery have tended to drop away.[34] Those remaining connected with the Church have generally been from more educated and middle-class sections of society. The increased price of commitment on the part of both parents and children has favoured prosperous suburban churches.[35] Thus the genuine and widespread success of the more family-orientated emphasis of the Church often hides a failure to reach beyond a relatively narrow section of society. Indeed the developments associated with a family emphasis in the Church may well have caused this: 'Despite the fact that there appears to be a great variety of work with children in many churches, the tendency is to be involved with an ever smaller percentage of children from mainly socially privileged backgrounds.'[36]

The Limitations of 'Family'

Evangelicalism has invested heavily in the concept of the family. Evangelical churches often set a high priority on bringing people of all ages together in an expression of the church as family. A programme of education is set up for children which generally links with the teaching programme in the whole of the church in the belief that the family needs to learn together. Increasingly congregations aspire to creating an intimacy which is seen to reside in the ideal family church. At the same time greater emphasis is also being placed on the role of the natural family as the basic unit of Christian care, intimacy and nurture. Criticism of these developments has generally focused upon the way in which certain groups, such as those without children, or single people, feel excluded. Added to this, despite recent developments, many feel that churches have not done enough to include children.

Discussion of church worship seems rarely to question the wisdom of 'family' or the assumption that the best church is one where everyone meets together to worship at the same time. It is received wisdom in the present-day church that it is good for everyone to attend one service. To suggest otherwise is to court a good deal of criticism and suspicion. Yet increasingly, youthworkers are finding that

the only way forward for their work is to establish some
kind of youth church.[37] Within a youthwork setting there
are a number of reasons why the Church seen as family is a
significant problem. The idea that it is the norm that all
ages should worship together puts tremendous pressure on
any young person or youth leader. Church, even when it is
family, is an alien place to the vast majority of young people.
The emphasis on one service could be seen as causing more
problems than it solves for people working with teenagers.
The Church as 'family' is problematic in the following ways:

(1) *Loss of diversity*: The concentration on one main service
either kills off other sorts of service in a church or in effect
devalues them. It used to be common for Anglican churches
to hold various services on a Sunday and mid-week. The
emphasis on the Church as family has affected this pattern
dramatically. If the key value of the Church is that we want
everyone to be together, then choice of service or worship
style is less possible within the one Church. Evangelical
Christians often exercise choice by moving churches. But
once that choice has been made there is generally only one
main liturgical dish on offer each Sunday. The lack of a
varied menu, and indeed the closing down of choice, affects
young people, especially if they want to experiment with
worship and youth culture.

(2) *Pressure to attend*: For evangelicals, belonging equals
attendance. To be a part of the family it is necessary to share
in worship. The theology of the Church as family lays great
emphasis on being with people of all ages at one service on
a weekly basis. The child, we are confidently told, 'belongs
within the group and is part of the faith family'.[38] Leach is
concerned that everyone feels a part of the worshipping
community.[39] Perham is very clear that every group 'needs to
be prepared to worship with every other group on a Sunday';
if this is a problem, he says, then they need to be '. . . helped
to see that their commitment to worship of the whole body
comes first and their sectional interests second'.[40] When
such sentiments hold sway it is a brave adult who tries to

remain a part of the church whilst sitting light to attendance at the main service. For teenagers, a good many of whom might want to be fully part of the church but cannot cope with the prevailing style of worship or the 'family emphasis', the pressure to attend is too much. Given the choice between belonging and attending or not attending they choose the latter.

(3) *Control and attendance*: The main Sunday service acts a kind of roll-call of the faithful. Concentrating everyone in one place at one time makes it easier to know who is there and who is not. This is important because attendance at church in the evangelical context does not simply indicate belonging, it also is a sign of spiritual health. The net effect of concentrating worship into one Sunday service is that clergy and others are quickly able to tell what the current spiritual state of the congregation might be. Sunday worship is therefore not only a means of building people up in the faith; it is also a method of social control. It is too a weekly reward for clergy, who have relatively few other tangible signs of success. Attendance as a sign of belonging is import-ant because it offers a clear definition of who is part of the group and who is not. To see the same faces week in, week out is reassuring. We know we belong to each other because we are part of the same church; we know this because we see each other every week. For young people, however, this aspect of attendance and social control is particularly diffi-cult. Many Christian young people find regular church attendance difficult, especially on a Sunday morning. A committed Christian young person may miss church for a variety of reasons; this may simply be the result of a night out, or a weekend away, or the pressure of exams. Sporting activity, or involvement with theatre productions or orches-tras might also produce some conflict. In the ordinary run of things most parents and clergy would be delighted to see Christian young people engaged in creative and constructive activities. The problem is that when attendance equals spiritual health the weight of expectation on young people to be in the church can be all-consuming.

(4) *Church without children*: The experience of many Christian young people is that they come under considerable pressure from their own parents to attend church as a family together. In part the need to attend together arises from the idea of a family church. There is something forlorn and dispiriting in being a parent attending a family-orientated service without your own children. But as children enter adolescence there is often a need for them to find ways of expressing their own individuality and identity in relation to their parents. Attending church together may present real problems for young people. This may in no way reflect badly on the spiritual state of a young person, but the close association of family and church and the pressure to attend one service may push young people away from the church. The close association of children and church can tend to reinforce precisely the roles that teenagers are seeking to break out of. Religion in many situations therefore militates against growth and change rather than encouraging it.

(5) *God and family combine*: The developments in church worship have tended to link closely concepts of family and of the Christian life. For many Christian young people their family lives have been so taken up with church organizations and activities that they find it difficult to separate faith from family. With the onset of adolescence significant problems emerge in finding ways to change from the previous relationship of child to parent and to establish a new relationship with the family. Such change will often mean that there is a period where some of the values and behaviours of the family are questioned or even rejected. When family and Church become almost synonymous the net effect is that many Christian young people feel the need to turn away from the faith in order to assert themselves. To grow up they require space but the Christian context within which they find themselves has seemingly squeezed out alternative places to be Christian.

(6) *Asking questions*: Many young people need some freedom and indeed permision to question and test belief. The all-age

nature of worship in many churches leaves little room for such enquiry when simplicity, certainty and clear teaching are core values. As *Unfinished Business* puts it:

> It must be acknowledged frankly that congregations in the main have not been particularly good at enabling young people to question values and beliefs and activities of the Church. It seems almost as though while it is acceptable for children to be given a sense of belonging in the congregation and so have experience of faith, however unexamined, and while they may be encouraged to affiliate to the life of the congregation by joining in the worship and other activities of the Church, while it is hoped for and prayed for that these children will progress to the point of making personal commitments in faith, yet there is a nervous reluctance to encourage any form of doubt or questioning.[41]

To own the faith there is some need to question and to search for the truth for oneself. This should be part of the adolescent period of religious development.[42] The concentration on one main service necessarily means that many of these needs are not reflected in the context of the weekly teaching and worship of the church. Consequently many young people may feel the services are irrelevant.

(7) *Cultural imperialism*: In any group of people meeting to worship over a period of years, a common culture begins to evolve. The assumption of many evangelical churches is that it is possible to create a service which can be accessible to everyone in a given community or area. The idea that we should all meet at the same time, in the same place and do the same things is of the essence in modern church life. To do this we inevitably have to have something of a shared culture. This might nod in the direction of certain styles and interests, but on the whole the message is that this 'culture' is for everyone.

For many young people without a church background the way that we worship and the cultural norms of the church community are a serious stumbling-block. The concentration on one main service as the mark of acceptable church attendance leaves these young people with a clear choice: fit in with our way of doing things or leave. Widespread experimentation with worship and culture in services such as JOY, The Late Late Service in Glasgow, or Holy Disorder based in Gloucester, can be seen as a reaction to the assumption that one common culture is an acceptable medium for Christian worship. The reality of current society is that the Church is surrounded by a number of different subcultures. Young people themselves are well aware of the existence of different groups which exist even within one neighbourhood or school. The church's insistence that fellowship and the worship of God should be conducted using only one subcultural medium flies in the face of increasing cultural diversity. When this subculture is so manifestly middle class and relatively privileged, the implications of narrowing worship options become even more disturbing.

The Family Church and the Subculture

The centripetal tendency of evangelicalism has been compounded by its embracing of an emotive concept of 'family' to describe church life. The search for security and intimacy has often brought with it an increase in control. The drive to meet together has somehow led to the marginalization of diversity. The search for family has closed down cultural diversity with the result that the subculture of evangelicalism has increasingly provided the medium within which worship and church activity take place. These developments have been extraordinarily powerful and all-embracing in most areas of the evangelical church. Evangelical concern for young people and children has therefore brought about a church context which is paradoxically a significant problem for many teenagers. Modern Christian youthwork, however, has largely adapted itself to exist within this particular context. On the fringes of the evangelical world there is some indication that the strong emphasis on one self-referential subculture within the Church has led many young people to look for more satisfying cultural forms within which to worship. The future agenda of those working with young people, it seems, will increasingly focus on developing patterns of church life which are able to embrace cultural change and diversity whilst maintaining a gospel commitment to the unity of the Church. If some advance is to be made in this direction then the impact of a theology of family may need to be unravelled from much of our church life. The present indications seem to be that it will again be young people who will be leading the whole Church forward on these issues.

The family emphasis of modern church life has had a considerable impact on the ability of the evangelical churches to reach out to the unchurched. The problem with being a family is that it sets a very clear order of priorities. Family members tend to come above those who are outside the family. The children of family members are seen as more important, or in need of being cared for first. The church-based youth fellowship has come to play an important role for precisely this reason. Such attitudes are rarely 'official' policy but they lie behind the emphasis in many evangelical churches at the moment. The family emphasis of the church means that it is important to be 'accepted' as part of the family. Such acceptance is the gateway to Christian care and nurture. The problem comes, however, when people who are socially unacceptable seek entry to the church or to the youth group. The family feel of the church in this instance is more likely to move people to protect vulnerable family members from a perceived threat. In these ways the feel of the modern church has served to isolate Christian youthwork and keep it 'in the family'.

PART III

Safety and the Subculture

Chapter 7

Safety: The Function of Evangelical Youthwork

Many evangelical Christians experience aspects of contemporary society as extremely threatening. This threat often arises from elements within youth culture. Clive Calver, head of the Evangelical Alliance, probably speaks for a good many when he says that:

> Many of us have genuinely had to bury our heads in the sand because we just could not cope with a syndrome of change which resembled a railway locomotive hurtling brakeless down a steep gradient with a hairpin bend at the bottom! Youth culture has proved to be too horrendous and we've had to turn our heads in distaste.[1]

This sense of alarm is by no means uncommon; one evangelical youthworker has referred to 'a Godless society in which God's name has largely been forgotten and for the present generation is just a swear word'.[2] The evangelical holding such views is likely to feel a deep sense of alienation from many aspects of contemporary society and youth culture is frequently the cause. The clothes young people wear, the music they listen to, the way they behave, the influence of the media and the spread of information technology – one or all of these is likely to figure in the concerns expressed by evangelical Christians.

A generalized fear of much of present-day youth culture becomes more concentrated as parents see their children entering the teenage years. James Dobson, the American evangelical family expert, starts his advice book for young Christians, *Preparing for Adolescence,* by telling a short parable. Adolescence is a journey from childhood in the 'womb-like' comfort of the Christian family, to the eventual goal of 'adultstown'. When puberty sets in each young person is driving along a road and has to keep going because there is no reverse gear. Part way down this road they are stopped by a man waving a red flag. This man, whom Dobson identifies as himself, warns the young person that ahead lies a dark gorge. Only by travelling slowly and with a good deal of care will the young person avoid falling into this gorge and wrecking their life.[3]

For many evangelical Christians such a view of adolescence has become commonplace. The teenage years are seen as being full of perils, and in parents of teenage children the language of alarm and fear seems to abound. Peter Brierley, in his survey of Christian work with young people, *Reaching and Keeping Teenagers,*[4] does little to allay these fears. According to Brierley there are hidden malign spiritual forces at work influencing young people. In this he is drawing heavily on the ideas of Winkie Pratney, who is closely linked with YWAM (Youth With A Mission). Chief amongst these forces, we are told, is the god Moloch. The book discusses at some length the practice of human sacrifice to Moloch. Moloch was first mentioned in Leviticus as a 'deity of unnatural cruelty' who demanded the sacrifice of children. The Moloch, we are told 'lives today'.[5] Brierley describes what he calls the Moloch principle which involves 'war on the child'. There are a number of aspects to this war which can be identified in present-day society, including: 'War on the womb: abortion', 'War in the home: divorce', 'War in the home: child abuse, incest', 'War on the mind: media exploitation of children', 'War on the mind: hidden agendas', 'War in the streets: violence'.[6] While he points out that many young people grow up never experiencing problems such as these, it is clear that Brierley is expressing, albeit in an extreme form, the concerns of many evangelicals. Pratney again spreads alarm when he says: 'Understand that the crux of the spiritual war today is over children; that the focus of the enemy is for little minds and hearts; that the dragon waits by the woman not to kill her, but her baby.'[7] Such language reflects considerable unease and even fear in the evangelical community.

Brierley's work, which was supported by a number of evangelical youthwork agencies and organizations, has been extremely influential, not least in its claim that large numbers of young people are leaving the Church. Andy Hickford, writing the foreword to *Reaching and Keeping Teenagers*, was moved to pronounce that the decline in numbers was 'a damning indictment'. If the Church remains complacent to these facts it will mean that 'a generation of young people is betrayed and the Church has no future'.[8] The emphasis on 'keeping teenagers' is particularly pertinent to Christian parents who fear that their children will desert the safety of the Church. This fear is made all the more real by the sense that all around are what Steve Flashman, using a phrase first applied to advertising, refers to as 'the hidden persuaders': rock music, the fashion industry and the sexual revolution.[9] Youth culture, along with the effects of what is generally termed 'peer pressure', is seen as being one of the powerful forces set to draw Christian young people away from the faith.

The Fears of the Parents Passed on to the Children

The concerns of evangelical Christian parents are probably not dissimilar to those of their neighbours who do not share the faith. Bookshops are full of advice books for parents and young people. Evangelical Christians, however, have tended to turn to their own experts in the field who share their beliefs. Christian bookstores have a surprising number of handbooks written to help parents and young people cope with adolescence. These books give an important and revealing insight into the way that evangelicals have sought to deal with the perceived threat of adolescence. In a good many cases Christian youthworkers have been seen

as those with the insight and experience to help young
people and adults through the teenage years. The advice
books vary as to their exact purpose, but they speak with a
remarkably similar set of values and fears. The material in
this chapter is based on a survey of evangelical advice books
for parents and young people.

Evangelicals are above all concerned to help young people
'survive adolescence'. Gilbert's *The Teenage Survival Kit* is
billed as presenting 'Everything you need to follow Jesus in
the modern world'.[10] Survival will mean that young Christians need to beware of the modern world where, as Gilbert
explains, 'we live our lives on illusion instead of reality'.
There may well be a number of attractive experiences out
there just waiting for us, but these ultimately do not work.
The key is that young people should commit themselves to
God. To this end, it seems, Gilbert sets out to exert as much
influence on the reader as he is able. If the teenagers find
their faith to be a little lacking in energy or excitement then
the answer is very clear: 'So if my experience is different
from what God promises in this world, who is wrong? I've
discovered it's always me . . . Either Christianity works or it
doesn't. Either God is at fault or we are.'[11]

Whilst there is a good deal to be said for the clarity and
directness of this approach to the faith, in practice the kinds
of decisions that young people face are rarely so simple. It is
hard to see how such advice might avoid inducing a good
deal of guilt in even the most conscientious Christian
teenager. There is something of the emperor's clothes quality
to this argument which says that 'If you can't see it, then you
are ignorant, or even worse a sinner.' It is easy to see how
armed with such arguments a church leader or youthworker,
who is at best mistaken or at worst in serious error, could
seek to control young people. For while God is always in the
right and we constantly need to approach him in a spirit of
humility and repentance, Christian leaders can very easily
get things wrong. Most young people will experience the
'word' of God through the ministry of youth leaders and
ministers who, it must be said, are far from infallible. The

problem with Gilbert's tone is that it does not allow for this possibility. In addition to this the heavy-handed advice seems to rely on the use of guilt and emotional pressure for its effect, arguing that we are always in the wrong if the Christian life lacks excitement, so we should feel badly enough about that to turn back to God. This argument, of course, would have something to commend it, if it were not for the weakness of the Church and youth leaders. It is right to challenge young people but in challenging young people Gilbert's book continually verges on the authoritarian and at times there is a distinctly manipulative tone:

> Is this your reality? Is this the Christian illusion that you're living out, swaying from apathy, through faked spirituality to despair?[12]

> A good maxim is, 'if in doubt, cut it out!' If it is doubtful (be it girlfriend, your fashion, your social life), then stop, say sorry, decide to move in the opposite direction, because it's not worth risking your walk with Jesus over anything.[13]

Gilbert makes every effort to lay down clear and authoritative guidelines for young people to follow. There is, however, an urgency here. Young people, it is feared, could very easily go off the rails and harm themselves and others. It is therefore of the utmost importance that they are warned of the perils. Satan, the reader is told, can influence you, and 'If ever Satan calls the tune in your life, you can be sure it will sound horrible. And unfortunately he is very good at knowing where we are weakest.'[14] Survival is a serious matter indeed.

Gilbert is an experienced and well-respected Christian youthworker who has worked for a number of years for Youth For Christ. *The Teenage Survival Kit* illustrates how the fears of Christian parents and the concerns of Christian youthwork interlock. Youthworkers and young people form a part of the same evangelical community, and will to some extent share a common perspective on the world. It is the argument of this chapter, however, that evangelical youthwork in recent years has been motivated by the widespread sense of alarm felt by Christian parents. This has meant that youthworkers have been in danger of losing a correct balance as we are energized by the fears of parents. Parental concerns give a emotional charge to the direction of Christian youthwork. One such example can be seen in the extreme nature of the comments made by Gilbert and others. The fear of parents has so affected the attitudes and practice of evangelical youthwork that we have begun to abandon education and nurture and enter the realms of social control.

The energy which has brought about this change lies in the needs of Christian parents. Parents are concerned that their children should be protected and kept safe from what they regard as the disturbing and dangerous world which threatens to engulf them during their adolescence. In this context youthwork becomes the means by which Christian parents seek to extend their influence on teenagers who are seeking more independence and freedom from the home. The youth fellowship offers a safe haven, a little distant from the home, but with the guarantee that young people will be supported and encouraged to continue in the faith. It is this which forms the main 'function' of evangelical youthwork. In responding to these fears by offering safety Christian youthwork walks a fine line. Safety and mission sit uneasily together.

Gilbert's *Teenage Survival Kit* may well be extreme but it is by no means the only book of its type. A good many other Christian youthworkers have extended their youthwork by offering advice to young people through writing books. *The Chocolate Teapot* is a humorous and, at times, hilarious guide to surviving at school. The author, David Lawrence, was for some time a schools worker with SU. The book, says Lawrence, is for those young people who look fine at church or in the youth group, but when Monday morning and school comes round they shrink into the crowd. As the going hots up they seem to melt, and, according to Lawrence, it is like pouring boiling water into a chocolate teapot. The book has a keen insight into what school life is like, and its author is straightforward in challenging young Christians to stand up for their beliefs. As he puts it, 'Sometimes life gives you a basic choice; please your friends or please God. The decision is yours.'[15] The stark reality of the choice sets out the agenda of evangelical youthwork; that is, to try to keep young Christians faithful to the values and lifestyle associated with evangelical Christianity. Clive Calver, who was the Director of BYFC, makes this aspect of youthwork clear:

> The youth leader needs to know of these pressures and give good sound teaching on the dangers of each of them, so that when put under pressure, the Christian adolescent will have a powerful answer to give, and not hide, run away or even compromise out of fear.[16]

Fear and survival are fundamentally linked in evangelical work among young people. Phil Moon, who was the head of CYFA, is also concerned to keep young people faithful. His 'Christian survival kit' is called *Hanging in There*.[17] Moon sets out to encourage Christian young people to seek a biblical faith, but this, we are told, is 'a serious business'. Being a Christian is not a religious rave or a spiritual Sega game or just a hobby. It is much more important than any of these things:

> It's about who your friends are (and aren't), and the things that really matter to you. It's about the biggest decisions you ever have to make in life, and how you're going to cope with the next sixty years and more. And it's about where you spend eternity, and how useful your life is going to be here on earth.[18]

It would be wrong to disagree with Moon when he encourages young people to weigh the importance of the Christian faith because, as he says, 'becoming a Christian is the biggest thing you could ever do.' Christian youthwork has got to have close to its heart the desire to see young people coming to faith and growing in relationship to Christ. What the writings of Moon and other Christian youthworkers illustrate is the extent to which these concerns are affected and often overshadowed by a desire among Christian families for their children to remain safe. There is a pervasive sense of fear, if not alarm, which comes through these books. This alarm is shared by the parents of Christian young people. Feelings are running high, and how the Church ministers to young people has to be affected by these emotions. The extent to which this may be the case is illustrated by the recurring themes in advice books for Christian parents and young people.

The Pressures of the World

Pressure is a key word when evangelicals discuss young people. It is a universally held view that young people are subject to considerable 'pressure'. Pressures come from all around but wherever they come from they are likely to be extremely dangerous.

Peer Pressure

Advice books are very concerned by the way that young people might be influenced by their peers. Sue Rinaldi is clear that 'without doubt the temptation to conform to peer pressure is enormously strong.'[19] Young Christians are very likely to give in to the 'pressure' to conform because in the teenage years the need to be 'approved by peers' is so important. According to Rinaldi, young people are surrounded by an atmosphere in which 'new age spirituality' is considered more fashionable. Gilbert also sees the dangers in the world of young people and he is forthright in his assessment of 'peer pressure':

> Peer group pressure is a very dangerous snare. Let's just define our terms. Peer group pressure occurs when you are moulded/persuaded/threatened to conform to the standards of your peer group of friends or colleagues. The

group you most want to be in with dictates the nature of your behaviour, fashion trends, choice of music, attitude to life, way of thinking etc.[20]

The problem, according to Gilbert, is that we have a 'kind of' herd instinct.[21] Young people will seek to fit in with a group, because they are naturally inclined that way. The problem with wanting to be accepted is that many young people, while looking for acceptance and friendship, end up selling themselves to achieve it, 'only to find it was a hollow temporary belonging'.[22]

Friendship in the view of many of these commentators is therefore dangerous. The alarm experienced by evangelical Christians is deeply felt as the YWAM worker Oliver Nyumbu makes very clear: 'The onslaught of peer pressure on today's young people is relentless. Casualties are with us in great numbers.'[23] Clearly it is possible that young people can be led astray by the activities of friends at school and elsewhere. But it is also the case that friendship is a very important and indeed a formative aspect of life. The dire warnings do not give a clear balance to the Christian view of friendship and peer group relationships. From the advice books it is hard to discover a strong sense of the positive role that friendship and the peer group might play in the lives of Christian young people. On the contrary, the overall impression is that friendship, especially with those outside the youth fellowship and the church, is highly dangerous. It is my view that this lack of balance is an indication of the effect that increased parental anxiety has begun to have on evangelical youthwork.[24]

Fashion

Young people, according to many evangelical commentators, are put under pressure by a feeling that they need to keep up with fashions. The media are accused of creating the impression that teenagers need to adopt certain styles of dress. This is a particular problem for girls: 'There is pressure from TV, radio, magazines, comics and advertisements for girls to act and dress in a grown-up way before they are ready.'[25] Such pressure needs to be handled carefully. According to Gilbert the teenager does not need an image; they already have an image which is God's. When choosing clothes young people should therefore actively avoid trying to impress other people. Instead they should simply ask, 'Do I really like this?'[26] Gilbert sets out two principles which should govern the way young people dress. First, their choices should not be conforming to peer pressure. Second, they should check that they are not rebelling in any way against their parents.

Once again there is a possibility that in advocating such caution young Christians who wish to explore their identity, and indeed their sexuality, through the way that they dress are made to feel guilty. Dress is an important aspect of the search for an independent identity in many adolescents' lives. A positive and balanced approach to these issues needs to shape Christian youthwork.

Music

Evangelicals have reserved particular disgust and invective for popular music. Nyumbu sees much rock as 'unashamedly promoting the profane'.[27] Many artists espouse a number of anti-Christian virtues, according to Nyumbu, which include: 'Devilish substitutes (for Christian virtues), sexual experience before marriage, self-gratification, sensual stimulation, taking care of No. 1, revenge, and criticism'. Given the extent of these negative influences, young people need to be instructed on how they are to listen to music. Nyumbu is concerned that they should learn to ask themselves questions. Examples he gives include: 'What is this music doing for me?', 'What images does it conjure up for me ?', and 'How does it make me feel?' It is not unusual for authors to single out particular kinds of music for criticism, although Gilbert is concerned to say that specific rhythms or styles of music are not inherently sinful or evil. His criticism is based on 'the message'. On this basis, 'anarchic or violently aggressive music' should be avoided. Similarly those bands which can be seen as 'devil' worshippers are a definite no.[28]

Roberts, the editor of *Alpha* magazine, also examines the impact of the media, and in particular popular music, but he does so with a little more sophistication. He stresses that it is lifestyle which needs to be examined. He therefore analyses the media in terms of what he calls a lifestyle of idolatry. Idolatry happens when people take neutral and harmless things and worship them as a god. The youthworker needs to interact with the mass-media age to build an ethic which affirms God's creation while recognizing the reality of sin and rebellion. Roberts advocates that we should encourage young Christians with a Christian worldview to 'engage the culture' and seek to be 'culture formers'.[29] 'The media is not an evil place. It is often dominated, however, by people with idolatry on their minds.'[30] Roberts' positive approach is extremely helpful; however it is clear that his words should be seen as offering a necessary corrective – it is generally not the case that churches encourage such an approach. It is more usual for caution and suspicion of contemporary styles of music to act as a brake on young Christians experimenting and becoming culture transformers as Roberts advocates.

Sex

Evangelical Christians are extremely concerned about sex. The sexual activity of young people, especially those from a church background, is a cause for considerable worry. Once again the discussion is conducted in an atmosphere where fear and alarm seem to prevail. Roger and Christine Day make it clear to parents that their children will very soon be exposed to 'the most incredible details about sex, much of it perverted and confusing'. More alarmingly the authors continue by saying that these Christian children 'will also have been put under pressure from their peers to indulge in sexual activity of all sorts'.[31] Such sentiments reflect the real worry that many Christian parents feel as their children enter puberty. The sense of threat from the 'outside' world is palpable. Given such feelings youthworkers attempt to dissuade young people from sexual activity outside marriage in the strongest terms: 'Sex outside marriage is still a spiritual experience, but now it is of Satan.'[32]

Engaging in sexual activity outside marriage gives Satan what Gilbert calls 'legal territory'. His advice to young people is to avoid all situations where they might be tempted sexually. Those who are going out need to ask themselves if Jesus would be embarrassed to be with them when they are alone with each other. Such advice is well aimed at inducing guilt in even the most moral young Christian. Anxiety and early sexual experimentation are very closely linked. Young people feel extraordinarily vulnerable about these matters and Gilbert's attitude seems remarkably unhelpful.

Again a significant fear is that Christian young people will be influenced by the values and behaviour which prevail around them at school. Williams describes how in a school setting, where Christians will probably be in the minority, the majority of young people will set the ethos of the school community:

> If you are a member of that community, it is very hard not to be influenced in some way, even if it is only in no longer being shocked. It is impossible for the non-Christian teenager to find a way through the maze of moral rights and wrongs; for the Christian young person there is a way, but it's hard.[33]

Advice to young Christians often includes the need for a restriction on the kinds of clothes that are worn. In most cases girls are encouraged to think twice before wearing dresses with low necklines, or short skirts. *Help! I'm Growing Up* advises young girls to flick through a catalogue or magazine and ask the question, 'Are there ones there that you should avoid?' The authors are very detailed in their prohibitions:

> We should avoid clothing that might in any way be associated with sinful acts. That includes things that are usually worn by prostitutes or homosexuals, as well as

very revealing clothes that are obviously intended to cause others to sin. Girls, if when you are older you go around without wearing a bra you might be following the latest trend – but you might also be causing extra unnecessary temptations to boys and men.[34]

The weakness of the male sex is often used by the writers of evangelical books as an excuse to control how teenage girls dress. Gilbert also wishes to maintain gender roles which are defined by a dress code. To this end he goes out of his way to condemn cross-dressing. Boys should not dress like girls and girls should not imitate boys.[35]

Temptation is also seen by a number of authors to extend to the practice of masturbation. Whilst admitting that the Bible does not explicitly condemn masturbation, the Days ask us if we can imagine Jesus masturbating.[36] Gilbert also gives a complete 'no' to the practice.[37] Dobson, however, tries not to condemn it, while giving some heavy 'be careful' notices. The range of restrictions and the force with which they are expressed shows how deeply issues of sex and sexuality shape the evangelical youthwork world.

The Pressures of the Church

The pressures of the world are all around young people, and yet ironically the Church itself is not above pressurizing Christian young people. Evangelical Christians appear to have very few qualms about putting adolescents under pressure in order that they might remain within the Church. Pressure seems to be a bad thing only when it it pulls people away from the faith. The main function of pressure is that it aims to keep young people in the Church. One of the key ways that this pressure is delivered is through Christian youthwork.

Integrated

Like the use of the word 'pressure', most commentators repeat the term 'integrated' in relation to young people and the local church. The utmost efforts should be made to keep young people's ministry 'integrated' with the rest of the church. John and Sue Ritter regard this as an issue of particular importance for churches and so they regularly run workshops and seminars on 'Integrating eleven to fourteen year olds'.[38] Fenton is also concerned that work with young people should remain as close to the main body of the church as possible. A vibrant youth group is one which is 'fully integrated into the life of the Church'.[39] To this end he is suspicious of events which separate young people off for activities of their own which, he comments, have more resemblance to popular television than they do to Bible teaching. Buckeridge is similarly critical of larger programmes and events; the key to 'integrating youth into the wider worshipping community', he says, is to be found in the friendships offered by adults to young people. Moon however seems a little more mechanistic in pursuit of integration:

> If you are a Christian, Church is not an optional extra, like central locking, metallic paint or ABS. It comes as standard and always has done. You can't survive as a Christian and forget about Church. It may not be easy. You may have to take the initiative. But Christians need each other to survive. So hang in there.[40]

It has therefore been a major priority for Christian youthwork to try to persuade young people to stay linked to the Church. A key aspect of this has been to make sure that the youthwork itself does not become a separate empire. Jones is clear that the youth group should not seek to be a church: 'For it to achieve blessing a youthwork must be at all times operating and considered as part of the local body of Christ.' Young people are part of the body and so it is important for youthworkers to teach them that they must function as 'living members'.[41]

Given concerns over integration, the current trend for new worship services run by young people causes much discussion.[42] Brierley is clear that separate services for young people are a bad thing. In the past, he says, the Sunday school was separate from the life of the church and this proved to be a mistake. This must not be repeated in the new movement for young people's worship. 'The methods of integration will be totally different', from those used to bring the Sunday school closer to the church, but they are nevertheless extremely important.[43]

Witness

It is seen as extremely important for Christians in their teenage years actively to share the faith with their friends. *Keep in Step* is written with the main aim of being a practical handbook to help young people do this. A good deal of pressure is applied in the book to encourage young Christians into evangelism:

> Isn't it strange how we all want the privileges of being a Christian and yet we shun our responsibilities? We want all the fun and everything but without the effort. And, of course, while we are happy sitting around smiling and singing 'I am H.A.P.P.Y.' people who don't know Jesus are losing their souls.[44]

We are all called to 'go out there and win' people with our testimony, say the authors, John and Sue Ritter. This not an option, it is at the heart of what being a Christian is about. Both Moon and Lawrence give the advice that it is better to let people know right from the start that you are a Christian. Lawrence says that 'the longer you keep your mouth shut about Jesus the harder it becomes to speak out.'[45] Young Christians, whether they like it or not, are witnesses because they have encountered the living God. The key question is whether they are a good or a bad witness: 'Good witnesses give an accurate account of what happened. Bad witnesses keep their mouths shut.'[46] Moon is characteristically blunt in the reasons why young people should speak out: 'Jesus

Christ was bothered enough to die for you and me. Surely we can be bothered enough just to tell our friends what he has done.'[47]

The necessity for young Christians to act as witnesses to their non-Christian friends is not simply a 'gospel' imperative. The fact is that evangelical youthwork is largely built on the principle that this will happen.[48] The nucleus approach to outreach, adopted by most youth fellowships, depends on the willingness of young Christians to reach out to the 'fringe'. According to Williams young Christians are the best placed to act as evangelists in a school setting, because they are in relationship with non-Christians. They already 'speak the language, they understand the trends in fashion and music; they share the same concerns and interests'.[49] Young Christians are therefore seen by evangelicals as being essential to the future growth of the Church.

Dating Non-Christians

Many parents and youthworkers are extremely concerned when young Christians go out with non-Christians. Gilbert uses St Paul's comment about being 'unequally yoked'. While some Christians eventually convert their partners, we are assured by him that in the majority of cases the opposite is the case: 'The fact is that for every story that ends happily, there are five more Christians going out with non-Christians who eventually lose touch with their God.' One rotten apple in the barrel, we are told, is sure to make the others also go bad.[50]

Moon kicks the unequal yoking argument nicely into touch by pointing out that 2 Corinthians 6.14 refers to mixing worship of idols with Christian worship. The Bible has no specific command for believers to avoid forming relationships with non-Christians. However Moon makes it clear how difficult it is to live in a close relationship with someone who does not share the deepest part of your life. The wise person 'will not even consider going out with someone who isn't a Christian'. Christianity is not train-spotting, a hobby or a spare-time activity. It takes over your whole life: 'If you think you can go out with a non-Christian and survive as a Christian I'm afraid you've got the wrong idea of what Christianity is.'[51]

Problems with Safety

This brief survey of evangelical books written to help young people and their parents cope with adolescence offers a revealing insight into the concerns that lie at the heart of much Christian youthwork. Many youthworkers are clearly deeply concerned to guide young people through a difficult period of life. The safety of young Christians is an important and weighty matter. The number of books dealing with this area is evidence of the seriousness with which the evangelical community is treating the nurture of young people in the faith. For parents there is a deep concern that their children should pass from childhood to adulthood in safety. This is understandable and indeed should be seen as a God-given responsibility.

Youthworkers are right to try to respond to the needs of Christian parents as well as those expressed by young people. The desire to see young people grow in the faith and in maturity lies at the heart of all Christian youthwork. There are, however, a number of problems which arise directly from the desire for Christian young people to remain safe.

All attempts to influence young people and Christian youthworkers have generally been fairly clear about the main aims of their youthwork:

The first aim of Christian youthwork must be to present a young person with the claims of Jesus Christ.[52]

Our aim is evangelism and the nurture of young disciples. . . . The goal that we have as Christians and the goal we should set before our young people is to be like Jesus.[53]

These stated aims are, on the face of it, extremely obvious. The Church is anxious that young people are encouraged, as

much as is possible, to follow Christ. This 'religious' answer
to what the role of the youth fellowship may be is, as far as
it goes, correct.

Christian parents and youthworkers often express their
wishes in these kinds of terms. Having said this, there is more
to this kind of comment than generally meets the eye. In
Young People and the Bible Moon gives us his summary of the
aims of Christian youthwork:

> Our aims are as long as they can be. The end in sight is
> presenting members of our youth groups to Jesus Christ
> when he returns, or when they die – whichever happens
> first. The aim which Paul had for Colossian Christians
> was that they would be 'perfect in Christ'. So, for our cur-
> rent youth group, our aim is that we should be working
> hard to help Simon, Russ, Jenny, Neil, Rachel and the rest
> to grow to Christian maturity, so that when Jesus returns
> we will be able to present them to him 'perfect in Christ'.
> Of course that involves young people becoming
> Christians first, and then going on growing as Christians.
> This involves a long-term view, and seeing youth work in
> the context of the work of the rest of the Church in the
> rest of their lives.[54]

Most Christians would be anxious to see young people
mature in the faith and remain true to Christ. The problem
with Moon's attitude is the 'total life plan' approach to nurturing in the faith. In this way youthwork and then church
life become a series of 'groups' which keep us until we end
our days. Talk of 'our' young people being presented 'perfect
in Christ' has more than a hint of of a protectionist and
paternalistic feel to it. The work of the Church appears to
be something which is done to us, rather than something we
participate in as adults. There is therefore an issue here in
the way that the need for safety and protection acts against
the young person's need to develop and grow. When the
desire to keep young people safe is charged with anxiety
from Christian parents, youthwork can easily lose a sense of
balance between these dual needs. Youthwork which gets

this balance wrong can foster a dependency which militates against growth towards maturity.[55]

The Need for Safety and Outreach

Ashton and Aiken are in little doubt that the main aim of Christian youthwork should be evangelism. The conviction that there is a gospel and that this should be shared with others with a view to seeing them converted is a fundamental evangelical value. While these convictions are deeply held by evangelical youthworkers, parents, and young people they are often subverted by a fear of the outside world and a desire for safety and security.

As youthwork reacts to the worries and fears of present-day teenage life by providing places of safety and refuge, its evangelistic capabilities are blunted. Clive Calver, while being concerned at the direction of modern culture, is also worried by the tendency for young Christians to become distanced from their peers. He speaks of the cultural isolation which many church-based young people seem to choose.[56] The cultural isolation of Christian teenagers is compounded by the tendencies within Christian youthwork which contrast the dangerous outside world with the safe inner world of Christian fellowship. A good example of this dynamic can be found in the school Christian Union as it is described by Williams:

> Outside, the school seemed full of noise, hostile faces and disturbance. In this dusty little room where the sun shone in showing up the desk carvings to their best advantage, there was peace. Twenty-five faces turned towards us. This was the Christian Union.

> The group was made up of both boys and girls, ages ranging from about fourteen to seventeen. There was a quiet burble of conversation as people talked and listened and shared lunch together. The contrast with the world outside this room was stark. They knew I was a Christian, but to begin with there was a wariness in their eyes as

though they found it difficult to trust anyone from outside
their group. In the midst of this intensely secular environment, their ties of friendship and fellowship were strong.
For them the Christian Union was the rock which allowed
survival in a very turbulent and often frightening world.
There was a defensiveness about the group. Their struggle
made them suspicious, even of visiting Christians.[57]

The sense of threat felt by these young Christians is palpable in everything Williams says. It is hard to believe that
she is describing a British school and not an American inner-
city ghetto or a visit to Beirut. The members of the Christian
Union clearly feel that they are on alien territory surrounded
by angry natives with 'hostile faces'. Williams, interestingly,
is not entirely free of this fear herself. She goes on to record
how glad she was to be able to leave this school which she
found to be such a threatening environment. The intimidat-
ing 'outside' is contrasted throughout the story with the
'sunlit' inside: outside there is noise – inside there is peace;
outside there is disturbance – inside there is a small group
who talk and listen to each other. It is clear that Williams
sees the 'insiders' as a faithful group of courageous followers
of Christ. Inside the Christian Union they are safe, but she
and they know that very soon they will have to 'go out there'
where disorder and hostile faces hold sway. For a few brief
and undisturbed moments they huddle together for support.

Williams has chosen a particularly 'rough' inner-city school
to describe, but despite this her portrait of a Christian Union
is recognizable in a good many other schools today. Many
Christian young people do feel under threat and insecure in
the school environment. The role of a Christian Union is
often to be as a place where support and encouragement can
be found in the midst of this threat. Williams is rightly
concerned to help these young Christians as much as she
can, but it is hard to see how a group which is in such fear
of their fellow pupils will be able to reach out with the faith.
Williams is reacting to young people who are feeling very
alienated, but there is also a question as to the extent to
which the alienation felt by young Christians in a school

setting is a creation of parents, church and youthworkers. If young people have been cautioned on the dangers of adolescence in the terms used in the advice books at home, at church and in the youth fellowship, it is understandable why these young people might be less than open in a school setting. In many cases Christian Unions and church groups simply provide a refuge and escape from teenage life for hard-pressed Christian young people. Of course life as a teenager can be extremely demanding. Christian youthwork, however, should be helping young Christians to engage courageously with their own culture.

Safety and an Alternative Subculture

Evangelical Christians have tended over the last two or three decades to produce an alternative Christian subculture of bands, records and festivals.[58] Clive Calver points out how the interests which lie behind these activities have begun to be extremely influential in the Christian world: 'So our youth groups have been trained to find their own world, their own music, their own scene while the real one travels along happily beside – unsettled and in utter darkness.'[59] The alternative Christian subculture offers a set of heroes and consumer items with which to construct a safe identity. Parents, churches and youthworkers are keen to see young people adopting the products of this subculture because it is Christian. Thus a wide variety of youth-orientated products are marketed on the understanding that they are positive and good.

It is easy for young people to keep within a rarified Christian environment. A separate subculture lessens the need to engage with 'the world'. The result is that Christian young people are in danger of becoming more and more isolated. The separation of Christian teenagers from their peers, however, seems to be one of the chief aims of the Christian subculture. Outreach is then limited to brief forays into the outside world to encourage non-Christians to join the youth group. The Christian subculture becomes an aid to this process, with, say, Christian bands playing at school missions and acting as an attraction for non-Christians. The result of this approach to mission is that Christian young people remain safely in their world and non-Christians are invited 'in' to appreciate the subculture for themselves. Those who find Jesus do so within the prevailing subculture.

It is questionable to what extent this approach to outreach has been formed by the desire to reach non-Christian young people or whether it has been simply designed to keep Christian young people safe. The relatively small number of young people attracted to the Church through these methods, however, would indicate that safety has perhaps been more important than successful outreach and the possible risks which might be associated with it.

Safety and Friendship Evangelism

The dire warnings against the impact of 'peer pressure' must have an effect on the kind of relationship Christian young people build with their friends at school. Such a negative view of friendship will almost certainly tend to influence young Christians towards the safe friendship which they experience with their Christian friends at the youth fellowship or the CU. If the central task of evangelical youthwork is to preach the gospel and the favoured strategy, the nucleus model, involves building friendships between Christian and non-Christian then there is a tension. The need for safety will tend to limit the ability of Christian youthworkers to encourage young people in friendship evangelism. The atmosphere of caution and maybe of fear is less than helpful to the building of outward-going youth groups. Real friendship grows out of shared activity and intimacy. If Christian young people are going to be helped to build such friendships they will need to feel that what they are doing is not only 'OK' but also a calling from God.

Youthwork and Sex

This chapter has argued that the anxiety of evangelical parents has a fundamental impact on the ethos of Christian youthwork. Nowhere is this seen more clearly than in the warnings concerning sex and in particular Christians going out with non-Christians. I probably need to make clear that I am not expressing a view on the rights or wrongs of the advice given. What I think it is important to note is the extent to which Christian youthwork has an energy for these issues. Such energy, I would argue, has its origins in the needs and fears of parents.

Sex is a 'primal' issue. Parents are deeply concerned with who their children marry and how they eventually shape their adult family lives. It is during adolescence that sexual orientation and the choice of eventual partners takes place for the majority of people. For evangelical Christians the church youth fellowship provides a safe place where their children can begin to take their first experimental steps in building sexual relationships. The view that many youth groups operate as a kind of approved dating agency has much going for it. Christian parents are rightly concerned that their children form Christian families for themselves. They are much more likely to do this if they go out with Christians. The youth fellowship offers an informal place to meet possible spouses. It is hard to think of any issue or issues which parents will feel more deeply about than these.

The Hidden Agenda of Evangelical Youthwork

Christian youthwork needs to come to terms with the extent to which its agenda is formed by the legitimate concerns of Christian parents. The uncovering of this agenda and the deep feelings which surround it will help youthworkers to begin to understand some of the tensions and problems which surround their work. This perception is particularly important where churches are investing heavily in youthwork by employing a full-time worker to run the youth fellowship. There is a need to recognize that the extent to which the growth in full-time youthworkers has come about is because Christian parents want to see their children being nurtured in a safe environment. Suddenly money and an emotionally charged agenda are being drawn together and the result has been the development of full-time youth ministry in this country. If this scenario is even partly true then the sooner this is made explicit the better. Youthworkers in a church setting often feel that they are torn between the needs of young people and the concerns of adults. It is important that youthworkers, while acknowledging the needs of parents, also balance the needs of young people. Risk-taking is part of adolescence. Growth to maturity involves making some mistakes and learning from them. When the need for safety is made explicit and understood by churches, parents, young people and youthworkers, there will be more possibilities for balanced discussion of the process of Christian discipleship. The integrity of evangelical work among young people demands that youth ministers and churches bring these issues out into the open.

One further issue arises from this discussion. It seems inevitable that the need for Christian parents to feel that their young people are safe will at times run contrary to the imperative to reach out to unchurched young people. Where churches embark on outreach projects to young people who do not socially fit the existing youth group tensions easily arise. I take one scenario as an example. Young people who are from an 'unchurched' background who come to faith may well have a whole host of everyday behaviours which would be regarded as being unacceptable among young people from a church family. They may smoke, swear, be involved in crimes, be sexually active, take drugs, and so on. When young people such as these come to faith they rarely change overnight into the 'normal Christian young person'. More often than not God chooses to work gradually in their lives, challenging them towards a holy and renewed lifestyle. The Spirit is gentle with them, slowly helping them to see the challenge of following Christ in particular areas of their life. The Christian youthworker who is in touch with these young people should respond to the way that God is working, encouraging change but also accepting a certain degree of ambiguity in behaviour. This is a slow and gradual process which will take a number of years.

The problem for the church-based youth fellowship is that 'unchurched' young people can easily be seen as a significant threat. If ten or even five such young people attached themselves to a youth fellowship, within a short period of time parents and church leaders would begin to get very worried. Ambiguity, which may be a normal part of the gradual work of God in an unchurched young person's life, is hard to marry with the need to keep Christian young people safe. The mere presence of a group who are perceived as being 'rough-looking' around a church group is enough to cause parents unease. If these young people are rumoured to be taking drugs, or if children from church families start to date them, the protests are liable to become very heated indeed. Christian youth groups, as we have seen, operate according to a set of rules which are very tight. Unchurched young people are often not allowed the time to adapt their lifestyle and faced with the clear boundaries of the youth group they often fall away.[60] In these ways the need to ensure the safety of church young people can dictate an atmosphere which prevents those whose lifestyle does not yet fit from joining the church, despite the fact that God is at work in their lives. In other words, the chief means for outreach among young people which is adopted by evangelical churches is also a means by which those who are not suitable are excluded.

Chapter 8

Dependency vs Growth

Adolescence is a crucial developmental stage. The word itself comes from the Latin *adolescere* which means to grow up.[1] The adolescent is growing from being a child to being an adult. Teenagers are therefore people 'in transition' and adolescence should not be regarded as a permanent state. To stay at an adolescent stage is to have failed to make it into adult life. Young people must grow up. Christian youthwork is defined by this period of adolescent transition from the world of the child to that of the adult. It is economic and social forces which have brought about 'adolescence' as we know it. The Church has tried to respond and different styles of youthwork have emerged.[2] Christian youthwork has therefore evolved in the realization that young people passing through adolescence need particular help as they negotiate the change from childhood to adulthood. Central to these developments in youthwork has been the desire to see young people reaching a spiritual maturity which they can take into adult life.

As we have seen in the last chapter the prevailing atmosphere of fear and a concern for the safety of young people within the Church raises significant problems for youthworkers who are concerned to help young people grow towards adulthood. Breen sees the influence of Christian parents as being of particular concern:

> So often the children's and youth programmes in the Church are there primarily to appease and encourage anxious parents. The parents are fearful that their children

will be unfulfilled and leave the Church and so apply pressure to the leadership to spend Church resources to meet their needs.[3]

Breen is critical of much youthwork which results from these pressures because it fosters what he calls a 'provider/client' relationship, in which youthworkers, in an attempt to keep young people, lay on events and activities and thus fall into the role of being 'providers'. Young people are encouraged to consume these activities and they therefore become 'clients'. The problem is that as young people seek to establish their own identity and independence, i.e. grow up, they tend to drift away from the church. Offered the choice between being dependent and seeking an adult identity outside the church the young Christians choose the latter.[4]

Angiers also identifies a pattern of parental influence on the shape of Christian youthwork:

> It is not only Churches that keep our young people in childhood: parents often do it. Youth leaders are viewed by some as people who are there purely to 'entertain' their offspring and keep them on the rails. Church youthwork has become the nice alternative to the rougher secular youthwork institutions and clubs. Once again we as leaders are being pushed towards a no-win situation. 'We give them what they want – entertainment – and they give us what we want – attendance at our events.'[5]

Entertainment, according to Angiers, is the real enemy of youthwork which seeks to help young people grow into mature and responsible Christian disciples. In response to pressure from parents Christian youthwork often gives in to the temptation to keep young people in a dependent child-like role in relation to church life. Under pressure from the culture within the church, positive policies which affirm the need for young people to grow become diminished by the weight of anxiety for their safety above all else. Christian youthworkers in responding to this pressure find themselves being like Canute – attempting to turn back the tide of adolescent growth.

Evangelical Faith and Childlike Dependency

Youthwork is not alone in seeking to keep those connected with the faith in a dependent, childlike relationship. Hull identifies the tendency within the whole of the Church to foster childlike dependency. This aspect of church life means that many Christian adults find it hard to learn and grow within the faith. Religion for a good many people, according to Hull, can act as an escape from the complexities and demands of adult life. To be adult in modern industrial society is to find an accepted place in present-day economic and bureaucratized structures. Church, however, has increasingly placed itself in the private, personal world associated with the family – it has functioned as a retreat away from adulthood and towards childhood. This process is described by Hull as the 'puerilization' of present-day church life.[6] The culture which often prevails in our congregations is one which socializes adults into a 'perpetual childhood'.[7]

Stackhouse also acknowledges that many religious communities encourage adherents to think and act as if they were children. While some play the role of the child a few act as parents. Such patterns, according to Stackhouse, are most prevalent within cults, but within modern evangelicalism he recognizes features which he terms adolescent. He argues that the emerging culture of North American evangelicalism is that of a 'perpetual adolescence' and identifies a number of parallels between the adolescent culture and church life. These include the move towards simplistic forms of expression in worship: 'The moronic "baby, baby, love, love" of MTV gets baptised into "Jesus, Jesus, love, love" with approximately the same effect: warm fuzzies.'[8]

Adolescents tend to exaggerate their feelings and the scale of their problems. They have a tendency, according to Stackhouse, to become self-obsessed and distort reality around their own self-importance. Within evangelical culture there is a growing industry which provides self-help literature, seminars and workshops. Young people also tend to identify strongly with heroes. Stackhouse compares this to the growing status of present-day evangelical 'stars' who write books or speak at conferences. These heroes occupy a position which means that their words are often held in uncritical regard by many evangelicals. A further aspect of youth culture is that it revolves around what is current. It is the new film or CD which has priority of place because it is 'hot'. Stackhouse argues that modern evangelical culture increasingly responds to what is new and trendy. What is important and worthy of note is what is 'hot'.

Hull and Stackhouse analyse the culture of the Church from very different theological and cultural situations. Their work, however, highlights the tendency for the Church to absorb believers, be they young or adult, into dependent worlds. Characterized as puerile or perpetually adolescent, these attitudes are as true of the character of Christian youthwork as they are of the wider Church. Indeed in many respects the attitudes described might be the result of concentrating on youthwork. For Hull, maintaining childhood in the church inhibits adult learning; for Stackhouse it inhibits a mature engagement with the church and the wider community. The culture of the church, however, has a tendency to restrict the development of an adult and mature faith. The one exception to this is where people are willing to enter into leadership. Both authors talk of leadership in the church as the primary route to responsibility and growth. Within a church context it is the leaders who act as parents and authority figures. To be adult therefore is to become a responsible church leader.

Youthwork and Leadership

Christian youthwork seeks to help young people grow in the faith. Growing in the faith is generally linked to a well-defined career of leadership. Starting with leading a few prayers in a service or a meeting, and going on to running a Bible study, leading on a Christian camp or becoming CU president at university, the successful evangelical route is well-trodden. Life in the average youth fellowship, houseparty and CU is structured so that Christian young people can begin to take on responsibility. Responsibility, however, also equals leadership. Within the youth fellowship, and within evangelical church life in general, the more responsibility you take on the more you become an accepted part of the leadership team. Thus the route to being accepted as an 'adult' on the youthwork scene is by being willing to adopt a leadership role. This aspect of Christian youthwork is illustrated by Steve Chalke in *The Complete Youth Manual*. Young people clearly need to develop and to grow, and Chalke tries to channel this development within the activities of the youth group. 'The youth leader must continually be asking such questions as "Does this person have the maximum responsibility and authority I can give him? Are his achievements acknowledged by me and by the group?"'[9]

It is hard to see how such responsibility and authority can be given to a young person in areas outside the life of the youth fellowship. The result of this policy is that it encourages the impression that growth, and therefore acceptance as an adult, only come through leadership within the group. If within the youth fellowship responsibility is framed solely by the activities of the local church, the impression given is that any activity outside the group lacks importance. Ashton is also keen that young people should be given responsibility and encouraged to participate in the life of the youth fellowship. Such activities should, he emphasizes, be restricted to ministry aspects of the work. Young people should not be involved in the planning of events, but in the building of personal relationships. As he puts it, 'We should make them responsible for people, rather than programmes'. Angiers also is a keen advocate of involving young people in the life of the group. Empowering young people involves getting them into activities which include setting up lights, moving furniture, and designing and painting banners.[10] His vision does however extend beyond the practical when he describes what he calls 'peer leadership': 'As youth leaders, when we empower our young people, we need to involve them totally in the process. . . In view of this we are always involved in the process of gradually giving our young people more responsibility and leadership and of taking less ourselves.'[11] There is obviously much to be said for the need to encourage young people to take responsibility and to help them to achieve within the context of a youth fellowship. Youthwork which failed to address this issue would be very wanting indeed. The problem with this solution to the problem of helping adolescents to grow up is that it focuses on the life of the group and of the church.

The emphasis on training and developing leaders has been for some time a characteristic of successful evangelical youthwork. David Winter, referring to his own experience of being involved in a youth fellowship in the 1960s, raises significant questions as to the inward-looking nature of youthwork. During this period the Church was quite confident in talking about establishing an alternative Christian lifestyle for young people. The problem with this, says Winter, was that it resulted in a separated Church. Youthwork at that time '. . . created a strong vibrant Christian Ghetto. The culture of the group was definitely Christian – it was the thing to be.'[12] Young people who joined a local church youth fellowship were encouraged to see their church activities as the centre of their social as well as their spiritual lives. Getting involved in the youth fellowship became almost an end in itself. This was a Christian activity and therefore it had to be good. To be active in the youth fellowship often meant that other interests and enthusiasms were overshadowed by religious life. Winter describes how from being a fairly left-wing thinker he moved in almost the opposite direction once he became a Christian and joined the church youth fellowship: 'If you became a Christian this is what you were expected to do. You didn't concern yourself much with the affairs of the world.'[13]

The prevailing attitude among evangelicals during the 1960s was that you could not change society. All the Church could do was change individuals. So the best thing that evangelical people could do was get on with changing individuals by leading them to faith in Christ[14] and linking them up with the youth fellowship. The real place of service was within the Church and it followed from this that young men would be encouraged to enter the ministry and particularly that of the Church of England. According to Winter there was a certain measure of expectation about this which meant that some felt that this was something which they 'ought to do'.[15]

In the 1990s, although the stress on ordination may have declined somewhat, the growth in short-term service such as the work run by Youth For Christ or Oasis Trust and Cracker carries some parallels with the situation described by Winter. The patterns which prevailed in the 1960s have to a large extent continued into the 90s. There may well be, as in the ministry described by Angiers, a concern for social action,[16] but this is tackled as an activity of the youth fellowship. In this and other ways evangelical youthwork may offer young people a well-defined pathway to responsible Christian adulthood, but in general this focuses on involvement in the group. The net result of this approach is that, while it may service the work with new leaders, in the long run when teenagers enter into adult life they are faced with a choice between accepting a dependent role and acting as leaders within the life of the church. Those accepted as responsible become leaders and act as parents within the organization.

Youthwork therefore socializes young Christians into a two-tier system within the church. There are the adult leaders and there are those who are led. If such a socialization is predominantly the case then it goes some way to explaining why many young people who do not wish to enter the leadership role find problems in remaining within the Church. This would especially be the case if they are of an independent or free-thinking frame of mind. This pattern of leaders and led, as well as explaining the drop-out of some young people from the Church, has been responsible for a number of severe problems which affect religious life.

Dependency and Religious Abuse

The impact of religion on some people's lives can be very traumatic indeed. *Healing Religious Addiction*[17] argues that it is possible to regard some religious activities and dynamics as 'religious abuse'. Within the Church, the authors argue, in some situations leaders abuse their followers. One of the chief means by which this takes place is when religion is used to inhibit freedom. To be healthy in a spiritual sense is to be free to think and explore problems, to trust our own questions and to be open to surprise.[18] As Fowler[19] and others have noted, faith needs to develop and grow. *Healing Religious Addiction* claims that it is abusive to restrict the development of an individual. Equally unhelpful is any religious practice which demands that the individual is pushed beyond a stage at which they are comfortable.

Similar themes are explored in *The Codependent Church*, which draws parallels between relationships within the family of a drug addict and the patterns of behaviour within the Church. These patterns have become known as 'codependency':

> Some churches are more codependent than others; it is a matter of degree. To the extent that any church – whether local community or international body – values persons without centers over healthy individuals or rewards reactive behaviour but punishes responsible action, it is dysfunctional and teaches codependence. To the extent that a church assigns its members roles to play and expects them to live by rules that rob them of their inner selves, it is dysfunctional and teaches codependence. To the extent that a church is a closed system, it is dysfunctional and teaches codependence.[20]

Terms such as codependency and religious abuse are alarmingly extreme. I introduce these ideas at this point more as a warning than as an accurate analysis of Christian youthwork in Britain. In churches up and down the country young people are treasured and cared for in genuinely Christian ways. The question we need to ask is whether we are as balanced in our approach as we can possibly be. Events within the Sheffield-based Nine O'clock Service would seem to indicate that a measure of caution and accountability needs to be built into all Christian work among young people to ensure safety. Some within the evangelical movement might distance themselves from NOS, seeing it as an extreme group; but if even some of what is described in this chapter as spiritual abuse and codependency causes us to feel uncomfortable, then we surely need to re-examine youthwork practice. Hoffman and the authors of *Healing Religious Addiction* come from the United States, but closer to home there is one account of the effects of evangelical youthwork which would support the view that we might not have escaped these issues entirely.

Jo Ind's moving and witty account of her battles with bulimia and the spiritual life in *Fat is a Spiritual Issue*[21] has some tough things to say about life in the evangelical church. She gives an intimate record of the inner world of a teenager dealing with an eating problem. She describes how her personal wrestling with her own self-image and sexuality was compounded by the teaching she received within the Church. As a young teenager she became a Christian and attended a large evangelical church. With her new life in Christ, she says, she began to learn a new moral code. This code was apparently derived from the Bible. As she began to walk more closely with God the rules seemed to become stricter and stricter concerning the things she was expected to do and not to do. 'Holiness', she says, 'was about formulating a mode of behaviour and sticking to it.'

> When I became a Christian I learnt that sex outside marriage was sinful, but as I became more like Jesus I realised that so too was kissing until you had prayed together and made some kind of commitment. Further more, even imagining kissing before you had prayed together and made some kind of commitment was as sinful as if you had actually done it.[22]

This kind of teaching about the faith meant that Jo was prevented from accepting her eating problem. The patterns of her disorder were mirrored in the teaching she was receiving. She describes how her faith began to work in her in two ways. On the one hand she felt a crippling guilt which consumed her, but at the same time she was paralysed by self-congratulation when she succeeded. She goes on to say that she also was led to view those around her through the same moral code. People who had casual sex deserved to get pregnant, while those who did not work deserved to fail in their exams. Those who rejected Jesus deserved to go to hell.

Jo Ind's interpretation of the faith, and the impact it had on her, may well owe a good deal to her own personal issues; but for a number of years she was closely involved with a CYFA houseparty. While her story may not give an entirely balanced reflection of the teaching she received, it should at least make us pause for reflection. How successful is our youthwork in seeking to help young people grow into Christian maturity? When the desire to keep young people safe is translated into a number of rules for behaviour, have we perhaps missed the point? Are we heading towards some kind of religious abuse?

Valuing the Need for Growth

Christian youthwork has not always been marked by a sense of panic and alarm in the face of adolescence. Frederick P. Woods, who was the founder and director of the National Young Life campaign in the 1940s, was able to balance his desire to see young people embrace the faith with a coherent and well-defined understanding of the process of arriving at maturity. In *Christian Maturity*, a small booklet written to help young people come to a conclusion concerning the faith, he makes it clear that it is an integral part of growing up to question and even to depart temporarily from Christian convictions. He bases this analysis on the four stages of development described by Eucken. In the first stage children believe all that they are taught. In the second stage, he says to the reader, 'you turn on your beliefs and rend them and you are left with nothing certain'. The third stage arrives when the young person works through doubt and unbelief to return to 'a real bit of faith'. This faith needs to be 'tested in real life to see if it works', and this is the fourth and final stage.

The accuracy or subtlety of Woods' developmental theories are less important than the fact that he starts his work with the realization that young people in reaching Christian maturity need to pass through a process of growing up. He takes seriously the need for young Christians to question the faith for themselves and he allows for a space where this sort of activity should take place. Instead of an overriding concern for safety, he acknowledges that young people need to check things out for themselves and he consequently allows for some risk in youthwork. Instead of trying to focus the attention of young people on activities within the youth fellowship or in the church, Woods puts a high priority on faith making sense in the outside world. He has the confidence to say that the only real place to work out faith is outside the Christian community in 'real life'. So far from seeking to maintain young people in childhood or in a safe dependency Woods recognizes the importance of exploration and of taking the risk of 'rending' the faith on the way to owning faith for oneself.

A similar positive approach to growth is seen in *The Growing Years* which was written by Helen Lee in the early 1960s. Lee advises parents to be prepared to let go of their young people as they grow up. The key is acceptance of the fact that teenagers need to find their own way and this means they must be allowed to set off on the journey of life. Young people may well make mistakes, but there appears to be no real way round that in Lee's mind. In a down-to-earth way she encourages Christian parents to grit their teeth, keep praying and let young people have the space to set out in life for themselves. When it comes to sex there is, despite a certain quaintness in the advice she offers, a reassuring trust and human tone in her comments:

Once they reach physical maturity, children naturally enjoy exploratory friendships with the opposite sex, and do a good deal of showing off to their boy or girl friends in a way that seems self-conscious and ridiculous. However, not only can we accept this as a stage – albeit a tiresome one sometimes – in the normal development, but we have not the faintest hope of preventing it, if we are foolish enough to try. They will make friendships in secret if we show intolerance of them openly.[23]

Being the parent of teenagers is not without its problems and worries, but Lee sees the care, trust and openness of the Christian home as the real insurance against serious problems. Parents should take courage from the fact that their children are surrounded by protective prayer. Lee did not appear to be threatened or panicked by the onset of the 1960s. She argues that allowing young people the freedom to explore and expand their horizons actually carries with it real benefits. We must 'be still and trust', and often events will turn out right in the end. As an illustration of this she tells how once she badly burned a pan in the kitchen. Seeing the pan as a total write-off she gave it to the children to play with in the garden. Within a few weeks the dirt and muck of the garden had turned a messy pan into a shiny one which she promptly reappropriated for use in the kitchen. Her message is that Christian young people need to be allowed to journey out into the world. As she puts it, 'Sometimes it takes this contact with rottenness to prove the reality of their Christian faith, which up to now has been a second-hand garment, a leftover of our own.'[24]

Woods and Lee share with present-day youthworkers a genuine desire to see young people grow up within the faith. The difference however comes in their tone rather than their message. It is refreshing to see earlier evangelicals approaching their own times with a confidence which we appear at times to lack. Whilst neither author is complacent or unaware of the problems, they have both managed to balance their natural concern with a recognition that Christian young people need to grow and develop. It might be said that theirs were gentler times, but this seems to miss the point, and each generation faces unique challenges. The advice offered by Woods and even the homely Helen Lee may not be adequate for our own situation but their acceptance that young people need to get some distance from the Christian faith and the Christian home is refreshing. These authors also show that the fear which, in my view, has significantly affected current youthwork is not endemic to evangelicalism.

Chapter 9

A Consuming Subculture

A major characteristic of postwar evangelicalism has been the marked increase in Christian consumer products. A stroll around the local Christian bookstore will reveal a remarkable array of items which are on offer: videos, cards, leather goods, CDs and tapes, T-shirts, magazines, newspapers, pottery, jewellery, and of course books. Evangelicals are enthusiastic consumers. Evangelical church life, in this respect, is reflecting developments within the wider society. We live in a consumer society and evangelicals consume religiously.

Youthwork has often led the way in the consumer boom of postwar evangelicalism. This chapter is an examination of the way in which the marketing and consumption of Christian products has functioned for young people and for the wider Church. Central to these developments has been the emergence of Elm House Christian Communications.[1] From the early days of *Buzz* Elm House used their magazine to promote and encourage the growth in a distinctly 'Christian' youth-orientated subculture. In recent years the publishing house has evolved a number of titles aimed at specific sections of the Christian public. In 1992 *Youthwork* magazine was launched to cater for those involved in Christian youth ministry.[2] At the time its editor, John Buckeridge, estimated that there were 100,000 evangelical Christians actively involved in youthwork. *Youthwork* is therefore an important source for the analysis of the subcultural nature of evangelicalism.

Selling a Subculture

Youthwork is clear and upfront in its aims. The subtitle of the magazine offers 'Ideas, Resources and Guidance for Youth Ministry'. The introductory editorial in the first edition set out the objective of giving 'practical help in your week-in, week-out contact and ministry to young people'. 'I hope you find plenty to stimulate, encourage and challenge you', wrote John Buckeridge.[3] *Youthwork* in many ways has been successful in these aims. My survey of the last three years' output has convinced me how valuable its contribution has been in offering resources to youthworkers.

For many Christians responsible for the day-to-day programme of Christian groups around the country, *Youthwork* has been a very great help indeed. Probably the most popular aspect of the magazine has been the inclusion of 'Ready-to-Use Meeting Guides'. These are life-savers for many hard-pressed youth leaders. The 'Ready-to-Use Meeting Guide' sets out a clear and easily run meeting for the youth group which then often requires minimal planning. Over the years the number of pages devoted to this resource has increased due mainly to the demand. Buckeridge has few illusions about this: 'Most people buy it for what they can use with their youth group. The ready-to-use stuff is what sells the magazine. A lot of people don't even read the articles.'[4]

Some might criticize a heavy dependency on such instant solutions as encouraging an ideas vacuum in church groups. At the same time there is a great deal to be said for setting out meeting guides in this way. In the first instance, the magazine indirectly teaches people how to go about doing youthwork. One example of this is the setting out of a clear aim for each session at the start of the guide. The guides are a regular and clear reminder to the evangelical youthwork world of what might be regarded as 'good practice'. In this way they manage to educate by example. They are also important because they have tended to deal with topics which might stretch the youth group and indeed the youth-worker. Many of the sessions tackle head-on what many evangelicals would see as controversial or difficult issues. For instance one 1995 issue[5] included a session dealing with homosexuality and another on racism. In the past topics have included suffering,[6] prejudice,[7] the Passover,[8] and pre-marital sex.[9] Alongside the meeting guide a regular feature has been material for starting discussions called 'Talking Point'. This too has regularly encouraged youthworkers to get groups talking about a wide variety of issues. The magazine has also offered resources such as a section entitled 'Artworks' providing cartoons and graphics which are freely available for local churches to photocopy.

Youthwork is clearly an important boost to hard-pressed youthworkers, but it is not all quick-fix. Over the years the articles featured have dealt with a wide variety of important topics. These have always balanced practical 'how to' material with more in-depth, thought-provoking content. The August/September 1992 issue dealt with recruiting volunteers, the legal issues involved in running a minibus, and a two-part series on sexual abuse. In Britain, as opposed to the USA, there are relatively few books published which might be seen as foundational theory for youth ministry. Given this lack of material it is to *Youthwork* magazine's credit that many of the articles are relatively meaty and well researched. In one or two cases the articles published could be said to encourage a clear step forward in the discipline of youth ministry. This would be the case with Andy Hickford's piece on the year of Jubilee[10] or the extract from Gunter Krallmann's book *Mentoring for Mission*.[11]

Positive much of it may be, but *Youthwork* remains a consumer product. The meeting guides, ideas pages and indeed the articles are themselves marketed to a Christian public in the same way that any other magazine might be. *Youthwork* is also similar to other magazines in that its content and its finances depend on advertising. Taking into account that the content of the magazine – the ideas contained in the articles and other material – is itself a consumer product there is not one page of *Youthwork* which is not dedicated to selling something. The variety of products offered is itself bewildering. April/May 1995 offers the following:

> IVP books, youth ministry training, a youth mission team, the magazine itself, a drugs seminar, MAYC weekend, YFC weekend, Christian Resources exhibition, a ready-to-use meeting, ready-to-use meeting compilation, Greenbelt, AOG church planting, ideas on peer group work, Oasis frontline, training course for youth ministry (21 notices), Oxford Youth Works, OU, Moorlands College, Northumbria Bible College, ideas on bullying, resources on bullying, *Youthwork Ready-to-Use Meeting Guides* 1–3, ideas on integrating young people, CMS Holidays, Bible Colleges (2), *Sophie's World*, Christian Rock bands (10 notices); jobs including: accountancy, promotions, housekeeper, activity instructors, pastor, accountant, conference centre manager, nanny/housekeeper, personnel manager, actress, administrator, youthworker, managing editor; classified ads including: Gaines Youth Centre, Christian Mountain Centre, Canal Holidays, Barnardos Holidays, family day, Gospel Conjuring, Hospital Radio, Christian Computer Software, youth ministry books, *Youthwork* magazine, book reviews (7), reviews of videos (2) and albums (1), Bible life materials.

This issue of *Youthwork* is by no means unusual in the number or variety of products on offer. Each edition of the magazine is intimately bound up with the consumption of a number of specialist products. In this respect the magazine simply reflects a significant network of producers and consumers within the evangelical youthwork world. To say this, I must stress, is in no way to make any value judgement on the magazine. We all live and work in a consumer society. The key insight which arises from a study of this magazine is the realization that evangelicalism, and the youthwork world in particular, is a community which produces and consumes products.

Popular Culture, Subculture and Evangelical Consumption

According to Fiske popular culture arises from a dynamic relationship between producers and consumers. It is wrong to view popular culture as being controlled by big business or the advertisers. Popular culture arises from the people:

> Popular culture is not consumption, it is culture – the active process of generating and circulating meanings and pleasures within a social system: culture, however industrialised, can never be adequately described in terms of the buying and selling of commodities.

> Culture is a living, active process; it can be developed only from within, it cannot be imposed from without or above.[12]

These two quotations from Fiske indicate a direction for a cultural analysis of *Youthwork* magazine. The buying and selling seen within evangelical youthwork is an indication that a community exists within which it is possible to see the various products giving rise to identities and meanings. Consumption and the identity of Christian youthwork have become closely linked. As we consume products we create meaning. One important example of this is found in the variety of summer festivals on offer. In one issue there were details of twelve different Christian events and festivals happening during the summer which youthworkers might choose to attend with young people.

Choice and consumption therefore characterize the current youthwork scene, but to consume is also to begin to construct identity. For the youthworker the choice between Greenbelt, Taizé, CYFA camp, or Soul Survivor is as much about identity as it is about styles of youthwork. Of course youthwork activities reflect wider theological trends. It is a moot point whether Soul Survivor or Greenbelt are the products of a theological position or are themselves the producers of theology. Certainly for many young people and youth leaders they represent not only a source of inspiration but also a kind of identity. Of late there have been a number of gatherings where I have heard youth leaders take sides in an 'I am for Paul' and 'I am for Apollos' way when they discuss attendance, or non-attendance, at one or more of these events.

Evangelicalism is a subculture. In using the term subculture I simply mean that evangelicalism is a subsection of society which increasingly operates within the framework of popular culture. It is youthwork, more than any other aspect of its life, which has moved evangelicalism along this path. What we see in *Youthwork* magazine is a complex relationship between the producers of Christian cultural products, the interests of the evangelical tradition/morality, and young people themselves. One good example of the way this works is shown in an article on Christian bands by regular contributor Kevin Elliott.[13] Elliott makes it clear that most non-Christian young people will probably never have heard of 'even the best known Christian bands'. In other words Christian bands can often operate within a fairly closed world of gigs put on by churches, youthworkers and specialist promoters. In fact the world of Christian music may even be a fringe or marginalized aspect of the more mainstream Christian bookshops. As we are advised by Elliott;

> Although most Christian bookshops stock tapes and CDs they often have a very limited knowledge of the market outside of the most popular praise tapes. If you ask for the latest offering of Zero or enquire if the One Bad Pig video is still available then expect vacant looks.[14]

It may not be so well-known, but there are Christian versions of 'rap, metal, dance, folk, thrash grunge, indie and soul to name but a few', according to the article. Elliott ends his piece by encouraging youthworkers to lay on events using Christian bands. Apparently many bands 'are suffering from a lack of understanding, involvement and encouragement from churches and a seeming reluctance to pay for an

evening of Christian entertainment'. It is this last phrase
which gives such a profound insight into the nature of
evangelical subculture. Youth leaders over the last twenty or
thirty years have hit upon Christian bands, events, theatre
companies and so on as an alternative Christian option to
offer to their young people. The evangelical subculture has
emerged because youthworkers have bought into what they
believe to be more constructive entertainments. As Elliott
puts it, 'We need to educate ourselves and then our young
people on the Christian music scene giving them the choice
of a more positive musical input . . . the future of Christian
music and ultimately our kids will benefit as more of us take
the plunge and put on a concert. Rap, Rock or Rave – go
on – book a band.'[15]

The premise on which the Christian subculture is built is
that young Christians need to be encouraged to consume
'positive' cultural products. The need for Christian bands
arises from the desire to see young Christians listening to
music which will influence them in positive (that is, evangelical) ways. All around the country youth leaders and
Christian parents are making small decisions along these
lines. Christian young people, for their part, may well
collude with the desires of their parents and their youth
leaders. A Christian Metal band or Rap act may feel a little
less risky or open to condemnation. Greenbelt festival might
be a place for some adventure, but it is nothing like the
secular festivals at Reading or Glastonbury. The Christian
bands, festivals, T-shirts and magazines offer a safe and
approved source for forming an identity for many evangelical
young people.

The desire for a safe alternative subculture for young
people has led Christian youthwork to adopt more and more
aspects of popular culture. The key point here is not that
this kind of music or that kind is now being used in church.
Rather it is that the construction of identity within the
Christian youthwork world now operates in similar ways to
that seen in other youth subcultures. Evangelicalism con-
sists of a number of different 'subcultural styles', and they

operate in similar ways to any other kind of style. Whereas
in the past evangelical identity might have been invested
heavily with doctrinal affirmations or theological argument,
these now assume less and less importance as indicators of
the various streams within evangelicalism. In the new context
even the 'quiet time' is becoming a marketing opportunity.
Buckeridge has offered what amounts to a consumer guide
to nine different Bible reading aids for young people. These
include what he refers to as a new phenomenon in Bible
publishing – 'special editions aimed at young people. Bibles
used to weigh half a ton and have severe black covers with
the words "Holy Bible" carved in gold leaf down the spine.
A new generation of "youth friendly" Bibles have bright,
eye-catching, even jazzy covers.' The article goes on to explain
that this is not just the old text between new covers. These
new Bibles have adopted a magazine style of comment with
'teen friendly guides' to aim to help the young reader get
into Scripture.[16]

It might be thought that these developments are an indication that evangelicalism is moving with the times, adapting
to modern culture. This new approach to Bible reading and
even to the Bible itself could be seen as a refreshing development which makes the faith more accessible to young
people. Christian bands working within popular styles of
music are an indication of the relevance of evangelical religion to a variety of cultures. Unfortunately this is not
entirely true. The basic problem is that evangelicals have
tended to invest most heavily in creating a parallel but
essentially separate subculture.

The Magazine and the Subculture

Youthwork magazine is a part of the evangelical subculture,
reflecting the values of a much wider community. The magazine is, in an important sense, simply a product of the
Christian scene. As we have seen, a substantial proportion
of the articles and ready-to-use material in *Youthwork* is
designed to challenge its readers to think more deeply and

broadly concerning their work. Having said this there are important ways in which the magazine reinforces what I have termed the evangelical subculture.

Youthwork has a very distinct perspective on popular culture and on the world of Christian youthwork. This perspective may not be deliberate editorial policy, but it is possible to see significant sections of the material within the magazine falling into a basic pattern. The ready-to-use meetings and the articles are generally sandwiched between two other regular features. The first of these is the news section and towards the end of the magazine there is the 'Culture Vulture' (in recent issues this has been called 'The Lowdown'). A survey of this material shows that, with relatively few exceptions, it falls into three broad categories: scare stories, positive stories and negative stories. In adopting these labels I am hoping to show how the world looks from within the evangelical subculture.

Youthwork magazine, in my view, sits firmly within the evangelical youth world. It is financially and ideologically committed to maintaining a strong evangelical youthwork subculture. From a position set within the mainstream of evangelical life, the magazine, along with a great many evangelicals, views much of modern popular culture with a certain degree of alarm. The scare stories in general approximate to the treatment of various aspects of youth culture and the wider secular scene. The positive stories deal with the activities of those within the evangelical youthwork world. The negative stories are reserved for aspects of the Christian youth scene which have a high profile, but which are seen, for one reason or another, as a threat to real evangelical commitment. One way of describing the perspective of the magazine is as three concentric circles. The inner circle is the evangelical subculture which is safe. The outer circle is the world of popular youth culture which is dangerous. The middle circle contains Christian youth activities which are seen as being 'dodgy'.

Scare Stories

It is in the 'Culture Vulture' (or 'The Lowdown') section
that *Youthwork* generally deals with the wider youth culture.
Announcing the arrival of this new regular feature Buckeridge
says that it will 'keep you up-to-date with all that's new in
the fast-changing world of popular youth culture'. He adds:
'That's crucial because popular culture has a major influence
on the value systems and beliefs of young people.'[17] Each
'Culture Vulture' includes what is called a 'C.V. Street Cred
Test'. In this test questions on details of youth culture are
asked and according to your success in answering these a
score is given. It would seem then that Christian youthworkers are expected to know what is going on in youth culture. To this message however must also be added the caveat
that youth culture is a distinctly dangerous preoccupation.

The general approach of the magazine is to focus on the
violent, disturbing and destructive aspects of popular culture.
Negative stories covered include the expensive nature of
trainers,[18] teenage pregnancy,[19] and Mortal Kombat.[20] Death
Metal is seen as the 'disturbing rise of a new genre of heavy
metal music', which has 'spawned a new magazine'.[21] One
issue managed to treat every one of the short articles in the
'Culture Vulture' section in a negative manner. The article
on 'computer trends' warned of games which are 'unsuitable
for children'. The secular teenage bands 'Take That' and
'East 17' are reported as adopting sexually explicit sleazy
images. 'Jungle House' music is said to have a 'manically fast
beat', whilst the highlighted quote from the Scottish Drugs
Forum warns that '. . . People who take drugs like ecstasy
don't even see themselves as drug users'.[22] Occasionally
youth culture is reported in neutral tones, but it is very rare
for there to be any positive appreciation of youth culture.[23]
The more regular fare is well represented by a brief news
item on Keanu Reeves who, we are told, now espouses
Buddhism, news which could be said to be calculated to
alarm evangelicals.[24]

Scare stories are not just limited to the 'Culture Vulture'

section of the magazine. Occasionally what are seen as alarming developments in popular media and advertising are also exposed. In the August/September 1992 issue a special feature news story concerns the 'ex-sex mag editor' who is now advising teenagers. According to *Youthwork* the BBC children's Saturday programme *Going Live* had appointed a man who once worked for the adult magazine *Forum*.[25] The influence of advertising is another issue dealt with by the magazine. Buckeridge is concerned to encourage youth leaders and young people to stop swallowing culture and to start to decypher cultural messages: 'We need to get behind the messages in our culture. A lot of money goes into manipulating young people to spend money.'

There is much in these sentiments that is to be encouraged. However the tone of negativity, not to say alarm, which lies behind the treatment of popular culture and the media reinforces the isolation of Christians within their own subcultural world. While it is important for young people to be discerning and critical of the culture which surrounds them, this needs to be balanced with some positive appreciation of the creativity, concern and the celebration of life which characterizes much of our current youth culture. If the predominant line is that there are so many dangerous messages 'out there' in popular culture, then any encouragement to participate with other young people in a common youth culture is inevitably discouraged.

Positive Stories

The vast majority of the news output in *Youthwork* features youth events within the evangelical subculture. With two or three notable exceptions (see *Negative Stories* below), these are presented in the most glowing terms. News items covered over a three-year period have been wide-ranging. They have included items on the Shaftesbury Society,[26] SU,[27] Crusaders,[28] MAYC,[29] Covenanters,[30] World Vision,[31] the Children's Society,[32] Taizé,[33] and Billy Graham.[34]

The news section of *Youthwork* performs an important

function for evangelical youth ministry. It is vital to know what is going on in the youthwork scene. The items on particular people reinforce the sense of community and give an idea of the movement of important figures or of key ideas. To find that your own appointment is worthy of a mention, and I can say this from personal experience, gives a sense of being where it is at.[35] *Youthwork* therefore defines a constituency and informs as to the key events, appointments and developments. In this way the magazine operates as a kind of trade paper, but it also acts as an arbiter of what lies within the evangelical youthwork world and what does not. Over a year or so the items reported give an indication as to what is worthy of note, who is 'in' and therefore, by implication, who is 'out'.

Also of importance is the frequency with which particular events, individuals or organizations are mentioned. *Youthwork* has a definite bias towards reporting those items with which it has a direct link. Steve Chalke, Oasis Trust, Brainstormers, YFC, Spring Harvest, Dave Roberts, and the various activities associated with 'Cracker' appear with predictable regularity.[36] That the magazine has a right and a financial responsibility to promote the events such as Brainstormers with which it is associated seems indisputable. Buckeridge is fairly open about the impact of this coverage on his audience: 'Readers are sophisticated enough. They are well able to spot yet another Brainstormers plug. But they understand we need to make things work.'[37]

The bias of *Youthwork* towards a relatively small and select group of people on one level is very understandable. The key factor here, however, is the effect which this emphasis has on the evangelical subculture in general. The magazine reinforces by its news policy what could be seen as the mainstream of Christian youthwork. In effect it defines certain events, and people, as being of central importance, but this personal promotion is less important than the uncritical and unobjective view which seems to be taken. The news items serve to reinforce the sense that within the subculture there are a number of exciting products which can be consumed. In so doing it tends to reinforce a centripetal movement and a somewhat self-obsessed view of evangelical activity. The variety of youth organizations featured does temper this a little, but the concentration on a few limited activities and people does little to broaden the horizons of those caught up in the subculture. If one of the key messages of the magazine concerns outreach to the unchurched, the news items tend to subvert this by reinforcing the view among Christian youth leaders that to make it is to feature in a large Christian organization or event.

Negative Stories

The news reported in *Youthwork* is overwhelmingly, and in some ways refreshingly, positive. Given this stance, the items which are reported with a negative feel to them tend to stand out somewhat. This prominence is all the more marked by the frequency with which certain Christian activities are treated in this way. There is something of the soap opera in the way in which the magazine has repeatedly sought to 'shed light' on two major Christian groups; the Nine O'clock Service (NOS)[38] and Greenbelt festival.[39]

NOS and Greenbelt are similar in that they have been extremely influential in the evangelical world. When significant developments take place, there is some justification in claiming that the reporting of them is 'news'. In a regular magazine or newspaper that would of course be the case; but with both NOS and Greenbelt *Youthwork* has pursued a quite distinctive agenda. Distinctive in the sense that most other Christian events or organizations are generally reported in extremely positive tones, or ignored altogether. In commenting on stories concerning Greenbelt, Buckeridge sees the role of the magazine as informing the Christian public as to what is going on: 'We get told so many stories, half of which aren't true. We get quotes, we check them out . . . Any rumours about youthwork, we try to set the record straight.'[40]

It is editorial policy that all potentially contentious items are fully researched. Care is taken to ensure that those being reported get the chance to have their say and respond to the item in their own words. At this level there is really nothing unethical or underhand in the way news items are handled. The interesting aspect of the magazine's approach to 'negative stories' is its choice of targets. NOS and Greenbelt have their roots within the evangelical world, but they have both embraced perspectives from a broad range of theological positions. It is these aspects of their activities that appears to cause *Youthwork* concern. So the visit of the theologian Matthew Fox to NOS was reported with the headline 'NOS flirts with New Age Prophet'.[41] The article reminds the readers that NOS have a controversial past by repeating the story that 'NOS provoked an angry response with bikini-clad dancers and new age symbols at Greenbelt two years ago.' Fox is reported as being connected with a 'Centre for Creation Spirituality' in California which includes on its staff 'Starhawk the witch (alias Miriam Simos); Buck Ghost Horse, a shaman (mystic guide healer); Luish Teish, a West African voodoo priestess; Robert Frager, representing Sufism (Islamic mysticism); and New Age analysts'. The accuracy of this reporting is not really the issue. The point is that by featuring this aspect of the activities of NOS (and also indirectly Greenbelt) *Youthwork* was sending a clear signal to the evangelical world that what was happening in the Sheffield community was in their view 'dodgy'.

Subsequently disclosures indeed indicated that all was not well at NOS, and some might say that the caution expressed by *Youthwork* was vindicated by later events. This seems however to be a little neat and tidy. *Youthwork* was uneasy about NOS for more general reasons than the specific issues which emerged concerning its leader, Chris Brain. It is the departure from clear evangelical ground which causes concern. *Youthwork* was primarily signalling an unease with the overall direction of the group. The point is not really whether *Youthwork* was right or wrong concerning NOS. The argument about negative stories is included to give an insight into the way that the evangelical subculture operates.

The fact that similar kinds of messages are also contained in the reporting of Greenbelt shows the wider pattern.

At a time when Greenbelt was struggling to find a permanent site *Youthwork* reported the failure in full.[42] Once again the facts were largely accurate. The message, however, was that Greenbelt had perhaps lost its way and was seen as a nuisance by protesters who objected to the festival moving to their area. Problems at Greenbelt are clearly 'news' within the evangelical world, but one has to ask, in the absence of 'problem stories' concerning any other organization or festival, why this item? This news story is by no means an isolated case. In recent years the magazine has featured special reports on Greenbelt by different journalists. Kevin Elliott's report of the 1993 festival was extremely positive; however, the text introducing the article puts a note of controversy into the piece. We are reminded that Greenbelt failed to find a permanent site and are told that '. . . despite a rain-free August Bank Holiday weekend the attendance was a disappointing 15,000'. Sossie Kasbarian found much to praise at the 1995 festival but she makes a point of highlighting the fact that one contributor is 'sometimes controversial' and that some opinions expressed at the festival were 'downright heretical'. Again the editorial text for the piece puts what could be regarded as a negative spin on the article, asking the readers 'So was it [Greenbelt] lip-smacking good or stomach-churning bad?'[43]

That *Youthwork* should report events at Greenbelt or at NOS is not in dispute. To ignore an important festival or an innovative new service, both of which influence so many young people and adults within the evangelical constituency, would be a serious oversight. The question of influence, however, goes to the heart of what this analysis of *Youthwork* magazine is all about. In making a point of reporting the questionable aspects of NOS and Greenbelt the magazine performs an important defining function for the Christian subculture. Here again is the question of safety. If the function of the evangelical youthwork subculture is to offer a safe environment for Christian young people then the fear that influences which are considered to be questionable or even downright wrong are being brought to bear is of primary importance. This is especially the case for those who are committed to maintaining safety. NOS and Greenbelt receive attention because they are important within the evangelical subculture. A good many churches and young people look to these places for inspiration. The message that they might not be entirely 'safe' is sent out and repeated by *Youthwork* magazine precisely because these two are on the fringes of the subculture. *Youthwork* sees no need to deal with the Glastonbury or Reading festivals because they do not have any obvious evangelical youthwork connections.

Buckeridge sees the role of the magazine in biblical terms, likening his treatment of NOS to the discipline offered within a church context. He is concerned to speak face to face with the wrongdoer and then if no headway is made he prints the story.[44] From his perspective within the subculture this approach makes a good deal of sense. If some parts of the evangelical youthwork world appear to threaten the safety of young people then it is important that as wide a group as possible are informed as to the exact situation.

The Limitations of a Subculture

Adopting a subcultural approach to youthwork has severe limitations. In the first instance it prevents, rather than encourages, critical thinking. If our perspective on the Christian environment divides into safe and suspect areas, then the temptation is that youthworkers and young people need not think for themselves. If certain exploratory initiatives such as Greenbelt are labelled suspect, whatever the rights or wrongs of the case, the ideology of the evangelical mind set makes these 'no-go areas', which for safety's sake should be avoided. There is fear of them influencing young people's lives and this fear can limit experimentation and enquiry. Instead of opening up young people to a variety of styles of Christian thought and life, and building a strong sense of their own identity through a mature reflection on modern life and the Bible, there is a tendency to keep to safe pathways. Of course no-one wants young people to turn away from Christ or fall into sin, but there have to be ways of making room for exploration and a variety of experiences as part of normal Christian growth. The adoption of a safe subculture, it has to be said, militates against this.

Chapter 10

Implications

I am very much aware that the analysis of Christian youth-work undertaken in this book represents work in progress. I have written assuming that others will eventually temper, develop or even disprove the ideas I have presented. So there is a part of me that does not want to draw too many con-clusions at this stage. Having said this somewhere inside me there is a voice which says 'So what? You've written all these words and what real use are they to youthworkers?' I there-fore offer the brief summary in this chapter of what I regard to be some of the implications of my analysis.

The Centrality of Youthwork

I think the key message of this book is that what happens today in youthwork happens in five years' time in the main-stream life of the Church. The evangelical story shows how today's youth leaders are tomorrow's clergy and the day after tomorrow they become bishops and even archbishops. Similarly the songs we use in youthwork today in a very short time are incorporated into regular Sunday worship. Developments in youthwork are in this sense the creative force which moves the Church on. Evangelicals and indeed the Church as a whole therefore need to invest heavily in staying in touch with young people and with youthworkers. The clergy and the church hierarchy cannot afford to lose touch with such an influential area of activity.

Youthwork is far from being marginal to the evolution of evangelical identity. My reading of the postwar boom among evangelicals is that it was led by young people and clergy who had themselves been deeply affected by youthwork. But just as evangelical success is linked to youthwork, so too are our divisions. We have been to a large extent shaped by our ministry among young people. If this was the case in the past it may well also be true in the future. This means that ministry among young people is one of the key creative places where evangelicalism will renew itself (or not, as the case may be). Theological education therefore needs to take youthwork much more seriously – the future shape of the Church is at stake.

In festivals, youth fellowships, camps, missions, and worship services up and down the country young people are 'growing up evangelical'. The message of the past is that as they do this evangelicalism, and eventually the whole Church, is changed. We are in a period of phenomenal creativity where youthworkers are experimenting with new forms of worship, new approaches to Bible study and new areas of spirituality. There is a need for evangelical clergy and theologians to work creatively with these initiatives offering support, wisdom and, where necessary, caution. I hope that this book goes some way to demonstrating the seriousness of this relationship. Senior figures in the evangelical constituency need to reorder priorities so that the theory and practice of youthwork are brought to the centre of their agendas.

A Serious Discipline

The third part of this book has offered a glimpse into the tensions which characterize Christian youthwork. We feel the force of parents' concern for the safety of their children. We should not, however, allow this concern to deflect us from the God-given charge to reach out to all young people. It is my view that youthworkers who are primarily involved in youth fellowships need to recognize the limitations of the group with which they are working. One youth fellowship will not be able to bridge the many social groupings which exist in the local community. Youth fellowships work best when young people are set free to reach out to their friends. But the task of reaching beyond the fringe of the existing fellowship, in my opinion, demands fresh approaches. I am increasingly coming to the view that youth fellowship work is one 'discipline' which could be described as working from the 'inside out' to the fringe. There is another youthwork discipline which involves working from the 'outside in' to the church. Both approaches involve outreach and the nurture of young people in the faith. They just operate differently. If we as youthworkers are clear about which of these disciplines we are seeking to operate within, then it is my view that we will be more able to square the needs of Christian parents and the needs of the 'unchurched'.

The Church looks to those working with young people for the answers. Whether we like it or not youthworkers are seen as the experts. We therefore need to get a clarity in our work which we can then offer to the wider Church. Outreach, however, will mean that we will need to learn the lessons from those who have gone before us. The creative pioneers of youthwork were concerned to develop approaches to particular groups of young people which took full account of their social and cultural situation. In contrast, the lack of theological education and reflection among many present-day youthworkers has meant that often we have sought quick solutions. We see a method of work in one place and we seek to apply it uncritically in our own. The contextual sensitivity which was demonstrated by those in previous generations needs to be relearned in the present. This is especially important when we are seeking to reach young people who are socially and culturally distant from those currently in the Church. It is my view that the key to this is the development of well-resourced and well-run training programmes for Christian youthwork.

Full-time Youthworkers

The growth in the number of full-time youthworkers is

something to be welcomed. The implications of this development, however, need to be thought through. Many of these youthworkers currently have no official connection to the structures of the Church. As the network of full-time youthworkers grows, the Church is effectively fostering a group of highly skilled and yet independent practitioners. We need to find ways of incorporating these people, with their undoubted experience, into the permanent structures of the churches. One further aspect of this is that many of those who wish to work with young people, who in the past might have offered themselves for ordination, are now finding jobs as full-time youthworkers. Consequently whereas in the 1960s there was a generation of young clergy committed to developing church youthwork, at the present time the number of young clergy skilled in these areas appears to be going down. The churches need to address this issue to see if ways can be found which offer young leaders a recognized (and therefore probably ordained) status and the chance to specialize in youthwork. This will be easier for some churches than for others, but evangelicals with their history of commitment to youthwork need to lead the way in pressing for the necessary changes.

Balanced Youthwork

The sponsoring of adequate training and a continued place within the churches for full-time and volunteer youthworkers should have as its end better youthwork. Young people need to be led to faith and encouraged to continue as Christians in safe and balanced ministries. The analysis of Christian youthwork followed in this book points to three crucial areas where more work needs to be done if we are to achieve this end.

The first is in the area of worship. The chapter which deals with the development of theological themes in Christian worship songs points to the need for clear and considered thinking in this area. It is my view that the movement towards a more apocalyptic imagery found in *Songs of Fellowship*

Book One contributed to the sense of alarm felt by many Christian parents during the 1980s. The spirituality which we see in the worship songs was worked out in life and one of the consequences of this was the loss of a proper perspective in the advice offered to young people. Worship is crucial to the health of the Church and the images, language, and the ethos of its music need to be treated with the utmost seriousness. These matters must be the concern of the whole Church, not just of publishers, songwriters and the organizers of festivals or youth services.

The second area that has been considered is the tendency for evangelical youthwork to build an attractive alternative subculture. On one level it seems that this is inevitable. The proliferation of consumer items targeted at young Christian people is so much part of the current scene that I can see little turning back. We also need to accept that any community of people operating as a religious group inevitably need some shared cultural activities. The real question is not whether we should have an evangelical subculture (or subcultures) because in my view we cannot operate without one. The key question is what the nature, purpose and direction of the subculture is going to be. Those of us engaged in Christian youthwork need to take some time to reflect on the part we play in promoting and creating the evangelical subculture. If we truly want young people to live out their faith among their peers, we need to ask ourselves how much the subculture which we promote is aiding them in this. Somehow we need to foster an openness as opposed to a closed perspective. Our separate festivals and events may be places of encouragement, but they also need to be launching pads for genuine dialogue with the wider culture. It is in our hands to try to ensure that this is the case.

For evangelicalism at large the subcultural style of various youth-orientated Christian groups is a matter which requires some deliberation. I have argued that the evangelical scene is shifting towards new ways of forming identity and that many of these arise out of the activities and enterprises which characterize the current youthwork scene. Senior clergy and leaders need to take some stock of this and come to terms with the way things are developing. We need to react to these developments with our eyes open and in a well-informed way. The embracing of subcultural style within the evangelical constituency has far-reaching implications and only a few of these have been dealt with in this book. Evangelical theologians need to wrestle with the changes which are beginning to come about and offer their insights, support and critique of youthwork practice. To ignore the current trends is possibly to abandon a generation.

A linked issue relates to the need for a sense of balance as youthworkers deal with the complexities of adolescence, the third area for attention. There is an urgent need for thinking in the area of Christian growth and maturity. Youthworkers need to have a good grasp of what process of growth they are fostering in individuals and in groups. Those teaching youthwork need to make it a priority to work with the disciplines of psychology, sociology and biblical theology to gain a sophistication in this area. Religious abuse is not distant from our practice, it is frighteningly close. Only a considered and well thought out approach to the nature and process of spiritual, emotional and physical maturity will suffice in the education of youthworkers, be they full-time workers or volunteers. Those agencies committed to a staged developmental approach to Christian education need to take this agenda and lead the way with it.

Finally I should say that I recognize that 'growing up evangelical' is far from being a simple matter. Young people are beloved of God and they are his instruments for bringing change and renewal to the Church. The many youthworkers and clergy who give their time to help young people discover and grow in the faith are therefore central to the continued witness of the Church in this country. It is my hope that the ideas presented in this book might help in this process.

Notes

Notes to Introduction

1. M. Brake, *Comparative Youth Culture* (Routledge and Kegan Paul 1985), p. 3.
2. R. T. France and A. E. McGrath (eds), *Evangelical Anglicans* (SPCK 1993), p. 7.
3. M. A. Noll, D. W. Bebbington and G. A. Rawlk (eds), *Evangelicalism* (Oxford 1994), p. 6.
4. A. E. McGrath, *Evangelicalism and the Future of Christianity* (Hodder and Stoughton 1994), p. 11.
5. D. Wells, 'On Being Evangelical: Some Theological Differences and Similarities', in *Evangelicalism*, p. 392.
6. *Evangelicalism and the Future of Christianity*, p. 35.
7. M. Saward, *Evangelicals on the Move* (Mowbray 1987), p. 31.
8. D. W. Bebbington, *Evangelicalism in Modern Britain* (Unwin Hyman 1989), p. 258.
9. D. W. Bebbington, 'Evangelicalism in its Settings: The British and American Movements Since 1940', in *Evangelicalism*, p. 367. 'Young Life' is an American organization which was started by Jim Rayburn. Rayburn took the name for his quite separate ministry from the already existing British National Young Life Campaign on the understanding that his US work would never operate in Britain under the title.
10. W. Martin, *The Billy Graham Story* (Hutchinson 1991), p. 91.
11. *Evangelicalism*, p. 367.
12. O. Chadwick, *Michael Ramsey: A Life* (Oxford 1990), p. 234.
13. K. Hylson-Smith, *Evangelicals in the Church of England 1734–1984* (T and T Clark 1988), p. 313.
14. *The Billy Graham Story*, p. 96.
15. *Evangelicals 1734–1984*, p. 313.
16. The one serious discussion of this is perhaps that in J. Eddison (ed.), *Bash: A Study in Spiritual Power* (Marshall Pickering 1982).

17. For more on this see V. Samuel and C. Sugden (eds), *Sharing Jesus in the Two Thirds World* (Partnership in Mission 1983); D. J. Hesselgrave and E. Rommen, *Contextualisation* (Apollos 1989); H. Montefiore, *The Gospel and Contemporary Culture* (Mowbray 1992); L. Newbigin, *The Gospel in a Pluralist Society* (SPCK 1989).
18. *Evangelicalism and the Future of Christianity*, p. 30.
19. *Evangelicalism and the Future of Christianity*, p. 94.
20. *Evangelicalism and the Future of Christianity*, p. 94.
21. *Evangelicalism and the Future of Christianity*, p. 117.
22. *Evangelicalism and the Future of Christianity*, p. 93.
23. These points are explored further in chapter 1.
24. J. Davison Hunter, *Evangelicalism the Coming Generation* (Chicago 1987), p. 11.
25. N. O. Hatch, *The Democratization of American Christianity* (Yale 1989), p. 5.
26. *Democratization of American Christianity*, p. 9.
27. These issues are explored further in chapter 3.
28. P. Brierley, *Reaching and Keeping Teenagers* (Monarch 1993).
29. R. Holloway, 'Evangelicalism: An Outsider's Perspective', in *Evangelical Anglicans*, p. 179.
30. *Evangelical Anglicans*, p. 181.
31. N. K. Clifford quoted in *Evangelicalism*, p. 12.
32. *Evangelical Anglicans*, p. 180.
33. *Evangelical Anglicans*, p. 183.
34. For more on this see chapter 7.
35. See S. Adams, 'The Process of Change Through Relationships Between Adults and Young People', in P. Ward (ed.), *Relational Youthwork* (Lynx 1995).
36. This issue is dealt with more extensively in chapter 8.
37. *Evangelicalism and the Future of Christianity*, p. 126.
38. *Evangelicalism and the Future of Christianity*, p. 132.
39. *Evangelicalism and the Future of Christianity*, p. 135.
40. J. G. Stackhouse Jnr, 'Perpetual Adolescence: The Emerging Culture of North American Evangelicalism', in *Crux* Vol. 29, No. 3 (September 1993).
41. *Evangelicalism*, p. 6.
42. *Evangelical Anglicans*, p. 182.
43. *Evangelicalism*, p. 8.
44. *Democratization of American Christianity*, p. 126.
45. *Democratization of American Christianity*, p. 146.
46. *Evangelicalism*, p. 8.
47. For more on this see chapter 4.

48. The many books designed to advise young people and parents are evidence of an increasing sense of concern – for more on this see chapter 7.
49. M. Noll, *The Scandal of the Evangelical Mind* (IVP 1994), p. 34.
50. See Q. J. Schultze, R. M. Anker, J. D. Bratt, W. D. Romanowski, J. W. Worst and L. Zuidervaart, *Dancing in the Dark: Youth, Popular Culture and the Electronic Media.* (Eerdmans 1991).
51. These themes are explored more deeply in chapters 7 and 9.
52. For more on this from a US perspective see *Dancing in the Dark*, pp. 14–45 and J. F. Kett, *Rites of Passage: Adolescence in America 1790 to the Present* (Basic Books 1977).
53. For the US side of the story see M. Senter III, *The Coming Revolution in Youth Ministry* (Victor Books 1992).

Notes to Chapter One

1. A similar pattern has been described by Senter in *The Coming Revolution*, pp. 42–6.
2. M. Smith, *Developing Youth Work* (Open University 1988).
3. P. B. Cliff, *The Rise and Development of the Sunday School Movement in England 1780–1980* (National Christian Education Council 1986).
4. *Rise and Development of the Sunday School Movement*, p. 72.
5. C. Binfield, *George Williams and the YMCA: A Study in Victorian Social Attitudes* (Heinemann 1973), p. 101.
6. *George Williams and the YMCA*, pp. 14, 18.
7. *George Williams and the YMCA*, p. 120.
8. R. S. Peacock, *Pioneer of Boyhood* (The Boys' Brigade 1954), p. 24.
9. *Pioneer of Boyhood*, p. 42.
10. *Pioneer of Boyhood*, pp. 127–8.
11. *Rise and Development of the Sunday School Movement*, p. 168.
12. D. Borgman, 'A History of American Youth Ministry', in W. S. Benson and M. H. Senter III (eds.), *The Complete Book of Youth Ministry* (Moody Press 1987), p. 65.
13. *The Coming Revolution*, p. 98.
14. *Rise and Development of the Sunday School Movement*, p. 169.
15. *Complete Book of Youth Ministry*, p. 65.
16. N. Sylvester, *God's Word in a Young World* (SU 1985), p. 12.
17. J. C. Pollock, *The Good Seed* (Hodder and Stoughton 1959), p. 16.
18. *The Good Seed*, p. 21.
19. *God's Word in a Young World*, p. 18.
20. *The Good Seed*, p. 32.
21. *God's Word in a Young World*, p. 19.

22. Quoted in *God's Word in a Young World*, p. 25.
23. *The Good Seed*, p. 33ff.
24. *The Good Seed*, p. 42.
25. D. Johnson, *Contending for the Faith: A History of the Evangelical Movement in the Universities and Colleges* (IVP 1979), p. 169.
26. *God's Word in a Young World*, p. 45.
27. *The Good Seed*, p. 65.
28. *Contending for the Faith*, p. 80.
29. *The Good Seed*, p. 66.
30. *God's Word in a Young World*, p. 52.
31. Quoted in *God's Word in a Young World*, p. 24.
32. *The Good Seed*, p. 82.
33. *The Good Seed*, p. 83.
34. See *Contending for the Faith*, p. 28; also J. E. Orr, *Campus Aflame: A History of Evangelical Awakenings in Collegiate Communities* (International Awakening Press edn 1994).
35. *Contending for the Faith*, p. 14.
36. *Contending for the Faith*, p. 52.
37. See *Contending for the Faith*, and O. Barclay, *Whatever Happened to the Jesus Lane Lot?* (IVP 1977).
38. *Contending for the Faith*, p. 301.
39. *Contending for the Faith*, pp. 93–4.
40. *The Story of the Crusaders' Union: These Fifty Years 1906–1956* (Crusaders 1956), p. 8.
41. *Crusaders' Union*, p. 8.
42. *Crusaders' Union*, p. 8.
43. *Crusaders' Union*, p. 28.
44. *The Good Seed*, pp. 73–4.
45. *The Good Seed*, p. 102.
46. Pollock and Eddison are at variance here: Eddison puts the Seaford camp in 1930 (*Bash*, p. 12).
47. *Bash*, p. 19.
48. *Bash*, p. 20.
49. *Bash*, p. 12.
50. *Bash*, p. 19.
51. Quoted in *Bash*, p. viii.
52. Quoted in *Bash*, p. 93.
53. Quoted in *Bash*, p. 33.
54. *Bash*, p. 21.
55. *Bash*, p. 27.
56. D. Watson, *You are my God* (Hodder and Stoughton 1983), p. 39.
57. *Bash*, p. 8.
58. For more on this see chapter 3.

Notes to Chapter Two

1. *Evangelicalism in Modern Britain*, p. 225.
2. *Evangelicalism in Modern Britain*, p. 226.
3. See P. Ward, S. Adams and J. Levermore, *Youthwork*.
4. Letter to the author, 1995.
5. D. E. Taylor, *Youth Fellowship Work: The Handbook of Scottish Episcopal Youth Fellowships* (SPCK 1946), p. 8.
6. *Youth Fellowship Work*, p. 11.
7. *Youth's Job in the Parish* (AYPA 1939), p. 11.
8. *Youth's Job*, p. 13.
9. *Youth's Job*, p. 41.
10. S. H. Evans and E. W. Southcott, *Unto a Full Grown Man* (AYPA 1942).
11. *Unto a Full Grown Man*, Vol. 1, p. xiii.
12. C. H. Plummer, *The Parochial Youth Group* (SPCK 1948), p. 28.
13. *The Church and Young People* (CEYC 1955), p. 30.
14. *Youth in the Country* (CEYC 1945).
15. Plummer in *The Review*, Vol. 4, No. 3, back page.
16. *The Review*, Vol. 3, No. 4, p. 2.
17. The CEYC in its early days advocated similar ideas on youthwork to those of AYPA e.g. 'Worship, study, service, witness and recreation' as a pattern for activities.
18. D. Winter, *Old Faith, Young World* (Hodder and Stoughton 1965), p. 44.
19. For more on Covenanters see R. W. Pinchback, *Christian Leadership of Boys: A Practical Handbook for Covenanter Leaders and Others* (Covenanter Union 1949).
20. See S. N. Wood and J. R. Hill, *Bible Class Teaching and Leadership* (SU 1964).
21. *History of Pathfinders*.
22. *History of Pathfinders*.
23. *History of Pathfinders*.
24. Young Churchmen's Movement, *Minute Book*, minute, 24 October 1930.
25. YCM minute, 17 December 1930.
26. YCM minute, 11 May 1930.
27. YCM minute, 18 February 1933.
28. YCM minute, 31 August 1931.
29. YCM minute, 23 November 1934.
30. *History of Pathfinders*.
31. Brochure, *Pathfinder Camp for Boys at Teignmouth*, 1954.
32. Habershon interview with the author, 1994.
33. See article by R. Warren, in *CYFA Bulletin*, November 1968; also

description of youth fellowship in CYFA soundstrip, *The Aims of a Youth Fellowship*.

34. This point was made to me by current CYFA staff members Steve Tilley and Bob Clucas.
35. *God's Word in a Young World*, p. 123.
36. I am indebted to Michael Eastman for these insights.
37. *God's Word in a Young World*, p. 124.
38. *God's Word in a Young World*, p. 126.
39. Brochure, *Inter-School Cambrian Camp*, 1955.
40. Letter to the author, 1995.
41. Arthur Marwick, *British Society Since 1945* (Penguin 1982).
42. Letter to the author, 1995.
43. R. Hoggart, *The Uses of Literacy* (Chatto and Windus 1957).
44. H. Loukes, *Teenage Religion* (SCM 1961); R. Goldman, *Readiness for Religion: A Basis for Developmental Religious Education* (Routledge and Kegan Paul 1965).
45. Letter to the author, 1995.
46. Letter to the author, 1995.
47. *God's Word in a Young World*, p. 126.
48. *Old Faith, Young World*, p. 63.
49. D. Watson, *Towards Tomorrow's Church* (Falcon 1965), p. 27.
50. M. Saward and M. Eastman, *Christian Youth Groups* (SU 1965), p. 48.
51. For more on this see chapter 4.
52. *Christian Youth Groups*, p. 49.
53. *Christian Youth Groups*, pp. 70, 71.
54. Barnett, quoted in *Christian Youth Groups*, p. 49.
55. *Old Faith, Young World*, p. 46.
56. *Tomorrow's Church*, p. 24.
57. *Christian Youth Groups*, p. 24.
58. For more on this see chapters 5 and 6.

Notes to Chapter Three

1. *God's Word in a Young World*, p. 234.
2. P. Watherston, *A Different Kind of Church* (Marshall Pickering 1994), p. 127.
3. A more comprehensive history of evangelical urban youthwork and FYT is beyond the scope of this work.
4. *A Different Kind of Church*, p. 45.
5. D. Sheppard, *Parson's Pitch* (Hodder and Stoughton 1964), p. 160.
6. D. and J. Hewitt, *George Burton: A Study in Contradictions* (Hodder and Stoughton 1964), p. 96.

7. *A Different Kind of Church*, p. 46.
8. G. Burton, *People Matter More Than Things* (Hodder and Stoughton 1965), p. 34.
9. *People Matter*, p. 30.
10. Quoted in *George Burton*, p. 14.
11. Quoted in *George Burton*, p. 126.
12. *A Different Kind of Church*, p. 53.
13. *People Matter*, p. 34.
14. Eastman quoted in *A Different Kind of Church*, p. 88.
15. Eastman letter to the author, 1995.
16. Letter, 1995.
17. *FYT in the UK: The Formative Years* (FYT 1985), p. 5.
18. *A Different Kind of Church*, p. 88.
19. T. Dunnell, *Mission and Young People at Risk: A Challenge to the Church* (FYT 1985), back page.
20. *FYT in the UK*, p. 5.
21. FYT, *Christians in the Youth Service* (SU 1967), p. 2.
22. 'The Aims of the FYT', in *Christians in the Youth Service*, p. 2.
23. Eastman letter to the author, 1995.
24. *A Different Kind of Church*, p. 89.
25. *Christians in the Youth Service*, p. 10.
26. R. Sainsbury, *From a Mersey Wall* (SU 1970), p. 46.
27. FYT, *Making a Start*, p. 2.
28. *Towards Tomorrow's Church*; see also H. Wilson, *The Parish Youth Club* (SPCK 1963).
29. *Making a Start*, p. 21.
30. *Making a Start*, p. 1.
31. Letter to the author, 1995.
32. P. Wilson, *Gutter Feelings* (Marshall 1985), p. 31ff.
33. Quoted in *A Different Kind of Church*, p. 154.
34. *A Different Kind of Church*, p. 136.
35. *Making a Start*, p. 2.
36. *Christians in the Youth Service*, p. 3.
37. *Making a Start*, p. 3.
38. *A Different Kind of Church*, p. 174.
39. *A Different Kind of Church*, p. 123.
40. P. Stow with M. Fearon, *Youth in the City* (Hodder and Stoughton 1987), p. 80.
41. See *Mission and Young People at Risk*.
42. *A Different Kind of Church*, p. 152.
43. *Gutter Feelings*, p. 112.
44. Letter to the author, 1995.
45. E. Neale, *Go Down in the City* (SU 1974), p. 55.
46. Letter to the author, 1995.

47. *Gutter Feelings*, p. 26.
48. *Gutter Feelings*, p. 25.
49. Eastmen interview with the author, 1995.
50. *George Burton*, p. 100.
51. *Mission and Young People at Risk*, introduction.
52. *Gutter Feelings*, p. 128.
53. *From a Mersey Wall*, p. 47.
54. Punton quoted in M. Eastman, *Inside Out: A Handbook for Youth Leaders* (Falcon 1976), p. 119.
55. See P. Ward, *Youth Culture and the Gospel* (Marshall Pickering 1992).
56. A. Bell, 'Reaching the Unreached in Youth Evangelism', in I. Green and B. Hewitt, *Collected Wisdom for Youth Workers* (Marshall Pickering 1988), p. 141.
57. *Mission and Young People at Risk*, section on 'Community and Youth Work'.
58. J. Benington, *Culture, Class and Christian Beliefs* (SU 1973).
59. *Culture, Class and Christian Beliefs*, p. 20.
60. *Inside Out*, p. 117.
61. *FYT in the UK*, p. 7.
62. Eastman in M. Fearon, *With God on the Frontiers* (SU 1988), p. 138.
63. *Gutter Feelings*, p. 124.

Notes to Chapter Four

1. *Evangelicalism in Modern Britain*, p. 264.
2. *Evangelicalism in Modern Britain*, p. 264.
3. R. M. Enroth, E. E. Ericson, and C. B. Peters, *The Story of the Jesus People: A Factual Survey* (Paternoster 1972), p. 14.
4. R. C. Palms, *The Jesus Kids* (SCM 1971), p. 19.
5. *The Jesus Kids*, p. 16.
6. *Comparative Youth Culture*, p. 90.
7. *The Jesus Kids*, pp. 16–17.
8. B. Wilson, *Religion in Sociological Perspective* (Oxford 1982), p. 138.
9. *Religion in Sociological Perspective*, p. 140.
10. *The Jesus Kids*, p. 20.
11. A. Blessitt, *Turned on to Jesus* (Word 1971).
12. Quoted in *The Story of the Jesus People*, p. 69.
13. *The Jesus Kids*, p. 31; see also K. Leech, *Youthquake: Spirituality and the Growth of the Counter-culture* (Abacus 1973), p. 116.
14. *The Story of the Jesus People*, p. 102.

15. *The Story of the Jesus People*, p. 103.
16. *Religion in Sociological Perspective*, p. 140; see also R. S. Warner, *New Wine in Old Wineskins: Evangelicals and Liberals in a Small-town Church* (California 1988).
17. *The Story of the Jesus People*, p. 87.
18. *The Jesus Kids*, p. 37.
19. *The Jesus Kids*, p. 32.
20. T. Jasper, *Jesus and the Christian in a Pop Culture* (Robert Royce 1984), p. 96.
21. *Youthquake*, p. 117.
22. *The Story of the Jesus People*, p. 14.
23. *Youthquake*, p. 117.
24. *Youthquake*, p. 117.
25. *Jesus and the Christian*, p. 147.
26. F. Dobbie, *Land Aflame* (Hodder and Stoughton 1972), p. 13.
27. *Jesus and the Christian*, p. 147.
28. *Youthquake*, p. 129.
29. *Go Down in the City*, p. 14.
30. *Go Down in the City*, p. 14.
31. A. Walker, *Restoring the Kingdom: The Radical Christianity of the House Church Movement* (Hodder and Stoughton 1985), p. 53.
32. Meadows interview with the author, 1993.
33. *Jesus and the Christian*, p. 88.
34. J. MacKenzie (arr.), *Songs for Jesus* (MGO 1972), back cover.
35. Quoted in *Jesus and the Christian*, p. 148.
36. *Jesus and the Christian*, p. 148.
37. Interview with the author, 1993.
38. T. Cummings, *Cross Rhythms*, No. 1, 1990, p. 4.
39. For more on this see chapter 9.
40. *Jesus and the Christian*, p. 134.
41. Quoted in *Jesus and the Christian*, p. 135.
42. Stone interview with the author, 1993.
43. *Jesus and the Christian*, p. 116.
44. *Jesus and the Christian*, p. 117.
45. *Jesus and the Christian*, p. 117.
46. Interview, 1993.
47. Interview, 1993.
48. S. Henderson, *Since the Beginning Greenbelt* (Greenbelt 1984), p. 2.
49. Interview, 1993.
50. Interview, 1993.
51. Quoted in *Jesus and the Christian*, p. 140.
52. Doney interview with the author, 1993.
53. See chapter 9 for reaction to the openness of Greenbelt.

54. For more on the ideas behind NOS see C. Brain, 'The Nine O'clock Service' in D. Gillett and M. Scott-Joynt, *Treasure in the Field* (Fount 1993).
55. *Jesus and the Christian*, p. 137.
56. For more on this see chapter 9.

Notes to Chapter Five

1. A. Dunstan, 'Hymnody in Christian Worship' in C. Jones, G. Wainwright and E. Yarnold, *The Study of Liturgy* (SPCK 1978), p. 462.
2. *Evangelicals in the Church of England*, p. 287.
3. D. J. Tidball, *Who are the Evangelicals?* (Marshall Pickering 1994), p. 31.
4. I limit the study to the first volume of each of the song series in part because these tend to exhibit in purist terms the particular characteristics of that group of songs.
5. *Study of Liturgy*, p. 456.
6. *Evangelicalism in Modern Britain*, p. 257.
7. *Evangelicals in the Church of England*, p. 288.
8. *Evangelicalism in Modern Britain*, p. 260.
9. *Evangelicalism in Modern Britain*, p. 249.
10. *Evangelicalism in Modern Britain*, p. 250.
11. *Evangelicalism in Modern Britain*, p. 257.
12. M. Saward, *Evangelicals on the Move* (Mowbray 1987), p. 52.
13. Baughen, letter to the author, 1995.
14. M. A. Baughen, and R. T. Bewes, *Youth Praise* (Falcon 1966), p. v.
15. *Youth Praise*, p. vi.
16. *Youth Praise*, p. v. According to Baughen considerable attention was given to covering the major theological doctrines. Indeed the project was delayed by Kenneth Habershon's insistence that songs should be written to 'plug the gaps' (Letter to the author, 1995).
17. *Youth Praise*, p. v.
18. *Evangelicalism in Modern Britain*, p. 258.
19. *Youth Praise*, p. v.
20. *Youth Praise*, back cover.
21. *Who are the Evangelicals?*, p. 52.
22. *The Charismatic Movement in the Church of England* (CIO 1981), p. 10.
23. *Evangelicalism in Modern Britain*, p. 233.
24. Quoted in *Evangelicalism in Modern Britain*, p. 241.
25. T. Walker, *Open to God – A Parish in Renewal* (Grove 1975), p. 12.

26. *Open to God*, p. 12.
27. *Evangelicalism in Modern Britain*, p. 241.
28. J. Gunstone, *Pentecostal Anglicans* (Hodder and Stoughton 1982), p. 212.
29. *The Charismatic Movement*, p. 38.
30. *The Charismatic Movement*, p. 36.
31. *Evangelicalism in Modern Britain*, p. 241.
32. F. Lees, *Love is our Home* (Hodder and Stoughton 1978), p. 161.
33. J. Punton, *The Messiah People* (Hot Iron Press 1993), p. 1.
34. M. Harper, *As at the Beginning: The Twentieth Century Pentecostal Revival* (Hodder and Stoughton 1965), p. 88.
35. T. Walker, *Renew us by your Spirit* (Hodder and Stoughton 1982), p. 41.
36. D. Wilkerson, *The Cross and the Switchblade* (Oliphant 1963), pp. 157–70.
37. *Love is our Home*, p. 54.
38. G. W. Pulkingham, *Gathered for Power* (Hodder and Stoughton 1972), pp. 71–7.
39. G. W. Pulkingham, *They Left their Nets* (Hodder and Stoughton 1974), p. 119.
40. T. Saunders and H. Sansom, *David Watson: A Biography* (Hodder and Stoughton 1992), p. 164.
41. *They Left their Nets*, p. 119.
42. *They Left their Nets*.
43. *David Watson*, p. 151.
44. *You are my God*, p. iii.
45. *Love is our Home*, p. 185.
46. B. Pulkingham and J. Harper, *Sound of Living Waters* (Hodder and Stoughton 1974), foreword.
47. *Evangelicalism in Modern Britain*, p. 241.
48. *Pentecostal Anglicans*, p. 212.
49. J. Fiske, *Understanding Popular Culture* (Routledge and Kegan Paul 1989), p. 5ff, and P. Willis, *Common Culture* (Open University 1990), p. 1ff.
50. *The Charismatic Movement*, p. 39.
51. *Who are the Evangelicals?*, p. 52.
52. *Pentecostal Anglicans*, p. 83.
53. I speak from personal experience here.
54. G. Kendrick, G. Coates, R. Forster and L. Green, *March for Jesus* (Kingsway 1992), p. 23.
55. *Restoring the Kingdom*, p. 35.
56. *Restoring the Kingdom*, p. 99.
57. A. Hastings, *A History of English Christianity 1920–1990* (SCM 1991, 3rd edn), p. 619.

58. *Songs of Fellowship* (Kingsway 1981), back cover.

Notes to Chapter Six

1. See P. Ward, *Worship and Youth Culture* (Marshall Pickering 1993).
2. *Something to Celebrate* (CIO 1995), p. 18.
3. *Something to Celebrate*, p. 63.
4. *Something to Celebrate*, p. 69.
5. *Something to Celebrate*, p. 70.
6. *Something to Celebrate*, p. 63.
7. 'Family', in D. J. Atkinson and D. Field, *New Dictionary of Christian Ethics and Pastoral Theology* (IVP 1995), p. 375.
8. *New Dictionary*, p. 375.
9. *Children in the Way* (CIO 1991), p. 1.
10. *Rise and Development of the Sunday School Movement*, p. 239.
11. *Rise and Development of the Sunday School Movement*, p. 238.
12. *Rise and Development of the Sunday School Movement*, p. 243.
13. *Rise and Development of the Sunday School Movement*, p. 245.
14. Quoted in *Rise and Development of the Sunday School Movement*, p. 245.
15. Quoted in C. Irvine, *Worship, Church and Society* (Canterbury Press 1993), p. 124.
16. *Worship, Church and Society*, p. 125.
17. *Evangelicals in the Church of England*, p. 325.
18. Quoted in *Evangelicalism in Modern Britain*, p. 256.
19. *Evangelicals in the Church of England*, p. 325.
20. *History of English Christianity*, p. 619.
21. *Evangelicalism in Modern Britain*, p. 256.
22. M. Botting, *Teaching the Family* (Kingsway 1994), p. 20.
23. *Teaching the Family*, p. 16.
24. *Evangelicals on the Move*, p. 52.
25. Quoted in *Teaching the Family*, p. 18.
26. *Teaching the Family*, p. 18.
27. M. Perham, *Liturgy Pastoral and Parochial* (SPCK 1984), p. 87.
28. The Consultative Group on Ministry among Children, *Unfinished Business* (CCBI 1995), p. 20.
29. *Unfinished Business*, p. 23.
30. *Children in the Way*, p. 51.
31. *Children in the Way*, p. v.
32. *Children in the Way*, p. 17.
33. *Something to Celebrate*, p. 89.
34. *History of English Christianity*, p. 666.

35. *Unfinished Business*, p. 19.
36. *Unfinished Business*, p. 19.
37. See P. Ward, *Worship and Youth Culture*.
38. *Unfinished Business*, 1995.
39. J. Leach, *Liturgy and Liberty* (Monarch 1989), p. 226.
40. *Liturgy Pastoral and Parochial*, p. 88.
41. *Unfinished Business*, p. 42.
42. *Unfinished Business*, p. 43.

Notes to Chapter Seven

1. C. Calver, 'Youth and the Church', in *Collected Wisdom*, p. 161.
2. T. Williams, *Christians in School* (SU 1985), p. 11.
3. J. Dobson, *Preparing for Adolescence* (Kingsway 1982), p. 11.
4. *Reaching and Keeping Teenagers*.
5. *Reaching and Keeping Teenagers*, p. 45.
6. *Reaching and Keeping Teenagers*, p. 50.
7. Quoted in *Reaching and Keeping Teenagers*, p. 231.
8. Quoted in *Reaching and Keeping Teenagers*, p. 15.
9. S. Flashman, *Closing the Gap* (Kingsway 1988), p. 19.
10. P. Gilbert, *The Teenage Survival Kit* (Kingsway 1986).
11. *Teenage Survival Kit*, p. 14.
12. *Teenage Survival Kit*, p. 15.
13. *Teenage Survival Kit*, p. 18.
14. *Teenage Survival Kit*, p. 57.
15. D. Lawrence, *The Chocolate Teapot* (SU 1991), p. 12.
16. *Collected Wisdom*, p. 253.
17. P. Moon, *Hanging in There* (Monarch 1994).
18. *Hanging in There*, p. 6.
19. Quoted in L. J. Francis, W. Kay, A. Kerbey and O. Fogwill, *Fast Moving Currents in Youth Culture* (Lynx 1995), p. 200.
20. *Teenage Survival Kit*, p. 102.
21. *Teenage Survival Kit*, p. 102.
22. *Teenage Survival Kit*, p. 102.
23. O. Nyumbu, 'Peer Pressure', in *Collected Wisdom*, p. 332.
24. For more on this see chapter 9.
25. R. and C. Day, *Help! I'm Growing Up* (Kingsway 1995), p. 58.
26. *Teenage Survival Kit*, p. 106.
27. *Collected Wisdom*, p. 335.
28. *Teenage Survival Kit*, p. 109.
29. Roberts in *Fast Moving Currents*, p. 132.
30. *Fast Moving Currents*, p. 132.

31. *Help! I'm Growing Up*, p. 13.
32. *Teenage Survival Kit*, p. 121.
33. *Christians in School*, p. 27.
34. *Help! I'm Growing Up*, p. 86.
35. *Teenage Survival Kit*, p. 107.
36. *Help! I'm Growing Up*, p. 52.
37. *Teenage Survival Kit*, p. 126.
38. J. and S. Ritter, *Keep in Step* (Kingsway 1987), p. 64.
39. Fenton in *Fast Moving Currents*, p. 171.
40. *Hanging in There*, p. 58.
41. M. Jones, 'Where to Start and Where to Go', in *Collected Wisdom*, p. 62.
42. For more on this see P. Ward, *Worship and Youth Culture*.
43. *Reaching and Keeping Teenagers*, p. 233.
44. *Keep in Step*, p. 27.
45. *The Chocolate Teapot*, p. 53.
46. *Hanging in There*, p. 63.
47. *Hanging in There*, p. 64.
48. *Youthwork*, p. 17.
49. *Christians in School*, p. 14; for a contrary view see *Youth Culture and the Gospel*, p. 30.
50. *Teenage Survival Kit*, p. 121.
51. *Hanging in There*, p. 97.
52. M. Ashton, *Christian Youth Work* (Kingsway 1986), p. 68.
53. N. Aiken, *Working with Teenagers* (Marshall Pickering 1988), p. 4.
54. P. Moon, *Young People and the Bible* (Marshall Pickering 1992), p. 6.
55. These issues are explored more deeply in chapter 8.
56. *Collected Wisdom*, p. 162.
57. *Christians in School*, pp. 9–10.
58. For more on this see chapters 4 and 10.
59. *Collected Wisdom*, p. 163.
60. See *Culture, Class and Christian Beliefs*.

Notes to Chapter Eight

1. R. Hurding, 'Adolescence' in *New Dictionary*, p. 143.
2. See *Dancing in the Dark*, p. 14ff and *Developing Youth Work*, p. 1ff.
3. M. Breen, *Outside In* (SU 1993), p. 49.
4. *Outside In*, p. 43.
5. P. Angiers, *Faith Builders* (Marshall Pickering 1994), p. 24.
6. J. M. Hull, *What Prevents Christian Adults from Learning?* (SCM 1985), p. 7.

7. *Christian Adults*, p. 9.
8. Stackhouse, 'Perpetual Adolescence' in *Crux* Vol. 29, No. 3, p. 2.
9. S. Chalke, *The Complete Youth Manual Volume 1* (Kingsway 1987), p. 65.
10. *Faith Builders*, p. 12.
11. *Faith Builders*, p. 26.
12. Winter interview with the author, 1993.
13. Interview, 1993.
14. Interview, 1993.
15. Interview, 1993.
16. *Faith Builders*, p. 196.
17. M., L., F. and D. Linn, *Healing Religious Addiction* (Darton Longman and Todd 1995).
18. *Healing Religious Addiction*, p. 10.
19. J. W. Fowler, *Stages of Faith* (Harper San Francisco 1981).
20. V. C. Hoffman, *The Codependent Church* (Crossroad 1991), p. 28.
21. J. Ind, *Fat is a Spiritual Issue* (Mowbray 1993). I should perhaps point out that Jo Ind is my sister-in-law.
22. *Fat is a Spiritual Issue*, p. 35.
23. H. R. Lee, *The Growing Years* (Falcon 1963), p. 145.
24. *The Growing Years*, p. 146.

Notes to Chapter Nine

1. For more on this see chapter 4.
2. The first separate bi-monthly edition of *Youthwork* came out in June 1992; preceding this three supplements were published in *Alpha* magazine.
3. June/July 92, p. 2.
4. Buckeridge interview with the author, 1995.
5. June/July 95.
6. June/July 94.
7. December 93/January 94.
8. February/March 95.
9. April/May 95.
10. December 94/January 95.
11. February/March 95.
12. *Understanding Popular Culture*, p. 23.
13. April/May 95, p. 26.
14. April/May 95, p. 26.
15. April/May 95, p. 28.
16. December 93/January 94.
17. April/May 92, p. 3.
18. April/May 93, p. 35.

19. June/July 93, p. 26.
20. December 93/January 94.
21. October/November 94, p. 28.
22. December 94/January 95, p. 27.
23. For an isolated example see 'Teens Back Live Export Ban', April/May 95, p. 24.
24. June/July 93, p. 34.
25. August/September 92, p. 4.
26. August/September 95.
27. August/September 92.
28. June/July 93.
29. August/September 93.
30. February/March 95.
31. October/November 94.
32. October/November 94.
33. April/May 95.
34. October/November 94.
35. April/May 94, p. 6.
36. I should also add that I found Oxford Youth Works and my own name appearing fairly regularly.
37. Buckeridge interview with the author, 1995.
38. See June/July 93, p. 5; August/September 93, p. 4; April/May 95, p. 7.
39. April/May 93, p. 5; December 93/January 94, p. 7.
40. Buckeridge interview with the author, 1995.
41. April/May 94, p. 7.
42. April/May 93, p. 5.
43. December 94/January 95, p. 6.
44. Buckeridge interview with the author, 1995.

Bibliography

S. Adams, 'The Process of Change Through Relationships Between Adults and Young People', in P. Ward (ed.), *Relational Youthwork* (Lynx 1995).

N. Aiken, *Working with Teenagers* (Marshall Pickering 1988).

P. Angiers, *Faith Builders* (Marshall Pickering 1994).

M. Ashton, *Christian Youth Work* (Kingsway 1986).

D. J. Atkinson and D. Field, *New Dictionary of Christian Ethics and Pastoral Theology* (IVP 1995).

O. Barclay, *Whatever Happened to the Jesus Lane Lot?* (IVP 1977).

M. A. Baughen and R. T. Bewes, *Youth Praise* (Falcon 1966).

D. W. Bebbington, *Evangelicalism in Modern Britain* (Unwin Hyman 1989).

J. Benington, *Culture, Class and Christian Beliefs* (SU 1973).

C. Binfield, *George Williams and the YMCA: A Study in Victorian Social Attitudes* (Heinemann 1973).

A. Blessitt, *Turned on to Jesus* (Word 1971).

D. Borgman, 'A History of American Youth Ministry', in W. S. Benson and M. H. Senter III (eds.), *The Complete Book of Youth Ministry* (Moody Press 1987).

M. Botting, *Teaching the Family* (Kingsway 1994).

M. Brake, *Comparative Youth Culture* (Routledge and Kegan Paul 1985).

M. Breen, *Outside In* (SU 1993).

P. Brierley, *Reaching and Keeping Teenagers* (Monarch 1993).

G. Burton, *People Matter More Than Things* (Hodder and Stoughton 1965).

O. Chadwick, *Michael Ramsey: A Life* (Oxford 1990).

S. Chalke, *The Complete Youth Manual Volume 1* (Kingsway 1987).

The Charismatic Movement in the Church of England (CIO 1981).

Children in the Way (CIO 1991).

The Church and Young People (CEYC 1955).

P. B. Cliff, *The Rise and Development of the Sunday School Movement in England 1780–1980* (National Christian Education Council 1986).

The Consultative Group on Ministry among Children, *Unfinished Business* (CCBI 1995).

J. Davison Hunter, *Evangelicalism the Coming Generation* (Chicago 1987).

R. and C. Day, *Help! I'm Growing Up* (Kingsway 1995).

F. Dobbie, *Land Aflame* (Hodder and Stoughton 1972).

J. Dobson, *Preparing for Adolescence* (Kingsway 1982).

T. Dunnell, *Mission and Young People at Risk: A Challenge to the Church* (FYT 1985).

M. Eastman, *Inside Out: A Handbook for Youth Leaders* (Falcon 1976).

J. Eddison (ed.), *Bash: A Study in Spiritual Power* (Marshall 1982).

R. M. Enroth, E. E. Ericson and C. B. Peters, *The Story of the Jesus People: A Factual Survey* (Paternoster 1972).

S. H. Evans and E. W. Southcott, *Unto a Full Grown Man* (AYPA 1942).

M. Fearon, *With God on the Frontiers* (SU 1988).

J. Fiske, *Understanding Popular Culture* (Routledge and Kegan Paul 1989).

S. Flashman, *Closing the Gap* (Kingsway 1988).

J. W. Fowler, *Stages of Faith* (Harper San Francisco 1981).

R. T. France and A. E. McGrath (eds), *Evangelical Anglicans* (SPCK 1993).

L. J. Francis, W. Kay, A. Kerbey and O. Fogwill, *Fast Moving Currents in Youth Culture* (Lynx 1995).

FYT, *Christians in the Youth Service* (SU 1967).

FYT, *FYT in the UK: The Formative Years* (FYT 1985).

FYT, *Making a Start.*

P. Gilbert, *The Teenage Survival Kit* (Kingsway 1986).

D. Gillett and M. Scott-Joynt, *Treasure in the Field* (Fount 1993).

R. Goldman, *Readiness for Religion: A Basis for Developmental Religious Education* (Routledge and Kegan Paul 1965).

I. Green and B. Hewitt, *Collected Wisdom for Youth Workers* (Marshall Pickering 1988).

J. Gunstone, *Pentecostal Anglicans* (Hodder and Stoughton 1982).

M. Harper, *As at the Beginning: The Twentieth Century Pentecostal Revival* (Hodder and Stoughton 1965).

A. Hastings, *A History of English Christianity 1920–1990* (SCM 1991, 3rd edn).

N. O. Hatch, *The Democratization of American Christianity* (Yale 1989).

S. Henderson, *Since the Beginning Greenbelt* (Greenbelt 1984).

D. J. Hesselgrave and E. Rommen, *Contextualisation* (Apollos 1989).

D. and J. Hewitt, *George Burton: A Study in Contradictions* (Hodder and Stoughton 1964).

History of Pathfinders (Pathfinder Papers).

V. C. Hoffman, *The Codependent Church* (Crossroad 1991).

R. Hoggart, *The Uses of Literacy* (Chatto and Windus 1957).

J. M. Hull, *What Prevents Christian Adults from Learning?* (SCM 1985).

K. Hylson-Smith, *Evangelicals in the Church of England 1734–1984* (T and T Clark 1988).

J. Ind, *Fat is a Spiritual Issue* (Mowbray 1993).

C. Irvine, *Worship, Church and Society* (Canterbury Press 1993).

T. Jasper, *Jesus and the Christian in a Pop Culture* (Robert Royce 1984).

D. Johnson, *Contending for the Faith: A History of the Evangelical Movement in the Universities and Colleges* (IVP 1979).

C. Jones, G. Wainwright and E. Yarnold, *The Study of Liturgy* (SPCK 1978).

G. Kendrick, G. Coates, R. Forster and L. Green, *March for Jesus* (Kingsway 1992).

J. F. Kett, *Rites of Passage: Adolescence in America 1790 to the Present* (Basic Books 1977).

D. Lawrence, *The Chocolate Teapot* (SU 1991).

J. Leach, *Liturgy and Liberty* (Monarch 1989).

H. R. Lee, *The Growing Years* (Falcon 1963).

K. Leech, *Youthquake: Spirituality and the Growth of the Counter-culture* (Abacus 1973).

F. Lees, *Love is our Home* (Hodder and Stoughton 1978).

M., L., F. and D. Linn, *Healing Religious Addiction* (Darton Longman and Todd 1995).

H. Loukes, *Teenage Religion* (SCM 1961).

J. MacKenzie (arr.), *Songs for Jesus* (MGO 1972).

W. Martin, *The Billy Graham Story* (Hutchinson 1991).

A. E. McGrath, *Evangelicalism and the Future of Christianity* (Hodder and Stoughton 1994).

H. Montefiore, *The Gospel and Contemporary Culture* (Mowbray 1992).

P. Moon, *Young People and the Bible* (Marshall Pickering 1992).

P. Moon, *Hanging in There* (Monarch 1994).

E. Neale, *Go Down in the City* (SU 1974).

L. Newbigin, *The Gospel in a Pluralist Society* (SPCK 1989).

M. Noll, *The Scandal of the Evangelical Mind* (IVP 1994).

M. A. Noll, D. W. Bebbington and G. A. Rawlk (eds), *Evangelicalism* (Oxford 1994).

J. E. Orr, *Campus Aflame: A History of Evangelical Awakenings in Collegiate Communities* (International Awakening Press edn 1994).

R. C. Palms, *The Jesus Kids* (SCM 1971).

R. S. Peacock, *Pioneer of Boyhood* (The Boys' Brigade 1954).

M. Perham, *Liturgy Pastoral and Parochial* (SPCK 1984).

R. W. Pinchback, *Christian Leadership of Boys: A Practical Handbook for Covenanter Leaders and Others* (Covenanter Union 1949).

C. H. Plummer, *The Parochial Youth Group* (SPCK 1948).

J. C. Pollock, *The Good Seed* (Hodder and Stoughton 1959).

B. Pulkingham and J. Harper, *Sound of Living Waters* (Hodder and Stoughton 1974).

G. W. Pulkingham, *Gathered for Power* (Hodder and Stoughton 1972).

G. W. Pulkingham, *They Left their Nets* (Hodder and Stoughton 1974).

J. Punton, *The Messiah People* (Hot Iron Press 1993).

The *Review* (CEYC 1945–7).

J. and S. Ritter, *Keep in Step* (Kingsway 1987).

R. Sainsbury, *From a Mersey Wall* (SU 1970).

V. Samuel and C. Sugden (eds), *Sharing Jesus in the Two Thirds World* (Partnership in Mission 1983).

T. Saunders and H. Sansom, *David Watson: A Biography* (Hodder and Stoughton 1992).

M. Saward, *Evangelicals on the Move* (Mowbray 1987).

M. Saward and M. Eastman, *Christian Youth Groups* (SU 1965).

Q. J. Schultze, R. M. Anker, J. D. Bratt, W. D. Romanowski, J. W. Worst and L. Zuidervaart, *Dancing in the Dark: Youth, Popular Culture and the Electronic Media* (Eerdmans 1991).

M. Senter III, *The Coming Revolution in Youth Ministry* (Victor Books 1992).

D. Sheppard, *Parson's Pitch* (Hodder and Stoughton 1964).

M. Smith, *Developing Youth Work* (Open University 1988).

Something to Celebrate (CIO 1995).

Songs of Fellowship (Kingsway 1981).

J. G. Stackhouse Jnr, 'Perpetual Adolescence: The Emerging Culture of North American Evangelicalism' in *Crux* Vol. 29, No. 3 (September 1993).

The Story of the Crusaders' Union: These Fifty Years 1906–1956 (Crusaders 1956).

P. Stow with M. Fearon, *Youth in the City* (Hodder and Stoughton 1987).

N. Sylvester, *God's Word in a Young World* (SU 1985).

D. E. Taylor, *Youth Fellowship Work: The Handbook of Scottish Episcopal Youth Fellowships* (SPCK 1946).

D. J. Tidball, *Who are the Evangelicals?* (Marshall Pickering 1994).

A. Walker, *Restoring the Kingdom: The Radical Christianity of the House Church Movement* (Hodder and Stoughton 1985).

T. Walker, *Open to God – A Parish in Renewal* (Grove 1975).

T. Walker, *Renew us by your Spirit* (Hodder and Stoughton 1982).

P. Ward, *Youth Culture and the Gospel* (Marshall Pickering 1992).

P. Ward, *Worship and Youth Culture* (Marshall Pickering 1993).

P. Ward, S. Adams and J. Levermore, *Youthwork and How to Do it* (Lynx 1995).

R. S. Warner, *New Wine in Old Wineskins: Evangelicals and Liberals in a Small-town Church* (California 1988).

P. Watherston, *A Different Kind of Church* (Marshall Pickering 1994).

D. Watson, *Towards Tomorrow's Church* (Falcon 1965).

D. Watson, *You are my God* (Hodder and Stoughton 1983).

D. Wilkerson, *The Cross and the Switchblade* (Oliphant 1963).

T. Williams, *Christians in School* (SU 1985).

P. Willis, *Common Culture* (Open University 1990).

B. Wilson, *Religion in Sociological Perspective* (Oxford 1982).

H. Wilson, *The Parish Youth Club* (SPCK 1963).

P. Wilson, *Gutter Feelings* (Marshall 1985).

D. Winter, *Old Faith, Young World* (Hodder and Stoughton 1965).

S. N. Wood and J. R. Hill, *Bible Class Teaching and Leadership* (SU 1964).

Young Churchmen's Movement, *Minute Book* (1930).

Youth in the Country (CEYC 1945).

Youth's Job in the Parish (AYPA 1939).

The Society for Promoting Christian Knowledge (SPCK)
has as its purpose three main tasks:

- **Communicating the Christian faith in its rich
  diversity**
- **Helping people to understand the Christian faith
  and to develop their personal faith**
- **Equipping Christians for mission and ministry**

SPCK Worldwide runs a substantial grant programme to
support Christian literature and communication projects
in over 100 countries. Special schemes also provide books
for those training for ministry in many parts of the world.
All gifts to SPCK are spent wholly on these grant
programmes, without deductions.

SPCK Bookshops support the life of the Christian
community by making available a full range of Christian
literature and other resources, and by providing support
to bookstalls and book agents throughout the UK. SPCK
Bookshops' mail order department meets the needs of
overseas customers and those unable to have access to
local bookshops.

SPCK Publishing produces Christian books and
resources, covering a wide range of inspirational,
pastoral, practical and academic subjects. Authors are
drawn from many different Christian traditions, and
publications aim to meet the needs of a wide variety of
readers in the UK and throughout the world.

The Society does not necessarily endorse the individual
views contained in its publications, but hopes they
stimulate readers to think about and further develop
their Christian faith.

For further information about the Society, please write to:
SPCK, Holy Trinity Church, Marylebone Road,
London NW1 4DU, United Kingdom.
Telephone: 0171 387 5282